Somebody Else's Mama

ALSO BY DAVID HAYNES:

Right by My Side

*S*omebody *Else's Mama*

DAVID HAYNES

MILKWEED
EDITIONS

The author wishes to thank the Ragdale Foundation and the Virginia Center for the Creative Arts for their generous support in the completion of this work, and also Paul J. Hintz, for his skillful reading and guidance.

The characters and events in this book are fictitious. Any similarity to real persons, living or dead, is coincidental and not intended by the author.

Published in 1995 by Milkweed Editions
Printed in the United States of America
Book design by Wendy Holdman. The text of this book is set in Minion.

95 96 97 98 99   5 4 3 2
First Edition

Milkweed Editions is a not-for profit publisher. We gratefully acknowledge support from the Dayton Hudson Foundation for Dayton's and Target Stores; Ecolab Foundation; General Mills Foundation; Honeywell Foundation; Jerome Foundation; John S. and James L. Knight Foundation; The McKnight Foundation; Andrew W. Mellon Foundation; Minnesota State Arts Board through an appropriation by the Minnesota State Legislature; Musser Fund; Challenge and Literature Programs of the National Endowment for the Arts; I. A. O'Shaughnessy Foundation; Piper Family Fund of the Minneapolis Foundation; Piper Jaffray Companies, Inc.; John and Beverly Rollwagen Fund of the Minneapolis Foundation; The St. Paul Companies, Inc.; Star Tribune/Cowles Media Foundation; Surdna Foundation; James R. Thorpe Foundation; Unity Avenue Foundation; Lila Wallace-Reader's Digest Literary Publishers Marketing Development Program, funded through a grant to the Council of Literary Magazines and Presses; and generous individuals.

Library of Congress Cataloging-in-Publication Data

Haynes, David, 1955–
    Somebody else's mama / David Haynes.
        p.   cm.
    ISBN 1-57131-003-7 : $21.95
    I. Title.
PS3558.A8488S65   1995
813'.54—dc20   94-34999
                                                                                    CIP

This book is printed on acid-free paper.

When she saw that she was steadfastly minded to go
with her, then she left speaking unto her.

FROM THE BOOK OF RUTH

Somebody Else's Mama

1

PAULA HATED THE RIVER. SHE HATED THE SMELL OF IT, the way it looked, all the old-timey, hocus-pocus, mystical nonsense about the Mississippi River. The river with secret ways. Old man river. The wise one. The river that got under your skin and into your soul. The river that did something to you. She hated that bull. These old black folks got on your nerves with all this mess—their "folk wisdom" and so-called life experiences.

This river was no more than the drainage ditch of North America. In summertime the Mississippi smelled of dead catfish and raw sewage. Old man river didn't flow by, it sort of boiled by, the color and consistency of weak chocolate milk. Drink some and you would probably die.

"You bout ready, Mother?" she shouted to her mother-in-law. At the very edge of the river, Miss Kezee stood, bent over, looking, Paula thought, like a shepherd's staff. Fifty feet away, through the paper-thin dress she saw the vertebrae on the old woman's back. Her bones looked razor sharp.

"Coach says we got to be to practice on time today. We're gonna be late." Tommy leaned out the window. His jaw was swollen out with a Tootsie Roll Pop, his baseball cap on backwards.

"Give her a minute," Paula said.

He threw himself back into the seat, roared with exasperation, and then crossed his arms. He whined to his brother Tim, but Tim was cool. That boy was always cool. He rolled his brown eyes and went back to his comic book. She loved all that cool on Tim.

"Fuck this shit," Tommy said. He reached across the seat and blew the horn.

"Whatsamatterwithyouboy," she scolded. "You want that old woman to have a heart attack and die? And I've warned you for the last time about your filthy mouth."

Tim had already yanked his brother back to his seat. They started to tussle. God bless eleven-year-olds, she thought. And their parents. She massaged her temples.

"Come on, Mother. We've got a lot to do today." What on earth did that old woman want at the river anyway. These daily trips to worship at the Father of the Waters had gotten old, fast. Every morning for the two weeks since she'd regained enough strength to stand and demand "take me to the river," Miss Kezee had toddled to that same spot, tiny feet planted on the last dry ground where the water lapped the shore. Not yet a month since Paula found her bedridden and disoriented in the house in Saint Paul. She had been so frail. Still seemed so. She was much older than Paula's mother had been when she died, and everything about her seemed ancient: the yellow gray hair, the arthritic stoop, the chocolate brown skin as transparent as petroleum jelly.

Would you be this way Mother? Were you like this when you passed?

The old woman turned and stumbled forward as if she were a punch-drunk prize fighter. Paula walked across the cobblestones to hold her by the arm. Miss Kezee clung to her arm as limply as an infant would.

I am doing this for me, Paula thought. I'm the one afraid she will fall. I'm the one who pictures her pitched face-first into the river, floating away like a length of hunchbacked driftwood.

She had imagined it, wished it—willed it even. More than once. Fall in, you old crow. Fall in and float away. Drift out of our lives forever.

~·~·~

I'm starting to get hot now. I don't stand for a whole lot of foolishness. We'll get you home in a minute, Mother, girl says. Got some more errands to run. Who this girl and who do she think she is? This Paula. Al's woman. We going to Saint Paul? I ask her. She said we was going home. This is River Ridge, mother. This is the road to Hannibal. We have shopping to do for the party. Al's running-for-mayor party. I stare at the wench a good long time. I know all that, I tell her. Why you want to talk to a person like they crazy? Tell me that? Why'd he marry a triflin gal like this in the first place. Boy never has had a lick of sense. Turn on the air in this car. Like to burn up in here. Cheap little gal. Stingy and ornery. Wouldn't give a drowning man a glass of piss water. Drive like a fool. Hundred miles an hour cross all kinds of lines in every lane. Why she haven't hit something, I don't know. Just a minute ago you complained…girl says. Fine, I say. Do what you want, I tell her. Y'all gonna do what you want despite me anyhow. And then she got the nerve to let out a big sigh. But see if she didn't roll up the windows anyway. I ought to knock that sigh right out of her. And knock some of them braids off her head too. What you got your head all knotted up like that for? You like it? she asks. Heifer shakes her head all around. Beads rattle like a dime store toy. Looks like hell, I say, and she say, Well, Al thinks it's pretty. Fool thinks a dog's behind's pretty, I say. And what he want to marry a ugly yella gal like this for anyway. Oh Mother, she says. Mother, really. Mother, can you be a little more careful what you say around the boys. Al and I try to set a good example.

Well, I'll be. She don't know who she messed with. Let me tell this little wench something. Look, wasn't my idea to come down here in the first place. You don't like my mouth then put me out with the garbage. I'll walk home. I'll open the door of this cheap ass car right here and I'll walk home. I'll leave now. You're getting tired, Mother, girl says. You got no right, I say. No right at all. I don't know who you think you are. We'll take care of you, Mother. Till you're better. It's a jail here, Charlie. I'll go home when I'm good and ready. Today if I want, and there ain't a thing you can do to stop me.

Paula turned her ears to the drone of the air-conditioning, let her breathing shallow until it smoothed with the rhythm of the road. I can handle this, she thinks.

"Them damn rowdy boys of yours left a mess in the back seat."

"They're boys, Mother. Eleven-year-old boys. Boys are noisy and messy." She sighed at that truth. She was trapped in a world of pre-adolescents. Twenty-eight sixth-graders at the Riverbluff Elementary School, two more at home.

And an old lady.

Somebody else's mother.

"My Al was never that way. Never. Never. Never."

Those clipped-off nevers sounded like barks, grated at her ears the same way the heavy metal music her students played did. A highway sign said "Hannibal — 8 miles."

"You heard me. I said never. Never."

She pictured the Al she knew: rowdy with his boys, rowdy as his boys. A man stumbling through life, his mind on another planet, enormous elbows that knocked lamps off tables at a turn, that had demolished every vase they ever had owned, none of which ever registered in his brain.

"I'm sure Al was a perfect child."

"Don't you patronize me, girl. Let me tell you something. I have cussed many a little heifer out in my time, and I will cuss you out too. Just cause you married to my son don't give you the right to talk to me any way you please. Just cause all I was saying to you was that them little heathens of yours put mess all over the back seat of my son's car..."

"My van, Mother. My van. My job. My money. My van. Mine."

The pressure pounded at her temples. She was exhilarated and sorry. Patting her mother-in-law's arm, she felt the withered tube snatched from her reach.

"Miss Kezee to you. Kuh-*zee*. That was Charlie's name. Use it. And let me tell you something else: I *will* get me a court order, I *will* be sent back to my own house, and you *will* be sorry."

"Fine."

She gripped the steering wheel tight to stop the tremor in her arm. She bit her lip and concentrated on the road. There was nothing to be said when Miss Kezee was this way. There she was, swallowed up in the bucket seat, her arms crossed through the leather straps of her large black purse, her jawline set. She snorted her anger and her owl head bobbed back and forth. What could Paula possibly tell this old woman?

She could tell her she didn't deserve this, that no one did. She could tell her to take her old ornery self back home and die alone. She'd tell her she's sorry. Sorry she's sick. Sorry she has to be this way. Sorry her own mother did.

Were you this way, Mother? Sorry, Mother. Sorry.

"Miss Kezee? I..."

"Where we going?"

A voice as thin as tissue.

"How you doing, Mother?"

"Cold in here. So cold."

"Here. Just a minute." She rolled down the windows of the van.

Paula wheeled the cart down the aisle of the National with Miss Kezee hung off her right arm. She remembered when the twins were little and shopping was a chore because there were never enough arms for all the babies and carts and purses and groceries. Hanging off her arm, the old woman walked with an almost military step: one foot forward, then bring up the other foot just far enough to meet the first. Then again. A slight warm smile parted her cracked and dusty lips. She could be so sweet sometimes and then immediately so hateful. Dehydration, the doctor had said. It's all chemistry, she said, and it's common. You throw it off and everything goes off. The brain. Everything. She made it sound simple, but here on her arm Paula had ninety-five pounds of the real thing, and there was nothing that doctor could have said to prepare her for the reality of this. She had talked about symptoms and treatments and timelines and prognoses. What she didn't talk about was that being sick was a life—a whole life. She hadn't talked about the eating and the drinking and the sleeping and the bathroom and the clothes and the hair and the everything else a person has to do to survive. She hadn't talked about the funky attitudes or the bad moods or the bad breath or the hurt feelings. She hadn't talked about it because she probably didn't know about it. Come over to my house and find out before you run your big mouth, Paula thought.

She rubbed her arm against the supermarket's cold. The aisles were full of the usual Saturday crowd: farm folks and people like herself up from small northeast Missouri towns to do their weekly errands. At Miss Kezee's pace she cruised slowly between the shelving, crammed to the lip with goods. She plucked from the counters like a robot would, filling her cart with the items on her list.

"What am I supposed to do with you?" she asked Miss Kezee. The old lady sniffed or snorted or made some other disgusting noise. Her face during her quiet times was oddly blank and a little frightened-looking. Her cloudy yellowish eyes wandered and searched. Paula dropped a package of black-eyed peas into the basket.

"What, indeed? Your son—my husband—that's the only reason on earth two people like us would be together. Isn't that right?"

No response from the old woman, a woman who bore so little resemblance to the man she claimed as a son that Paula strained to see any connection between them at all—this tiny person and her tall, solid man, this country-talking old thing and her college-refined gentleman. How could they be from the same planet, let alone the same family. She dragged whomever this was through another aisle.

For whatever reason the National was especially awful today. The farmers and their plain, thick wives carried the loud scents of tobacco and Ivory soap on their cotton work clothes. Their children, one or two of them Paula's students, clambered up and down the aisles and shrieked at their parents, demanding barbecue potato chips and sugar-coated cereals, hair, matted and greasy, that begged combing, fingernails clotted with dirt. A big-breasted mean-looking black woman in a purple tank top grabbed up a toddler and swatted his bottom.

"Boy, I told you to stay with me," she hollered. The baby squealed and threw himself on the floor. "All right, mister," the sister said. She picked the boy up and tossed him into the cart with the beer and soda and crackers. Food stamps fanned from a pouch on the side of her purse.

"I hate coming to the store when they act like this."

"I know what you mean," Paula agreed. Up closer she could see the woman was much younger than she first suspected: twenty-five, maybe.

"You having a little party, too, I see." The woman scanned Paula's basket. The toddler screamed again and received another swat on the bottom.

Paula looked at her groceries and felt embarrassed. You could read a person's whole life in a shopping cart. Bran cereal, tacky magazines, cases of beer, bags of junk food. She rolled her eyes and nodded "Yes."

"You take care now," she said and pushed on down the aisle, anxious to get away. One never knew: it might be contagious. Here, after all, was just the kind of woman her mother warned her she might turn out to be. Loud, fat, and common, swatting her kid's behind in the supermarket, wearing her food stamps as if they were marks of distinction. Paula would never even have a food stamp in her wallet, let alone consider using one. Her family would starve first. One saw these women all the time, these "Gerties" as her mother had called them. Back in Saint Louis her mother would pick them out by the dozens—along Delmar and sitting in Fairground's park. "Look at Gertie over there," she'd say. She'd point to some poor obese woman with uncombed hair, dangling a cigarette and trailing a bunch of kids. She never knew why her mother called them that name. Gertie must have been someone she knew. Paula got the message, though. Here was one of the ways your life could turn out: If you weren't careful, if you messed up, if you didn't do what Mama said.

Mama said be good. Mama said eat healthy foods. Mama said marry a sensible man and raise strong kids. Mama said be responsible, practical, and above all else, Mama said, whatever you do, don't end up like Gertie.

Here she was now, a mama herself, two boys—two half-grown men—that she often didn't have a clue what she was supposed to do with, and a husband who seemed sometimes overwhelmed by the simplest of things—finding a bowl for the leftovers, wringing out a washcloth. And this old woman—somebody else's damn mama, for God's sake. And she has followed every one of Mama's rules, consciously or not—she knows she has. And still, here, she has wound up with all this. And as she looks around the store she imagines many a one of these other women is in some place similar or worse. How could that be? And what was this family stuff supposed to be all about anyway?

She stopped in front of the frozen food case, shook her head, and giggled.

"Some days you just have to throw up your hands," she said. "Chocolate or vanilla ice cream, Mother?"

Wench standing there looking in that glass, laughing like she heard some kind of joke. I got a joke for her. And I'll be the only one laughing. Chocolate, I say. And if you don't like the way things are, you can always leave. I know I plan to. Walking around here sighing and carrying on like she's the only woman ever had the blues. And with all she got and had and gonna get, she better consider herself lucky. Many folks be happy with what she throw out. Oh Mother. Oh I beg your pardon, Mother. I didn't think, girl says. I know you wasn't thinking. Start thinking, get finished up and get me out of this sonnabitch fore I freeze to death. And then the gal take both ice creams anyway in which case why she ask me what I want in the first place? That's what I mean by triflin. I tell her, Wheel this cart on down to that last aisle away from some of these honkies. All the poor white folks in Marion county must be out today. Look at em. Buying all that nasty broccoli and rye bread and mess like that. I get sick of em anymore. That's the truth. Oh Mother, keep your voice down please, girl say. She better watch her step before I show out on her good. Always worried about what folks think. Treating me like I'm ignorant. What she don't know. Watch me. I'll say a word and look at her. Watch her flinch. Free show for me. That's the trouble with these young gals, all of them. They know too much. Been to school for thirty years and still ain't got sense to come in out of the rain. Can't do nothing right. I give her a whole list of things I need. Got my salve I ask her. I need my salve keep some motion in my elbow. Girl don't never get none. Yes Mother, I got some ointment. And I told her to get some Tabasco sauce because everything the girl fix taste like wheat paste. Yes Mother. A honeydew. Yes Mother. A couple of other things, too, but before I can check, girl goes off on me. Mother, I got everything on your list and my list and Al's list and the twin's list. If you need anything, we'll come back Monday night. See. Have the nerve to get short with you. Don't get short with me, girl, I tell her. A person is just trying to be helpful. Any decent person would. I strain myself reaching down in the cart to help out a little bit. Grab a few things and set them up on the belt. Don't you know everything I take out the basket she got to touch too, pretend to be sliding it along the belt, and I think to myself, store could save all that electricity her standing around sliding things along, don't need no conveyor belt. The real reason she got to touch everything is cause I don't do it right. This goes with those, Mother. Put all the Jell-O together, Mother. These are on special, Mother. Me, I drop it all back in the basket. Forget her. Next thing she throwing stuff out as fast as she can like this is some kind of a race. Or so she can get stuff before I do. Hell'll freeze over before I help her again. Me, I keep my eye on the white check-out girl. You can't be too careful with your money. I try and tell my girl something, I say Keep a real close eye on these white folks. They'll cheat you every which way to Sunday. I whisper, but girl says Mother—that Mother mess again, as if I said something nasty, and here I am having borne only one child and it wasn't even her. Shshsh, she says. But she don't fool me. I can see she's watching real good, too. Excuse me, miss, she says. These mixes are on sale. Four for three dollars. The white girl calls over a boy to go check for her. Of course she wasn't gonna trust no Negroes. And then when she's shamed cause my girl is right, she don't say she's sorry or nothing even though she's just about cheated my baby out of a dollar. I'll go over there and beat her ass if you want, I say. Oh Mother, shshsh Mother, and then she try not to laugh. How about these? These on special too. I hold up a can of cocktail nuts. No, ma'am, they are not, the white check-out girl says. I keep on holding up more stuff and asking. Paula, she grabs me round the waist and takes me to sit down. You can't be too careful, I say. I talk loud as I want. Then I hear her apologize to the white girl. Now I'm really hot. I'll turn this joint out if I want to.

And finally, of course, it comes down to public humiliation. On the bright side: everyone thought the old thing was funny and cute. Funny and cute: the way people thought Mammy was funny and cute in "Gone with the Wind." Paula remembered sitting in a repertory movie house in Saint Louis when she was little with her own mother watching Clark Gable and Vivian Leigh. She remembered Hattie McDaniel's gruff shouting. Her bellowing. She remembered that her spine felt as if it had a separate life, as if every nerve in her body were extra receptive to shame, or whatever she felt. She remembered a white man at the popcorn stand hectoring his girlfriend with the Mammy voice. "Do you be or don't you be wantin some popcorn." Some such nonsense. She remembered how her mother had squeezed her hand tightly when Mammy announced that Miss Meli was dead.

Highway N stretched in front of them in a silver gray band across the flood plain. Ahead the old state road rolled up and over some hills, and the river crept by below off to the right, a flash of blue-brown through the thick state forest trees.

"Real pretty along here," Paula said.

"Always has been," answered her mother-in-law. "I always did like this drive."

Miss Kezee hummed to herself, a slow, almost tuneless song that reached now and then a jarring crescendo and then dropped to a quieter drone. Her head beat back and forth in time to the rhythm. She stopped, folded her hands on top of her purse, and looked down at them.

"You wasn't embarrassed back there, was you?"

Paula thought she saw a smile. "No Ma'am," she said.

"Told you bout ma'aming me. Told you I don't like it."

"Sorry."

"You call me Miss Kezee. It's not personal, but it's what I like. Was my husband's name."

"I'll try to remember that." Just like she'd try to remember the rest: that she drank two-percent milk, craved horehound candies, would watch Dan Rather only, and preferred pink bath towels, please.

"I didn't mean to cause you no shame."

"You didn't."

"Yes, I did. You don't need to lie to me. I'm trying to say I'm sorry to you."

The old woman looked down at her purse. She seemed genuinely contrite. She chuckled.

"I do that sometimes. For sport. Charlie called them my

fighting ways. Said I could cuss out every damn navy on the seven seas and have some leftover for the marines, too." She reached over and patted Paula's knee. She pursed her lips. "You do all this running for that boy of mine. Bless your heart." Paula couldn't gauge the sincerity of that. She shrugged. "You make your little deals. You know how that is."

"He's doing pretty good, I guess," the old lady said and then mumbled, "but I wouldn't know." She turned her head to the side and let it loll back against the seat and roll with the rhythm of the road.

"You got tired today, Miss Kezee. I've had you out too long."

"I don't do much going out these days. Arthritis done whipped my ass."

"You did good."

"I wanted to come. Ain't been this way in fifteen years."

"We'll get you a long nap this afternoon. You'll be good and ready for the big party."

"I suppose everybody'll be there. All the important Negroes. You help me fix myself up in case I might catch me a new husband tonight."

After supper she would let down the yellowed hair and run a comb through it with a little oil. She'd fix it into a tidy ball on the back of her head, and she'd suggest the pink floral print that she'd found in Miss Kezee's closet in Saint Paul—the dress with the lace collar. On the hanger it was delicate, yet there was enough color that it didn't seem prissy or old-ladyish.

"We better talk now, baby. You know what I'm saying?"

"Yes, Miss Kezee."

"I love my family. Y'all know that. I love the time I have with y'all."

They were traveling parallel to the river. A string of barges rushed by, dividing the water, pushing the waves to shore. Paula knew the direction of this conversation. She had rehearsed her own lines in her head: now could remember none of them.

"We're happy to have you," Paula said. It was all she could remember. She tried to sound sincere.

"So, this is hard for me say, but I want to go home. To my own home. I need to go home."

"We just want to keep an eye on you here so we don't have to worry so much." She smiled to reassure her.

"I don't want an eye on me. I want to go home. You understand that?"

"You're four hundred miles away from us. You need somebody to look in on you. To help you when you're...out of sorts."

"I got my neighbors. The minister. A little nurse lady looks in on me now and then." Her bottom lip pulled at the top one. She leaned into Paula as if to emphasize certain words. She pointed north with one finger. "That's my home. Me and Charlie's home. You got no right."

Paula said nothing.

"I don't want to stay in that house. I can't stay in that man's house. I swore I wouldn't and I won't. You've got to help me. Will you help me?"

They crested the hill into River Ridge.

"Take it easy, please."

"You got to promise to help me."

"I promise, Mother. I do."

"I've gotta go. Oh, Charlie." Her head nodded forward and she fell into sleep.

A white sky like blue. Fish big as a skillet. I love you, Charlie. Love you like I ain't loved no man. Flashes of river through the trees. Goblins. Cold air. Hot air. Cold air. Cold air. Biscuits. Watermelon. Ivory soap. Tobacco. "This on sale too, ain't it?" Love you more than I love any man. "Come back to Saint Paul, Nobi." What about my boy? Al's woman. Paula. Al's boys. Twins. My grandsons. "Boy's grown, Nobi. He'll take care of himself." A white hot sun shining, water flowing slow. "Let's make a vow to the river we'll be together always." He treats me so bad, Charlie. He's mean to me. Here we are home. You awake now, Mother? I'll get you settled before I unload. Xenobia, I want you out of my house. I'll kill you before I let you go with him. Let me go, A. B.

"You've got to help me."

"I'll help you up the steps, Mother. Take your time."

"You're hurting me, A. B."

"I'm not A. B. This is Paula."

Al's wife.

Miss Kezee collapsed against Paula's arm on the top step of the wide wooden porch.

"I swore to that man. Swore I'd never set foot here. Look where I am."

She sat the old lady down on the porch swing. With her arms around Paula, Miss Kezee sobbed into Paula's chest.

"You're safe here now. We'll take care of you."

"Will you? Can you?"

Paula saw in her mother-in-law's face fear and anger and doubt, but something more than that, too. A dare: almost as if the old lady were willing her to fail.

"Yes," Paula said. "Yes, I can."

2

WHEN I GET OVER TO WALTER'S I'M ALREADY LATE. It's been one of those days where you are always behind the hundred-year-old driver who is going right down the middle of the street. Or whenever it is your turn to check out, that's the time they change the register tape. I'm not in any particular mood for foolishness.

Just my luck Walter and Berneice are into the middle of another one of their—I don't know what to call them. They have these things. When the moon is full or when the wind blows from a certain direction or when you couldn't even begin to guess when, you shouldn't go into that house without a suit of armor and some earplugs. Like a fool, I figure I'll just pop in and pick up the copy for the fliers and pop out.

So I come in the door and the first thing Berneice says to me is that I better get in there and tell that big ass nigger something. She shoves me down the hall towards their kitchen. I say "yes, ma'am," cause a person doesn't mess with Berneice when she is carrying on. Not with her temper, and not with her butt being every bit as big as Walter's, if not bigger.

I meet him coming back down the hall—right on by he goes. I might as well not have even been there. He's saying, "And here's another thing: who was it last time took the car all the way to Springfield, Illinois, didn't have but a quart of oil in it, almost burned up the damn engine, and then come back complaining because the car got all hot on her? Who was that?"

He comes charging back down the hall. He knows what's coming, and tries to get on the other side of me before it gets here. Before we get to the kitchen, here it comes.

"Look," she says. "Bring up the goddamn car one more time see don't I take down one of these skillets and knock you across your nappy head with it." She's reaching around me grabbing at Walter and he's laughing and pushing me between them.

"I'll knock both y'all out," she says. And she would too, her being only an inch or so shorter than me and with a good twenty-five pound advantage. She stomps out.

"You better take your big self someplace," Walter yells at her back.

I tell him I just came to get the copy.

"Damn these women," he says. He goes back to the sandwich makings he's got laid out on the counter.

I tell him, "Nigger, I told you you better slow up some on this food."

He layers on another slice of cheese and gives me the finger.

"Come on sit down over here," he says.

"I have to go," I say, and I do, what with everything needs to be ready for the party, and Paula already testy. Berneice comes back in spinning her car keys on her finger.

She says, "Nigger, my forty-five dollars better be stacked up nice and neat on that table when I get back, or the Lord help you."

He waves his hand at her. "Best get out my face," he mumbles through a mouthful of sandwich.

"I'll be back," she says, sashaying out.

"She can kiss my forty-five dollar ass," Walter says, taking another huge bite out of his sandwich.

These two can really carry on, and I tell him that. He says it ain't nothing, and I guess he would say that cause that was what it was like at his parents' house when we were kids. At Walter and them's house a free floor show came with dinner, and it didn't cost you extra, either. Survival around that kitchen was learning how to get your two cents in and then how to get out with your person and your dignity still intact. First of all you had to talk loud enough to be heard. Everybody in that house talked at the top of their voice, and at the same time, too. Nobody showed mercy, and if shouting wasn't good enough, you stood up and shouted, and if the conversation was going good, they would all be standing up, hands on their hips, full-throttled voices, talking at the same time. Me, I didn't do so well over there. I didn't know how to play the game. I was afraid if I said anything at all I would hear the standard "sit down, fool," which is what they said to Walter all the time. I didn't know that the first few times out, mom and dad were there to help you. They'd say things like, "listen to the boy," and "out of the mouth of babes." I didn't know that you got just enough support, until you were expected to hold your own and get out there with the big kids and take your lumps.

None of this went on at our house. At our house, children (me) didn't say anything at all, not unless you were asked to. No one spoke. My mother and father had nothing to say to each other or to me. I had all these ideas about what a family was supposed to be like. From watching TV and from being over at Walter's house. And I remember always having this vague sense of disappointment that we were not like the Cleavers. When I turned nine I remember my parents trying to throw me this birthday party. Actually, it was just the two of them and me. I remember my mother in the kitchen fussing around putting candles on a cake she'd baked and my father sitting in a chair telling her what she was and wasn't doing properly. It wasn't so much an argument as it was a man giving all kinds of unnecessary and not particularly helpful advice on how to decorate a cake to a woman who might have been dead from the expression on her face. When it came time to light the candles and sing the song, they were both cranky, and me: I was looking to find out if a big surprise was coming. None did. We sat there and ate the gummy yellow cake, looking at it so as to avoid looking at each other. A lot of times we were more like a painting of a family than anything else. Like a scene out of one of those beige Scandinavian films where the only sound is the ticking of a clock.

Thinking back I know that it was less a lack of color than that there was a cloud of unhappiness there. I always felt strangled when I was around them.

That has been over a long time now. My father died almost twenty years ago, suddenly, in a car accident. I was finishing graduate school and trying to figure out what to do with my life. My mother called to tell me he was gone and I remember the strangely detached and neutral tone she employed. She might have been reporting on the stage of the river or on the number of crows nesting in the trees out back. The news hit me hard at first.

I would like to believe that my mother was sad he was gone. I would like to believe that she salvaged something from their life together—some fond memories of her years here on the river and of whatever made her fall in love with him in the first place. Probably not. She left River Ridge almost immediately. She has mentioned his name to me only once since the funeral.

Once, up at her house in Saint Paul, she sat with me outside on the porch, and she asked me did I blame her for his death. I asked her why she would think such a thing.

"I was gonna leave him. He was mad." That was her explanation.

I reassured her, or I tried to. I told her that no, I didn't think it was anyone's fault. I remember she had that kind of look people get on their face when someone tries to keep them calm during tornado warnings—that rather childlike and simple look, as if you might just by your words convince them the world was flat and the moon made of green cheese.

"Good," she said, and she's never said anything more.

She has stayed away from here since his death. Afraid of his ghost, no doubt. Paula and I have made their house our house now and filled it with our lives and our boys. There are no ghosts. If anything, there is only the remote everyday evil that each of us carries: our foul attitudes and nasty moods. We try to keep it at bay.

"Where's my stuff?" I say to Walter, eager to be on my way.

"Ah, nigger, not you too. I'm sitting here trying to enjoy me a little snack and I got this one wanting this, and that one wanting that. A man couldn't catch a break to save his life."

"Nigger, all you do all day long is snack. That's why your butt weighs three hundred fifty pounds. All I'm asking you to do is get up off it and hand me my paper. I've got to go."

He tells me to hang on a second and then proceeds to tell me about how the folks he's been talking to tell him the election is getting too close to call. "They say Tyrone Turner's got all them old club men sewed up, but I think we can sway a few."

Bless his big self, Walter loves this political shit, especially all the maneuvering and scheming and gossip—the crap I'd just as soon do without. He would be out there running himself, except every time he gets up in front of folks he takes to stammering and stumbling over his words. Black folks, we'll put up with a lot from our leaders, but you got to talk good, that's for sure. I wouldn't really be in it at all if I didn't feel like I was burning out on the newspaper business, the small-town businessman business. It's something different, that's for sure.

"You really think we got a chance?" I ask.

Walter shrugs, inhaling the last bite of sandwich. "Hard to

say, these folks around here. You know how they is: One day they for you, the next day not. We got as good a chance as the next one."

"We. Nigger, what are you running for?"

"Oh. Now. Don't let me come over there and put a Berneice on your ass."

"I'll be in Saint Louis before you hauled your fat behind off that chair."

Before I even move he is up and got me in a head lock and is mashing all three hundred and fifty pounds on top of me.

"Saint Louis, huh?"

"Get off me."

"You just a pretty face. You know that? Say it. Say it."

"All right," I say. "Off me." The big fool. As big and as kind and as gentle as he could be. Knows this political shit—could be off running Jeff City, or Washington, for that matter. Hiding out here on the river. With me and the rest of us, I guess.

"Yeah, that's right. You getting slow and weak, old man."

"Fuck you," I say, though I know there's some truth in it. I am changing and my body is doing some interesting shit. Pains here and there, and yesterday I saw three more silver strands on my head. It turns out all those jokes about gray hair became personal and mean spirited and less funny. That's me they're talking about. I hardly eat half of what I used to and still I gain weight. Pretty soon I'll be Walter's size.

It's more than that, though—it's the . . . substance of my life, I guess you'd call it—that's changing. (What the hell is that? What is the substance of a person's life?) I know it's about more than my body and more than what I do everyday. And though I can't be completely precise, I know something is changing, and I know I don't feel the same way I did when I was thirty or when I was thirty-five. Where did the words go for this feeling? Maybe they were back there around Walter's table when we was growing up, there on the days when I was not there, when I was at home cutting up my meat, chewing, bathed in my parents' silent contempt for one another. Maybe somewhere in all the words that were never said around that table were the words to talk about what is happening to me now. What I can say is that it feels to me sometimes as if someone has taken my house and ever so slightly turned it on its foundation. My perspective has changed: I have a different view. I am scared and excited and distracted all at the same time, and I cannot wait to see what's going to happen next . . . that's it: the feeling that something is about to happen.

And frisky, too, I've been feeling. Like I want to make some trouble. Like I'm bored or something. We're almost forty, Walter and me. And his big ass is like when we were fourteen—carefree and as agile and efficient as hell when he wants to be.

"Wait right there," he says, and he finds me the copy, over in the family room at his desk. It's OK, I guess. A list of my so-called accomplishments and a list of promises. Looks like bullshit to me.

"Slap that picture of you and your woman and the kids right here on top. Print in cream or light blue. Got that?"

Walter uses his tone that makes me feel as if he thinks I am maybe twelve and he is the school newspaper editor talking to some eager but thick reporter. But I don't get into it with him. He has, out of that makeshift office and with these slapdash forms, elected a half-dozen representatives and almost all the local folks up and down the river here.

And I'm getting out of here before Berneice gets back. I didn't see forty-five dollars on the table, nor any sign it is forthcoming.

I stop by the paper to do the printing and then come on up here to the house.

Which made me wish I'd stayed at Walter's.

3

*M*ISS KEZEE DOZED QUIETLY. PAULA HAD COAXED HER up to the bed, helped her into her nightgown, and covered her with a quilt. She sat by the bed while the old lady trembled herself to sleep.

Poor old thing. So weak and frail. So frightened of everything. So alone. Paula had wanted to bring her here many times—for a visit, or to live, even. She'd thought about her often, all by herself up there in that house in Saint Paul. But she had refused to come, even for a short stay. Al had told her that his mother hated this house. He'd told her about his parents' terrible life together and about his father's death and his mother's guilt about it, but Paula never really bought it. How could you hate a house, especially a beautiful old home like this? And why would the woman feel guilty? The man died, and from what Paula understood she was well rid of him, glad to get on with her own life. Whatever, this was a woman with a story, and she'd like to hear it directly from the source. Maybe she'd get something out of the old girl—some tidbit, an anecdote or two. She'd ask her again. Before the party, maybe.

The party. Damn this party. The last thing she wanted to be doing was fussing around with some party, particularly a party for a bunch of politicians. She didn't even know most of the invitees, and the ones she did know she didn't particularly like. Oily, obnoxious louts. In her house.

She and Al didn't throw a lot of parties—except birthday

parties for the twins, which didn't count because all you did was run around wiping up messes and never got to talk to anyone, and lately she'd taken to the field trip-type number where you load a bunch of boys into the car and take them someplace like Six Flags and let them go. She certainly never had this kind of party—strangers standing around making small talk. This was her mother's kind of party: a party with a purpose. There had to be food around in little silver bowls for people to nibble on; a full bar, enough to support plenty of two-fisted drinking; quiet jazz playing. And a hostess to circulate. Circulate! her mother always said, and she would make a sweeping motion with her hands when she ordered Paula to get out there and get into action. Circulate! It meant moving from group to group and insinuating yourself into other people's conversations. It meant complimenting the women's dresses and the men's ties. It meant asking after other people's children. Circulate! her mother said. The same thing viruses and ugly rumors did. If someone had told her she would be circulating right here in her own house, she would have asked if they had lost their mind. Yet here she was, preparing, trying to remember her mother's prescription for a successful evening.

Number one, of course, was a clean house.

The Johnsons never had a clean house and Paula didn't give a damn. She didn't like housework: she didn't know anyone who did, except for maybe Walter's wife Berneice, who, if she *didn't* like it, at the very least made some sort of fetish out of it. You could eat off the floors over there, though God help you should you spill a crumb on her white rugs. She was worse than Paula's mother, what with all of her cleansers and schedules and routines.

Paula herself did as little cleaning as she could get away with, and apparently her family didn't mind. Al noticed only what particularly affected him, like when he couldn't find the mate to a sock or when he was thirsty and there weren't any more clean glasses in the cupboard. He'd grouse for a few minutes and then rinse something nasty out of the sink and use that. Maybe he'd load the dishwasher, if he didn't have anything else on his mind—but probably not. Tommy, well he was part hog—one of those children who liked a mess, who liked to wallow around in his own clutter. He reminded her of the cartoon character who trailed a cloud of dust, except in his case he trailed a cloud of eleven-year-old boy detritus: candy wrappers, G.I. Joe parts, cassette tape containers, mitts, balls, homemade swords. Once, he'd walked by her classroom trailing an old sock out of one pants leg. "I thought these pants felt funny," was his only comment. She remembered hoping her colleagues hadn't noticed. They already thought she was different, but to be labeled an incompetent mother to boot . . . Tim was the only fastidious one, and where he got that trait was anyone's guess. He would pick up after all three of them if he got disgusted enough. Now and then he would scold them about how disorganized things were. "People should take care of their own crap," he would say, hauling another bundle of everyone's dirty laundry to the basement. He'd wash them, too, but then afterwards, and for what Paula thought was spite, he would put his own things in the dryer and leave the rest balled up wet in the washer. Could she blame him? His idea about taking care of your own crap sounded like a good plan to her. She kept her bedroom tidy, cleaned up the kitchen on her nights to cook. Occasionally, she and Al got inspired and spent a day spring cleaning. Scrub, brush, and wax or vacuum every square inch of the house, floor to ceiling. She actually sometimes enjoyed her mother's favorite task: taking the dust mop and "squaring off those ceiling corners." It was one of those instant-results deals. Between times, there was a teenage girl, Charlotte from around the corner, who came in once in a while to baby-sit and to do some dusting and ironing, during the school year especially, when things were particularly hectic.

The truth was, Paula liked the house this way. She liked the clutter: the piles and layers gave the impression people actually lived here, unlike her mother's house, which always looked as if she ought to separate the riff-raff from the furniture with velvet ropes, the way museums did. And it wasn't call-the-department-of-health time: they wiped down the toilets often enough, and didn't leave food out to attract insects. But they sure weren't winning any good housekeeping medals.

She straightened up the parlor first—the large square space they called a parlor because that's what they called rooms like it on those old TV westerns. She hated this room. She hadn't done a thing to it, decorating-wise, since she moved into the house. Cave-like, it was cool and dark, with heavy furniture, thick draperies, and oriental rugs. Family photos clustered on the tabletops and mantelpiece: Johnsons, Fullers, the new Johnsons. There was a picture of Miss Kezee, or Mrs. Johnson, she was then, her arms around a portly smiling man. A. B. Johnson had been a darker, more sharply featured version of his son. Mrs. Johnson is drawn into her husband—he has her pulled up next to him as if she is some sort of stuffed toy he has captured at the state fair. She looks pained. Her smile, if she was smiling, is defiant and wry. There, in another photo, was a young Miss Kezee. Paula thinks she was Miss Taylor back then, and in the picture she is haughty and beautiful, the photo a half profile. Her hair was pressed and waved, tucked around her far shoulder. The picture was hand tinted with unnatural skin tones, and though her head turns away, her eyes meet the camera coquettishly and with a touch of suspicion. It was the most distinguished thing in the room, which was appropriate, because Paula always thought of this room as belonging to her mother-in-law. When she first came to the house she was charmed by this space, and she and Al had decided to leave it just the way his mother had, in all its antique, turn-of-the-century splendor. More recently, though, she felt completely unable to inhabit it, to make it in any way her own. She'd tried all kinds of things; she'd added pictures of her own family: there were her parents, there were her children, there was she. They looked as out of place there as she always felt whenever she entered. She read in here, wrote lesson plans, or just sat, as if somehow, by her mere presence, she could take possession. Still, the chairs would not fit her back and the colors did not please her eye. The previous winter she and Al had talked about doing the room over. "I don't like living in an antique store," she had said, but they had finally decided not to. The old things were too valuable to just dispose of, and there wasn't anywhere else in the house to put them. If she wanted comfort, she had her own living room across the entry: an airy and open space full of soft, welcoming chairs and sofas, the kind of furniture you could throw yourself on without the least bit of guilt. The parlor would remain Miss Kezee's.

Wiping along the window sill she was reminded how many ways the room was similar to Miss Kezee's house in Saint Paul: the preference for antiques (or at least replicas of antiques), the cumbersome window treatments, the dark, textured wallpapers. She ran the dust rag along the high and round dark wooden frame of a balloon-back chair, careful to whisk the dust away from the padded back and seat. This exact chair was in Saint Paul, though the one she dusted now was the real thing, purchased when such things went begging as junk up and down the River Road. The Saint Paul chair was a replica, a velvet back that was really Scotchguarded velour, and carved legs and arms molded from wood scraps that scratched easily to reveal a rough and ricey grain.

It was eerie visiting that other house. Though smaller and a frame house, not brick, inside were the same smells, mimicking this house the way an echo mimics a voice. They were the same, and yet not quite the same. One was diminished, somehow, flatter and mocking.

Neither house was like the other house Paula had known. Her mother had never embraced antiques, neither would she care to repeat the same style of furniture from one era to another. In the Saint Louis West End home she grew up in, she had endured Danish Modern, Mediterranean, Contemporary, Scandinavian, and various conglomerations. Her mother kept a lot of Saint Louis furniture merchants happy: she was never satisfied. Remnants of that house were relocated here, each a quirky surprise. There was the low, loose-cushioned chair with scratchy orange upholstery and rounded wooden arms, the one whose leather straps held the cushions, but just barely. There was the occasional table, a dark, oak-stained monster encrusted with carved grape vines and Corinthian columns. There was the glass cube her mother used as a plant stand. Paula had turned it over and used it for umbrellas.

She sat down on the parlor sofa, the one whose back arched away from you and forced you to lean back to relax your shoulders. You had to take care to catch the cushions at just the right spot with your butt. The stuffing rolled like waves, and the crests gave you a nasty poke. At least the Saint Paul version had a soft foam-rubber seat.

She worried about the house in Saint Paul. There was no one to house-sit, and there hadn't been time to close it up properly. Ms. Cole, the neighbor woman, said she'd look after things. She seemed responsible enough, though Miss Kezee called her an ignorant lazy slut. (But then she called a lot of people that, and worse names, too.)

Ms. Cole was the person who had called up in the first place to tell them how sick Paula's mother-in-law had become.

"I hadn't seen her in a couple days," the woman said, "so I let myself in to check on her. She been up in that bed for days."

Paula had asked if she was feverish.

"She don't look good at all. She's not eating, and she won't let me call her doctor. You know how she gets. I figured I better call you, since it seems like she don't even know who I am half the time."

She thanked the woman and told her she'd do something. The phone call had come back at the beginning of the mayoral campaign. Al and Walter were spending the days as exuberantly as school kids, planning slogans and posters. Al breezed in the door that night five feet off the ground with excitement.

"Who wants to be the first to give the future mayor of River Ridge a kiss." Tommy and Tim tackled him at the knees: Al fought back, pushing at the tops of their heads until they all collapsed in a heap.

"One of these days you'll knock this house down," Paula said. She beckoned Al to the kitchen with a finger. "I need to see you. In here."

He popped open a beer, plopped down a chair and put his feet up in another. The kitchen smelled of the onions she was frying with pork chops for supper.

"What's up?" he asked.

"Your mama's neighbor called from up in Saint Paul. Said Mother has been sick."

"She go to the hospital?"

"She's being stubborn."

"She's herself then. Don't you think?" He sipped at the beer and scanned the front page of the previous day's *Post Dispatch*.

She turned the chops. "Might be serious. Ms. Cole says she's bedridden. Says she's been disoriented."

"Hmm," Al said. He was engrossed in some article, probably

deciding whether to pick it up in the next edition of his own paper.

Paula pulled the paper from in front of his face with the fork she'd been using to turn the chops. A river of hot grease snaked down the page. "What should we do?" she asked.

"I don't know. Give her a couple of days, I guess. See how she feels."

She figured *fine,* that was that. It was his dear mama and she'd done her part. This, after all, was a woman she hardly knew. Miss Kezee had never returned to River Ridge, not since Paula married Al, and except for two brief visits they'd made to Saint Paul, their contact had been cordialities exchanged during the monthly calls between mother and son. "How are you, Mother? I'll put him right on. Nice talking to you, too."

Fine. If that's the way he felt.

Yet, all through dinner, as her sons and her husband ate—greedily, as usual, she thought—the pork chops and thick mashed potatoes, and after supper, when the boys played Nintendo and watched MTV, and as Al hammered away at his computer, she would look up from her dinner or from the stack of spelling papers she was marking and she would catch a shading of skin, the line of a nostril that reminded her of the old woman in Minnesota. She could be dying right now—dead right now. And here they sat: just another family, puttering away on a normal evening, doing everything and nothing. As if there were nothing that needed doing.

That night in bed she lay awake on top of the covers. She imagined she could see the ceiling fan turning, but the room was too dark for that. She concentrated on the almost inaudible sound of the blades and on the odd contrast between Al's nasal breathing and the soft whooshing of air.

She thought about her own mother. Gone for years now,

and she still remembered the promises she made to herself of what should be done, tomorrow.

Nobody in this house was helpless or stupid. They had learned a thing or two along the way. There had been sacrifices and a loss here and there. There was love—often—and compassion, too. They were better people than this. Someone was in trouble. Someone in their family needed someone. Needed them. Now.

"This is wrong," she'd said out loud.

In the morning she arranged for a short leave of absence, made lesson plans for a week, and flew to Saint Paul.

Even when the parlor had been vacuumed and dusted, still, to her eye, it looked dirty. She aimed the nozzle attachment toward the center of the room as if it might suck up the unrecalcitrant dust.

"A dump is a dump," she said.

2:30. To the living room, always easier to clean. They were never still enough in this room to allow the dust to settle. Mostly just clutter and crumbs here.

The violent chorus of a hand bell sounded from the second floor.

"Girl! Girl!" It was Miss Kezee.

Paula rolled her eyes and started carrying a box of junk up to the boys' room.

"Girl! Girl!"

"I'm on my way, Mother."

She set the box in the middle of the floor, between the beds, where she knew they could not ignore it.

"Girl! Girl!"

She checked herself for the right attitude before entering the guest room.

"I see you're awake. Feeling better, I hope."

"I been ringing this goddamn bell since Christ died. My arm's about to fall off. You been laying on your ass watching the baseball game, ain't you?"

"I was vacuuming. I didn't hear . . ."

"About nine hundred degrees up in here and I'm all covered up. You must want to cook me. A person would die before they got a cool drink."

Paula bit her lip, folded down the comforter and lay it across the rocker.

"Not that a person don't expect bad treatment in jail. Lips so parched I can't even swallow."

"How about some ice tea?"

"And someone like me might want to see a baseball game, too. But don't nobody never think about that."

Paula clicked on the portable set before she went down for the tea.

The cab from the Twin Cities airport dropped her at the house next door to 888 Iglehart. The houses on this block were identical: frame houses with the same dormer window in front. Miss Kezee's was blue, this one was brown. Paula had decided to talk to the neighbor first, but the truth was she was a coward. She didn't want to face Miss Kezee alone. If she was sick, bad enough, but, worse, what if she was well? How would she explain this impulsive visit? As long as she'd known her she'd said less than one hundred words to this woman.

Ms. Cole praised the Lord, relieved at Paula's arrival.

"I knew you'd come," she'd said.

She sat with the woman in her kitchen and listened to the struggles of the last few days. This Cole woman was larger than Paula imagined her. Her hair had once been pressed and styled, though today tangled clusters stood around her head and she wore a blouse and skirt that needed washing. She might be another "Gertie," but there was something about her that wouldn't let Paula lump her in with that lot.

"Excuse this mess," she said. "I got a lot of kids." When she asked her how many, the woman said eight.

Paula shook her head in sympathy. Too many. Another black woman working herself to death over a house full of babies. Even so, here in the kitchen, things seemed to be in fairly good shape. There were lists of tasks to be done on a chalkboard above a counter and names attached to each one. A magnetized clip on the refrigerator door held coupons. The jumble of breakfast dishes by the sink was the only mess that Paula could see. That, and Miss Cole's unkempt appearance. After 10:00 A.M. and she obviously had yet to do any sort of grooming.

There didn't seem to be any sign of a man around here—none of the things you would look for: no workboots or tool kits, no denim jackets on the hooks by the door. Eight kids: must have been men around at some point. She always wondered how this kind did it—how they got and kept the men in their lives. She figured every once in a while they must fix up nice, go out somewhere, and do something to reel them in. She couldn't guess what this Cole woman did. She didn't seem the type to go wild and pick up a lot of different men. She wouldn't walk herself up and down the streets like those Gerties did and drag in whatever followed her home. She seemed truly shamed at the way she looked. She was probably presentable when she tried.

"I wished I'd known you were coming this morning," she said.

Paula apologized. She knew the feeling of being caught off guard herself, surprised and exposed when she wasn't at her best.

Miss Cole told her about finding Miss Kezee "up over there" and then about how she'd been nursing her for a day or two.

"She's a sweet little thing, that mama of yours. We all love her a lot up here."

"She's my husband's mama, actually. And she is quite a woman," Paula said, but just to make conversation. What she knew about her mother-in-law would not fill the side panel of a cereal box.

"She has always been there for me. For the other ladies up in here, too. You know, if I have to run out, she will sit with the kids for an hour. She watches your house. Her husband, well, he was so active in everything before he passed. I felt so bad for her when he died."

"How long did you say she's been sick?" Paula asked. Al called his mother every month or so. He'd always said she sounded good.

"She been fading a little bit since the mister died, but that's been, what, two years now?"

Paula nodded to agree.

Miss Cole waved away a fly from the butter dish. "These last six months she's been very low and seems like she gets cranky with you. We been taking her soup and doing some cleaning for her. Just looking out, you know."

"We appreciate that. You don't know how much."

"Well, she's a good old soul. We got to see to our own, don't we?"

"That's true," Paula concurred, though she didn't know whether the idea was something she really agreed with. A rather simple way of looking at life, she thought.

"I hope somebody be looking after my mama if I couldn't. That's all I know."

Paula closed her eyes. She remembered that at some point she had had that same thought.

The bell clanged again, this time dully, like the slow striking of an anvil in a forge.

My bright idea: put a bell by her bed in case she needs anything. She filled a tall glass with ice cubes and tea and then stirred in three spoons of sugar—"you never make it sweet enough." This ought to keep her.

The clanging of the bell continued.

In the room Miss Kezee lay back on the bed, staring at the TV and mechanically raising and lowering the bell. She saw Paula and dropped it.

"Oh, Paula, you made me some tea. That's sweet of you." She sat herself up slowly and took a sip while Paula held the glass. "You made it the way I like."

"Lots of sugar."

She cupped her hands around the glass. "I can get it now."

"Sure?" She helped her set the glass on the night stand. "It'll be right there for you."

"What's happnin in this game?" Miss Kezee asked.

"I don't know. I haven't been watching."

"I used to follow the Cardinals all the time. Always catched the game on KMOX. Not at all since we moved up to Saint Paul."

Paula turned off the set. She pulled at the draperies and at the bedclothes. She played at rearranging the night stand—doing nothing, really. She was unsure what was comfortable, proper, needed. There was so much more to be done downstairs.

"Will you be OK for a few minutes?"

"Where's Junior?"

Miss Kezee called Al "Junior." Probably all his life, and he hated it. She patted the bed to indicate Paula was to sit.

"Out campaigning."

She patted the bed again. "Come on."

Paula sat and tried to forget the evaporating time.

"Campaigning, huh. I never figured Junior'd be one for politics. He wasn't ever too interested in that in school."

"This is something he and that Walter cooked up. They say it's like a fever you get, and he's got it bad. He's full of all kinds of ideas these days. I can't keep up with him."

"Crazy ideas, if you ask me." Miss Kezee took a sip of tea, sucked up a piece of ice, and chewed. "What's this . . . corporation . . . consideration . . . whatever mess?"

"Al wants to dissolve River Ridge and reincorporate a new town along with Cleta and Oak Grove."

Miss Kezee watched her while she spoke, her eyes drinking in the nuances. Paula could see in her hollowed cheeks the pieces of ice cubes rolling around.

"Sounds bad. Sounds like a bad deal."

"Al and Walter did all this research. They say it's the best thing for us."

"Don't sound right. Them's white towns, you know. Lots of these folks around here won't go for that."

"Al thinks they will."

"His daddy was the mayor, you know. A no-good, crooked son-of-a-bitch." Miss Kezee fake spat.

Paula laughed.

"That's what he was. Hmmph. I hated them days."

"Politics seems to get you excited."

"Depends on what you mean. If you mean folks having their say, being listened to, count me in. One thing about me is, I'm always gonna have my say."

"Takes a lot of work to keep on top of the issues."

"Ain't nobody said you have to know nothing to get out there and vote. You got a right. Now me, I ask all the questions I want. Then I pick the one looks like he's the least crooked." She picked up the glass and took a long drink.

Paula saw her opening. Smoothing the blanket with her hand, she asked, "Mother, tell me why you hate this house so much. Tell me about Al's dad."

"Don't you worry about that."

"You said you hated those days. You were . . ."

Miss Kezee raised her hand and closed her eyes. She shook her head, almost imperceptibly. "I'm a little tired now," she said.

"Can I get you something else? You hungry?"

She lay back and waved her hand. Paula rearranged the pillows and covers. She watched her as she slept again. Or pretended to.

The house in Saint Paul had an unoccupied feel to it. The air was stiff and musty, as if it had not been disturbed for ages.

Miss Cole shouted up the stairs, "Miss Kezee, baby," and to Paula she said, "She's sleeping a lot these days. Go on up."

In the large front bedroom Miss Kezee lay curled on her side, swallowed by the king-sized bed and by various blankets and sheets and towels.

"I brought you a visitor. Looka here."

"Hello, Mother Kezee," Paula said. She gave her a kiss on her hot, dry cheek.

She shook Paula's hand with her trembly, weak fingers.

"She's so frail. How are you feeling, Mother?"

A thick exhalation served as response.

"Has the doctor been here?" Paula asked.

Miss Cole answered, "She said she didn't want no doctor. I wasn't sure what to do, so I called you all."

David Haynes   39

"It's OK. She's too sick to know what she wants. I don't even know if she has a regular doctor."

"She sees Dr. Crawford up at Central Medical. I took her in a cab back in the fall. I'll find the number for you."

Paula rubbed the fragile, cold hand. Miss Kezee sighed and inhaled. She exhaled with a rattle, mumbled "Charlie" and "Throw it back" and "I'm comin."

The room was close, the air mentholated and stale. Tissues smothered the dresser tops and dotted the floors. The bedding was sour: she was sure it had been soiled.

"Here's Dr. Crawford's number. I got to be running. Kids'll be comin in."

"Miss Cole, I don't know how . . ." A hug rescued her from her inadequate words.

"We're right next door."

After arranging for the doctor to come by, she set to straightening the room. This wasn't supposed to happen. Nothing in all the home-ec classes and psychology classes and education classes and women's magazines, nothing she remembered told her what to do about a sick old woman— especially a sick old woman who was four hundred miles away. What should she do with her? Leave her here for the neighbors to see after? She wasn't Joanne Cole's mama. And what if there hadn't been a Joanne Cole? Maybe looking after her was the government's problem. Yes, maybe. But the government didn't seem to know about her, up in this room, dirty and sick. They could pay strangers to look after her. As if looking after your old relatives was just another job to give away. Like valet parking or washing windows. And what if there was no money? What if no one knew you were there?

I knew you were there, Mother. I did.

This was all wrong. All wrong. Forget about fair and

convenient and adequate and modern. Talk about right and wrong. This woman was sick and alone. That was wrong.

"I'll get you some more water," Paula said, but then, startled, she dropped the pitcher and froze.

"Goddamn thieves, I caught you this time. Get out of my house before I blow your muthafuckin brains out." Miss Kezee sat up in bed with a small revolver pointed at Paula's head.

Still no Al. She shook nuts into several bowls and filled others with sesame sticks and mints. This damn party. Walter said it was a good move—old big-bellied Walter Dawkins. Those two thought they were just the sort of enlightened, progressive young black men this town had been waiting for, with their college degrees, nice manners, and proper talk. Most of the other young folks and all the old ladies agreed, but Paula knew that the older men thought them arrogant, self-important troublemakers, full of crazy ideas. The party was one of those ideas. Bring together the old-timers, the county commissioners, the town councilmen, and the school board to spend an evening with the new blood. She didn't know how this was supposed to work. Maybe Al was supposed to dazzle them with fancy patter. The cool drinks and the hot conversation were supposed to turn heads, make them listen to reason. In suburban Saint Louis, maybe, but in River Ridge? In this backward backwater? But, what did she know. She'd put on a pretty dress, smile, and think about however she and Al would even the score for all this extra effort.

Ten to four. She grabbed her purse, her keys, and headed for the door. She remembered: she'd have to see to Miss Kezee first. That had become the newest rule of the house: see to Miss Kezee first. Before breakfast, on her prep period, during lunch, before fixing supper in the evening: see to Miss Kezee.

She called softly to her mother-in-law. There was no response. "I'll be back with the boys in a few minutes. Just rest." That would have to do. Maybe she'd just sleep. Maybe she'd wake and read the *Essence* or the *Jet* left there on the nightstand. Maybe she'd roll from the bed, hamstrung and helpless in a tangle of sheets and blankets, calling to no one, or, missing a step, maybe she'd tumble like a sack of soiled laundry down into the entry, breaking all her old bones. Maybe in a gentle breath she'd just pass.

"I'll be right back."

Doctor Crawford had discovered a low-grade fever and suspected a waning infection of some kind. She would have to run some tests. Miss Kezee was dehydrated, she said, and she was worried at her state of mind.

"I remember the old sister as being a bit more feisty."

Paula couldn't imagine Miss Kezee choosing to go to a woman doctor, even if she was black. She seemed familiar with the case, though Paula still felt unsure. These doctors had a way of performing on cue, and this woman seemed to be the smooth sort—more like a car saleswoman than a physician. And all these medical types knew how to put on the show.

"She's been in and out," Paula said and snorted a little laugh. "She pulled a gun on me." Paula had thought twice before telling about the pistol. She would never have told that sort of thing about her own mother. It seemed so niggerish. She went ahead and told it, though, one black woman to another, figuring maybe she would understand.

"That's our Miss Kezee," Dr. Crawford said. "Xenobia, I want you to cough a little more for me." She listened to her chest again. "Tell me what you mean by in and out.'"

"Who that girl you brought in here?"

"That's your daughter-in-law," the doctor shouted. As far

as Paula knew, Miss Kezee had never been hard of hearing. Dr. Crawford kept making faces and signs at Paula as if the two of them were in on some sort of joke. "She pulled a gun on you, huh."

"Yes, and then passed right out again."

"That a nurse you got with you?"

Paula shook her head. "It's Paula, Mother. Al's wife. One minute she's fine, the next minute she seems so weak."

Dr. Crawford gathered her things back into her bag. "Sounds like she could have had a small stroke. She's weaker on her left side. She's a tough old gal. She's fightin hard. At her age a lot can happen."

"She's only seventy-five."

"I heard eighty-two," the doctor said. She seemed surprised, made a little note in her chart. "No matter. With old age the numbers make less and less difference. Some go down in their sixties, others play along well into the nineties. There are no rules. She'll be fine. I've got an antibiotic there for her, and I want you to pump all the fluids you can into her. Watch the fever. If she still has a temperature in a day or two, call me."

That moment, Paula decided. Right as she spoke. "I want to take her home."

"I thought she was home."

"I want to take her to my home. My husband's and my home in River Ridge. Down north of Saint Louis on the river."

The doctor tapped her fingers on the chart. "That's a lot of travel for her."

"She needs someone to look after her. My husband and me."

"She does need someone for now. But—and let me emphasize this: she will get better. She's pretty sick right this minute, but folks her age get sick just like folks our age. She will recover."

"Can I take her home?"

"When the temperature goes down, yes, but be careful with her. Have your doctor call me when you get home."

Just then Miss Kezee coughed up some phlegm.

"Dr. Crawford," she wheezed.

"Yes, ma'am."

"You tell this bitch to give me back my gun."

Quiet in this damn house. Ring this damn bell till your arm fall off. Don't nobody come. Turn on the TV myself, I guess. Didn't never like this room no how. Not even when I lived here. Have a view out to nothing. Girl got this joint fixed up like a girl's room. Frilly stuff all over. Not even no little girls living here. Never was. Used this as the junk room myself. Put all the stuff in here I didn't know what to do with. Had me some boxes of old clothes. Awful old clothes. Ugly wool stuff the moths eat up. Some fancy big hats I useta wear back in Saint Paul, back in the old days. Had a box with some books and stuff and a bunch of old plates and dishes and things. Couldn't care what happened to all that old mess.

Don't really care none about this house. Hate this house. Got to get away. Gonna get away. Walk right away. Only thing to do. Get myself together, get myself up and get away. Go home. To my home. Me and Charlie's home. I gotta go.

That's what I'll do. I'm comin Charlie. Cold in here. Get away. Where that girl? Comin Charlie. Cold everywhere. River flowin. Where's Charlie? Didn't mean for him to die. What we gonna do Charlie?

Beautiful day.

Sky brighter than blue. It is a warm day. The sun is a lemon drop in the bright sky. There is a man beside the woman. He is a happy-faced man with salt-and-pepper hair around his head like a crown of laurel. He has a little mustache and some hair on his chin. He looks happy always. He is a dark-skinned man, the rich dark brown color of chocolate candy.

"Come on," the man says. He is wearing coveralls and carrying a fishing pole.

"Comin, Charlie," the woman says. A thin woman. Older than she looks. Her skin wrinkles at the neck, her hair is streaked with gray. She is pretty. She is stepping clumsily down the rocky bank. She did not dress for fishing.

"Careful," the man says. Like a schoolgirl she tumbles down and lets herself be caught.

"Snakes all up in here," the man says. "You watch yourself."

"Where are some snakes?"

The man points to a creek inlet, to some brush. "Probly a nest of copperheads up there. You afraid?"

"Not of you," the woman says. The man laughs.

They sit on the riverbank and fish. The river flows by silent. Sometimes it roils like a stew. They catch shy glances of each other now and then.

The woman is not supposed to be with this man.

"Got a bite," the man says. His pole is wobbling and bending, or he is making it do so. "It's a monster. You got to help me Nobi."

The woman reaches for the pole.

"Stand behind me," the man orders.

The woman grabs his shoulders. The man cranks back and forth on the reel.

"Get him! Get him!" the woman encourages. Her knobby knees press into the man's shoulders. They rock back and forth together.

"Hold on," the man says. He stands up. The woman hangs on to his shoulders.

"Get him!" the woman yells.

"I got him now."

The big fish breaks the surface. The man yanks back at the pole. The fish flies past them.

"Look out! Look out!" the woman yells. She jumps up and away from the fish.

The man laughs. It is an enormous fish. A catfish. A fish as big as a skillet.

The woman makes a pool on the shore for the fish. They sit close together and watch the fish flopping in the shallow water.

"Make mighty good eating," the man says.

"We got no place to cook him," the woman answers.

They are not supposed to be together.

They stare at each other's faces. The man has a kindness the woman sees that makes her feel new. She trembles. The man rubs the outside of his wrist across her breasts.

"Mens have been slapped for much less," the woman says.

The man does it again. The woman grabs some hair on his chin and tugs it gently. They kiss and she pulls away.

"Too old for this mess," the woman says.

"You're not old at all," the man answers.

The woman strolls away, down the bank. The man does not follow. She turns to look at him. He is looking at her with round, wet eyes. A round, dark brown man. Her heart is filled with love for him. He indicates for her to return to him and she does.

"Where were you thirty years ago?" the woman asks.

"It don't work that way."

She sits by him, puts her head on his shoulder, and lets her hot tears wet the front of his clothing.

"Seems like I never get nothing I want," the woman cries.

The man kisses her head, calls her Nobi. No one ever called her that before. Time doesn't move. Time speeds by.

The woman has a husband waiting. Or not waiting. It doesn't matter.

"I want you to come back to Saint Paul with me, Nobi."

"How I'm gonna do that?"

"He don't want you no more. Your boy's grown. He don't need you. You come on home with me."

The man encloses her in his arms. His soft padded body seems to absorb hers. He is clean and sweet smelling, all pipe tobacco and hand cream.

"I'm comin, Charlie," she says. "I really am."

The bright blue sky fills with noise. Swirling. Spinning. The house and the other man. It is dark.

Want to think about the river.

The house and the man. This house and the man. This house a house I lived in. Don't want that.

"I'll kill you first," the man says. Another man. A. B. Don't want that. Comin, Charlie. "Don't you do it, Xenobia." Darkness. Want the river. Want Charlie. Where are you, Charlie? Think of the river. The river.

The bell was ringing when they walked back in the door.

"Girl, damn you. Girl!"

"Better hop to it, Ma," Tommy said. He'd already dug into his bag of food. The grease from the French fries smeared around his mouth like a transparent beard. He'd finish his food, she knew, and be all over Tim for a share of the other bag.

"Sounds like she's off again," Tim said.

"Where in the hell are you, girl? Girl!"

Tim patted her arm by way of encouragement.

"Take that food to the kitchen. You," she pointed to Tommy. "Keep your hands out of my snacks. They're for the party."

Tommy saluted. "Yes, sir," he said.

"Girl!"

"Hurry up and eat so you can get to the chores."

Tommy was already unwrapping a cheeseburger and eating as he walked, tearing huge bites. He'd be done before he got to his chair.

"Lord help me!"

She ran up the stairs to see what had happened. "What is it? What's wrong, Mother?"

"Look at this shit you been making me watch. Oh my Lord."

A rerun of Beverly Hillbillies was on.

"Just look at that mess. Oh Lord. Look at that ignorant old white woman."

"Mother, I turned the TV set off before I left. A long time before."

"No, you didn't."

"Yes, I did." She pushed the off button again.

"Damn thing's been running all day long. Bout to drive me crazy. What you want to torture me for, girl?"

"Is there anything else you want while I'm here?"

Miss Kezee waved her hand as if to dismiss her.

Back in the kitchen she found the boys gobbling and slurping away at the burgers.

"How's Grandma?" Tim asked.

"Cranky." She saw Tommy—his food gone—spidering his fingers across the table to Tim's french fries. To the chips. To the nut bowls.

"You better tell this boy I'm not messing with him," Tim warned.

Tommy giggled. He lowered his head to his hands, fixing the food in his eyes like a crocodile.

The bell sounded again.

"Ten, hut!" shouted Tommy.

"Girl!"

"And I'm not messing with you either." She gave a little tug to each of Tommy's ears.

She took her time on the stairs. She walked to the bed with her hands behind her back.

"I smell food. Y'all eatin, ain't you. Didn't think about me up here."

"I'll get you some soup."

"Is that what y'all having?"

"I got the boys some hamburgers. I don't know what Al's having. I'm just snacking."

"Too selfish to think about me."

"I'll get you some soup." She walked back to the kitchen in time to see Tommy sneak a handful of nuts.

"I warned you."

"I couldn't help myself. He hit me." He gave his brother a pathetic, accusatory look.

"I told him to keep his hands off my food. Mom, he reached over and grabbed a whole bunch. He's a greedy dog."

"Well, sounds like somebody got what was coming to him. Here." She handed Tommy the cleaning bucket from underneath the sink. "Get busy." He took the supplies. Mumbling under his breath, he shoved his brother's shoulder as he passed.

"I'm gonna hurt you, boy," Tim snapped.

He would, too, she knew. Hurt him good one of these times. Sit on him, slap him around, twist his arms until he cried uncle. And Tommy would whine, have a good cry, and beg forgiveness. Or beg for more.

She heated the tomato soup. She made the thick red-orange liquid into a whirlpool with her spoon, then tried to reverse it. Some things just didn't figure. Like these twins. For so many years they'd been so alike: first steps together, chicken pox the same week. Now they were as different as two eleven-year-olds could be. This one here—Tim, coolly chewing each bite, careful, thorough. The other one: well, out in the bathroom she heard all the water running and the sloshing of the brush around toilet. She heard the toilet seat slam down.

"Son of a bitch," she heard him holler. Tim heard him, too, and they both laughed. Tommy came in, the front of his clothes dark with water, carrying the small trash can to be emptied.

"If you make a mess, you'll just be doing it over," Paula told him.

"Think I don't know that?"

The bell went off.

"Girl!"

"Ha!" Tommy sneered.

"Just a second," she said, hand on his arm. She filled the soup bowl and set it on the tray. The soup was good and hot to the touch. The old lady had fits over tepid soup. She handed the tray to Tommy. "You go," she ordered.

"Huh?"

"Girl! Hurry!"

"Take it. And be nice."

He shuffled off with the tray, and she and Tim had another good laugh. She was glad to have a child who shared her sense of humor.

"You want everything vacuumed, Mom?"

She was also glad to have at least one child who didn't mind a chore now and then. "Just do the hall and the stairs, please."

He wadded up all the wrappers—his and his brother's—and stuffed them into one bag.

The bell again.

"Uh oh," Tim said.

"Girl! Now, dammit."

They met Tommy at the bottom of the steps. There were

blotches of soup on his shirt and drips down his pants. She noticed a red blotch on her son's arm, a deep red blotch under his brown skin. The empty bowl sat on the tray.

"What happened?"

"What did you say to Grandma?"

"I didn't do anything. Honest I didn't." There was fear in his voice. "Man, she's crazy." He started crying.

"Girl!"

"You're OK. Just calm down. Clean the tray and finish your chores. I'll see to her."

"Ma," Tommy whimpered, sniffing his tears.

She kissed him on the head and hugged him. "It's OK, son."

"Damn you, girl."

Two days after the doctor's visit the fever had broken and her temperature was almost normal. She was sleeping a lot, and when awake she seemed alert, if only briefly.

How lonely and quiet that room seemed. And dark: its tiny dormer windows covered with thick heavy draperies. She loved her thick draperies; she had them in every window in the house.

The bedroom was formal, except for one thing. There on the dresser. A whole herd of them. Dozens of them. Day-glo plastic dinosaurs. Many sizes, dime-store cheap. A brontosaurus, tyrannasauri, a gentle pterydactl flying by a string. They were bizarre, ridiculous, and cute. They made Paula's heart want to break.

"You like my things." A tiny strained voice. Miss Kezee struggled to her elbows, smiling. Paula went to her and filled in behind her with pillows so she could sit up for a while.

"Why do you have these?"

"Charlie give em to me. Every holiday when Charlie give me a present, he stuck one of those in there for me." Her skin was still ashen, as if she'd been powdered with cocoa mix. Her lips looked cracked and painful, her eyes yellow and veined. Paula couldn't remember if her eyes had always been that way or not.

"Mother, I think you're gonna need to let us take care of you for a while."

Miss Kezee turned her head away.

"Al and me, we have a big house. . . . I guess I don't need to tell you that."

"I hate that house," she'd said in an almost inaudible voice. She stared out the window.

"We can look after you. It's hard for us with you up here. We worry so much."

Miss Kezee released a long breath that deflated and exhausted her. She covered her face with hands.

"What's wrong, Mother?"

Miss Kezee shook her head slowly. A frail, high-pitched moan came from somewhere in her throat.

"Hear me now. I won't say it again. I know you're right. I know you mean well."

"Thank you, Mother."

"I hate it, Paula. I hate it so much," she sobbed.

"I know."

"I'd fight you if I could. I'd fight you to my dying breath."

She tried to look calm for the boys. Still, she felt herself flying up the steps two at a time. The old lady sat up at the edge of the bed, her face set in anger. The red soup stain trailed down the side of the bedding to a puddle on the floor. She aimed the handle of the bell at Paula and started in.

"Goddamn you, girl, if I told you once I done told you a million times not to send no tomato soup up here. Goddamn nasty tomato soup. Look like blood. Told you not to cook that mess for me. I won't eat it. I told you I won't eat it."

The old lady talked so fast she spat and drooled as the words streamed from her mouth. The anger rose up in Paula till it burst. She shoved her words in the old cow's face.

"WHO DO YOU THINK YOU ARE?" Each word rolled out full and round.

"Never in my life have I eat no damn tomato soup and this bitch got the nerve to send some up here. Why, I don't know what I ought to do . . ."

"THROW SOUP ON MY BABY . . ."

"Damn person starve to death in this house before they get a cracker. One lousy soda cracker. Some damn tomato soup. Why, I wished I would see some more damn tomato soup."

"I'LL KILL YOU. YOU HURT MY CHILD . . ."

"Send that little ugly heathen up here with no manners and he like to throw some tomato soup in my face, talking bout 'here, Grandma, we made you some tomato soup,' and I don't even eat no damn tomato soup."

"YOU CLEAN THIS MESS UP . . ."

"Ugly little heathen. I'll knock all the black off him—off all y'all up in here. Some tomato soup. See if I eat some tomato soup."

"YOU GOT STRENGTH TO CARRY ON LIKE THAT YOU CLEAN UP YOUR OWN MESS . . ."

"What's that you say? Don't you holler at me, girl. Got the nerve to make some tomato soup and then gonna holler, too. Don't you turn your back on me. Girl! Girl!"

As Paula turned to leave the room she felt something sail over her shoulder. The bell hit and shattered a heart-shaped souvenir plate from Lake of the Ozarks. Paula snatched the annoying thing from the floor. She pushed hot air from her nostrils, pointed the bell at the puddle of soup and the new pile of glazed ceramic shards, turned her back, and walked out.

"Girl! Damn you girl!"

Down at the bottom of the steps, two identical round-eyed, closed-mouthed boys, one with a sponge, one with a vacuum hose, stared at their mother, mesmerized.

Composure, she thought. One step, then another. "Hide this," she said to the one with the hose. She handed him the bell and walked to the kitchen. She poured herself some coffee and sat down.

Composure, she thought. Poise. All those rules of her mother's. She tried to keep the cup quiet against the saucer. She hoped the coffee would quell her shivers.

The two boys stood at the hallway door. Still round-eyed. Again frozen.

"Oh! Oh! Oh!" From the upstairs.

Just stop the shaking. Don't blink: let the eyes dry. Stop shaking.

The boys stared.

They want me to do something. To do and say the right thing. Be strong. Be the mama. Sorry, boys. I don't know how. Just watch me, though. Watch me pretend nothing's happened.

The sponge pulled at the vacuum tube's arm. "Come on," Tommy said, but Tim hesitated. "Come on," Tommy insisted.

Miss Kezee screeched. The shriek was soon drowned out by the sounds of the vacuum and running water.

Her mind blanked from anger. The pounding of her pulse made the room vibrate. She breathed deep, hoping to slow everything down, but still: the bright walls with their cheerful wallpaper irises beat in time with her heart. The second hand on the clock leaped from second to second.

4:30.

The cleaning stopped. Just then she heard Al's voice and the simultaneous chatter of the twins. Then Al was in the dining room door, arms crossed. The back of his shirt was soaked and stained with sweat. He was holding the bell.

She shook her head, got up, and left the kitchen by the other door.

She had given Joanne Cole a check for twenty-five dollars and a notarized letter authorizing her to have access to the house until she and Al decided what was to be done. Maybe Miss Kezee would be coming back, but Paula thought not. She had her mother-in-law's valuables stored and then packed her necessities into an overnight bag and a worn-out old suitcase she found stashed in the back of the closet.

Once, while she was packing, Miss Kezee sat up in the bed and began screaming about how they'd finally come, how the black wenches had finally come to steal her blind. She had yanked a brass lamp by its cord and pulled it to the floor, and then passed out from the exertion.

For the most part she had been disoriented and benign. She ate and drank properly and helped make the arrangements to close up the house, packing her own things, often with a suspicious eye on Paula, as if she were afraid Paula would grab something and run off with it.

On the plane Miss Kezee forced the flight attendant to give her extra nuts by complaining of staleness. She accused one girl of holding out on her while she brazenly stashed the nuts down the front of her dress. Everyone thought she was "sweet."

She had talked loudly about the mostly white passengers around her. When a businessman glanced in her direction, she'd asked him, "What are you looking at?" She'd also asked had he seen enough and was there anything else she could show him. When he said, "Enjoy your flight, grandma," she'd asked Paula to go over there and kick the motherfucker's ass for her. Loudly, she'd asked it.

The businessman seemed to think she was "sweet," too.

Paula stared straight ahead at the *Time* magazine she had

grabbed. Through the one-hour flight she kept staring at the magazine page and tried to pretend she was having bad dream. It didn't work.

"She's asleep now," Al said.

Paula, who had been curled on her side, rolled up to a sitting position facing Al. He came to sit on the bed beside her. "Rough day?" He massaged her calf.

"I want you to promise me something."

He nodded.

"I want you to promise me that if I ever get like your mother is now you will take me out back and shoot me."

"That bad?"

"I'm gonna make the boys promise the same thing. I'll wait until they're older—out of college—so I can be sure they won't do me in just to be spiteful."

He reclined on the bed and eased her down beside him, perched his chin across her shoulder, draped an arm across her chest. "We could never do you in. Anyway—you'd just come back to haunt us. I know."

"She threw hot soup on your son."

"No doubt crippling him for life."

"It could have. What if it was something else. What if she got a knife. I don't know, I think she's . . . I don't know. She's stronger, but she goes in and out of these moods. Sometimes I just want to slap her.

"You read in the paper about helpless old people who get abused by relatives, and you think, How could someone do that? I know how: it would be easy. I feel the same way as when the boys are real bad: out of control. I don't like feeling that way."

"So maybe we place her out at the Manor."

"You mean 'the home?' It's OK to call it that, you know. Yes, maybe we should put her in the home."

"No shame in our not being able to care for her."

"But we *can* care for her."

"Even with the abuse? Even with all the time she takes? Paula, she's my mama, but I don't like coming home and having my boys tell me what she said to you. I don't want her upsetting you. I told her that."

"She doesn't mean to . . ."

"How do you know what she means?"

"I guess I don't. She was back on that not-meaning-to-kill-him stuff again today."

"That crap." He shook his head and sniggered. "You're gonna have to learn to ignore her. I do." He hopped up from the bed and leaned back against the dresser. He studied her a minute and then made his pronouncement.

"So here's what we do. We make the arrangements and get her set up out at the Manor."

Paula winced. "Those places . . ."

He shrugged. "It's not so bad. We can keep an eye on her. You take a run up there tomorrow and check it out for yourself."

Everything was simple for him. When he wanted to, he could be so cool. For things like this, especially. She let a few tears leak down across her temple.

"And it's not the same as with your mama," he added.

She rolled over, back to him, got up, and went to the window. "You don't know about me and my mama," she mumbled.

He came and hugged her from behind. "I don't like to think about Mother in that place, either. But I think it's for the best. I'll leave it to you. Whatever you decide to do." He squeezed her in a way that seemed to be requesting a response. She didn't have one.

He kissed the back of her neck. "I'll go finish up downstairs." He handed her the bell from the dresser as he left.

Driving home from the airport, Miss Kezee had been quiet and alert. The weather was already warm—hot for early May—and the air conditioner in the van droned away. Paula chattered nervously about the sights along the way: Here was the new Mid Rivers Mall. On that road you get the ferry to Illinois. Here is the Dairy Queen, the quarry, the Skylift.

Miss Kezee sighed now and then. She stared coolly out the window. Paula wondered if she was trying to get a glimpse of something familiar.

They stopped frequently during the hour-and-a-half drive for drinks and to get a rest from the rolling of Highway 79.

At the turn-off for River Ridge, Paula announced, "We're almost there."

Miss Kezee said quietly, "I give over twenty years of my life to this place. I know where we are."

Paula said nothing more. She pulled the van to the curb in front of the house and went around to help Miss Kezee from her seat. The old lady's face streamed with tears. She'd set her jaw hard. Their eyes met, and what Paula saw in those eyes pained her to her center.

"You've no right, damn you, girl. No right at all."

4

$\mathcal{A}$LL HELL HAD BROKEN LOOSE.

The way I figure it, I can never tell these days what I'll find when I come in the door here: half the time it's quiet as a morgue. You couldn't find a person if your life depended on it. The other half it's like today: chaos.

What happened? Hell, it's not even important. The boys are all upset, Paula's all upset. I go upstairs and my mother's muttering and sputtering and she's all upset. I hug this one and pat that one on the head and get another one to take a nap. You would think that civilized people could get through the day without this kind of carrying on. Me, I'm thinking I need to hire a camp counselor or something to keep a lid on things while I'm out. Mother was being herself is all it was. I tell Paula she ought to leave that old woman alone. I tell her that Mama is as cranky and ornery as they come, but you know how Paula is. She should have been a social worker. Not that she's thin-skinned: she can go a round with the best of them, and nine times out of ten she'll win.

I think she would have been fine had Mama not thrown hot soup on one of the boys. That's what upset her, I think. And the boy, he'll be fine. What's that old woman gonna do to a big strong healthy boy? Not much.

But Paula, she is one of those fierce mamas. She is a lioness, a mother bear. She is one of those "better not nobody mess with my kids" mamas, and woe to anybody doesn't take good warning.

She is on me all the time that I don't keep a close enough eye on them, that I am too permissive, that I allow too much roughhousing. What I figure is that young men need a little freedom, they need to test those limits. She will worry herself to death one of these days. If she don't worry me there first.

She says I play too much. She says I get too rough with them. Yeah, I like to wrestle around with my boys. I try to be careful, too, though sometimes you just don't know. Sometimes I'm wrestling with them and I pin somebody's arm behind his back, and one minute he's laughing and the next minute he's looking at me like he thinks I'm gonna break his damn arm. My own kid. As if I would. Paula says I don't know when to quit. She says I'm as bad as they are with my teasing and carrying on and that one of these days someone's gonna get hurt. I don't know. Some days I think she's right, but most of the time I figure, what's the harm in it? At least I'm spending some time, giving them some attention.

More than my daddy gave me.

And that's what boys like: all that rough stuff. These two anyway. They are boys, and boys like to test their strength, especially against the big boys. They like to see who is the toughest. It's a built-in thing.

And I want them to be tough. They have to be able to handle themselves out there. That's the least I can do for them.

No, I am not one of them bully dads who slaps their kids around to make them tough. A little horseplay never hurt anybody.

More and more I'm thinking that a woman don't know shit about what to do with boys. We been reading these folks who are raising a ruckus about the number of households headed by single mothers, and more and more I'm thinking that there is a problem. It's not that mothers aren't loving or aren't good parents, it's just that there are some things you need a daddy for. Yes, there's the physical stuff, including the getting out in the yard and batting the ball around stuff. But there's more to it than that. Some of it is inside stuff.

One thing is that boys are more private. They don't like to do all that talking and sharing shit that mothers want to do. They just like to let things be sometimes, to not smother everything with words. I see these women out here raising these boys by themselves, and I just have to shake my head and hope they turn out halfway decent.

No, I'm not perfect in the dad department. This twins business drives me up the wall sometimes. I can't even tell the two of them apart most of the time. Yeah, they have their little quirks and idiosyncrasies. For example, I come in today, they start telling me the terrible stuff that's going on with their momma and grandmomma, and I know that the one who is lying and exaggerating is Tommy, because that's how the boy is. He's a natural born comic: he'll spin out a tale for you to break your heart or make you bust a gut, and sometimes you just have to say to him, "Boy, get out of my face with all that bullshit." For the most part, one noisy kid is the same as the other, if you know what I mean, and we got two of them at the same time. Clattering around and slamming doors and pounding their big feet up and down the steps. Might sound a little cold, but that's the way it is. Kids is kids, and when they're noisy and on your nerves, they are noisy and on your nerves—even if they're your own and you love em.

These two lately are playing head games with me. I know they are. Intentionally trying to screw me up. The other day one of them comes up to me and he's talking in this strange gravelly voice, asking me for fifty cents or whatever it was. I ask him what the hell his problem was and he starts the "what problem?" routine, but he can't keep that shit-eating grin off his face. Like I wasn't ever eleven and didn't know all the scams. Chip off the old block, they say. My legacy.

Most of the time I think that legacy crap is just that: crap. A child has an independent life. He comes into the world and there should be no demands on him. No expectations. I shouldn't be expecting one thing or another out of these boys, and if they turn out to be bums or turn out to be presidents (same difference?) I shouldn't care about that one way or the other, right? Bullshit. They better turn out good. Otherwise it makes you crazy.

Poor Walter with just that one boy—Andrew—and he's already going crazy. Fourteen, and, well that probably says it right there. Walter, he's turning gray faster than me. We're sitting around shooting the bull last week and all the sudden he turns to me and says, "He's gonna fuck up. I just know it. He's gonna fuck up."

"Who's gonna fuck what up?" I ask, and he lays out how nervous he is about the big baseball game or whatever the hell it was. The man is about to lose his mind over this bull. And whenever he talks about his boy this way, he gets this look in his eye like he's drowning and somebody had better throw him a life preserver or something. Now if a strong intelligent brother like this goes off, what chance has some twenty-five-year-old gal got down in the slums chasing after some gangster she brought in the world way back when? Me, I just tell Walter things will be OK. And I wonder if I'm supposed to be getting that upset—over the grades and the fistfights and the other stuff? Am I supposed to be that scared?

These boys are growing awfully fast. Pretty soon them big feets will fit those big bodies. Seems like they just started school.

I miss those peanut-butter-and-jelly days, when they were in kindergarten and their mother had just gone back to teaching and I had to do a lot of afternoon baby-sitting. I miss that year. Yeah, I was pretty good at it. I made a decent sandwich and I was a pretty entertaining dad, if I don't say so myself. Tuck one under one arm and one under the other arm and take off to God knows where. Tom, he was the one liked his soldiers. He was the easy one. Give him that box of army men and he was gone for hours. Tim, though, that was a little boy could talk your ear off. Everything he did had a story to go with it. A twenty-minute story. Silly, bizarre shit, with no logic to it, shit that turned back on itself, asymmetrical psychedelic shit. But beautiful. Beautiful. Even though they came with study questions of the "What do you think of that?" and "Guess what happens next?" variety—the kind where I couldn't just say "Uh, huh, Uh, huh," but had to have a response of some kind, because when he didn't get one, I got tugged on and pulled on and generally badgered until I came up with one. I always looked interested and surprised and excited. Or tried to. Broke his little heart if I didn't. Which was the hard part—the little thin skins. And I never could—still can't—predict those weak places. If you could have some kind of a guide book that told you where they were vulnerable, told you what you had to look out for, it would be so much easier.

For example, Paula told me last week that Tim (I think she said it was Tim) had developed this justice thing, that he had this new obsession with fairness. She said he was keeping a keen eye on the size of portions and the amount of money that came out her purse. She told me I had to be careful, because even though he might not mention it right there on the spot, he was keeping a list, she knew, to the item, and he'd whip that list on you when it was the least to your advantage and the most to his.

Now, how would she know something like that? And how

many other traps are out there just waiting for me to walk into them?

Paula, that's what she puts all her energy into, figuring this kind of shit out. But that would drive a normal person crazy after a while: guessing what's on other folks' minds. I got enough trying to keep my own head in check.

I have to say I love this little family of mine. Having Mama here changes things. Rounds it out in a way, but makes it hard for us to just be ourselves. Everyone has to tiptoe around and make sure they don't disturb the old thing. Paula has been a champ—she's taken it on—more than I would have ever asked her to. The boys, they don't know what to make of her. They aren't used to a lot of family around. In fact with Paula and me both being only children, and both her parents gone, my mother is about the only family they've known, and they only saw her if we made a trip up to her house in Saint Paul—last time about three years ago.

I remember we'd gotten up early—about five thirty—and loaded into the van and were on our way by six. We drove all the way up the Great River Road. One of these days, what I want to do is take this crew and do the whole thing, both sides, from here to New Orleans and back. Stay in cheap motels, eat in a lot of greasy spoons and visit every tourist trap along the way. One of these days.

The river is incredible north of here, wide and meandering and lined with bluffs. The boys liked the parts in southern Wisconsin where it's filled with islands. They thought those were floating swamps out there and they wanted to stop and rent some boats and go paddling around. I was never the kind of person who liked swamps and bugs and all of that and neither is their mother, so don't ask me where they got that notion. Those two, they have always been ones to like to root around back in the woods. Paula, she has a fit. She says she knows they are going to get bit or stung by this or that, or fall down some well, or get lost in some cave. We've been lucky, I guess. A broken arm and a few bad cases of poison ivy is all we've had to deal with. I guess I'm a fatalist. I guess I figure what's gonna happen to them will happen, and there isn't a whole lot me worrying can do to stop it. They're pretty smart boys and don't do a lot of foolhardy crap like jumping off the roof or wading in the river. You have to hope for the best, don't you?

I did nix the canoes, though.

We had taken a car full of garbage. Chips and pop and homemade cookies. And still we stopped four or five times to eat, even though it was only an eight-hour drive. Every two hours or so we pulled into a McDonald's or a Burger King and loaded up with some more. Paula, she went right along with it, even though she pretends to be one of those balanced diet kind of gals, always making sure there is a vegetable with the meal and not too many sweets. Yeah, I guess french fries are vegetables too, and don't you know she was in that car grubbing on them goodies right along with the rest of us. A lot of her strictures are for show, anyway. You come up with all these rules and regs not because they make any kind of sense but, because they are "the right thing to do."

Mama and them fed us again, right away when we got to Saint Paul. Chili and cornbread. We stayed four days, and they kept us busy the whole time. The guy Mother was married to kept us going: to the zoo, to both downtowns, to the Twins game at that domed stadium. Big, weird, awful place that was, like being inside a beach ball. All blue and green inside.

Mama, she was very cool the whole time we were in her house. I don't know what kind of impression the boys could have had of her. She certainly did not fuss over them like some grandmothers do. None of that hugging and kissing and dipping into the apron for treats crap. Interesting thing about twins: they always have someone else around to entertain them. While we were in Saint Paul the boys stayed huddled together most of the time, whispering and furtive the way brothers can be. Mama and her husband could have been the owners of a bed and breakfast for all they cared.

Me, what I loved was the car trip itself. I liked being enclosed in that car for a couple of days with all that junky food and my people. I liked to pretend like I was the chieftain of some technologically advanced tribe and that we were out on some quest and it was us against the world. And though we might have our own squabbles—over who ate the last of the Doritos and who gets to choose the radio station—if we were attacked, we would hang together. I imagined us a hundred years ago, crossing the Iowa prairie, looking for a place to call our own. I am a hunter, stalking deer through silent forests, walking down bucks, my boys at my side. (I have caught many single-handedly, of course. Bison, too.) Paula knows which wild plants will sustain us: dandelion, sassafras, wild cucumber. She boils them along with the meat we bring, my boys and me, making savory stews. I tan the hides, she tailors the clothes. We don't need anyone. We build our home on a rise above a small winding river. We can see fifty miles in any direction. The sky turns pink at dusk, and at night we gather by the fire and contemplate our day. The native people are our friends. We live a long time.

It was the kind of trip where all of that seemed possible—or in my head it did—and for a moment, on the way home, as we approached I-80 just north of Davenport, I thought I might turn right, go west. We would go somewhere and start fresh. We would become some other people.

I guess we are lucky I am not that impulsive. We aren't the sort of people who do that sort of thing. So we came on home.

And the trip was perfect, except for one little thing I remember. I don't like to think about this.

We were south of Keokuk, in northern Missouri, where there is that long straightaway on the floodplain. We had been driving all day, stopping at a lot of scenic overlooks and historical sites. The Effigy Mounds. A few of the state parks. It was twilight, and out beyond the cornfields the sun had just dropped into the night. The boys were sound asleep: we'd had a long day. Paula was driving and I was riding shotgun. For some time now that particular piece of the road has needed repairing. Battered to cinders by a never ending stream of trucks and flooded regularly, that length of highway is tucked away in a corner of the state, anonymous and forlorn, and no one does a thing about it. We bumped along and sometimes felt as if we were driving on railroad ties. Paula was talking to me, or at me, the nervous way she does. She hates silence more than anyone I know, and a lot of times what comes out her mouth is just . . . crap. And she shifts topics too, so that one minute you are talking about the price of beef at National and the next minute about who was on Letterman last night. Half the time I just tune this shit out, and I cannot remember a thing she was saying at that particular moment.

The boys were snoring in the back—I remember that—and I remember their arms and legs were tangled and twisted together. I had been in and out of a dream since we left Burlington. I would drift away and then wake up down the road, and the monotonous Iowa scenery and the gentle stream of Paula's conversation flowed together seamlessly and had an almost intelligible logic that mystified me and made the time pass the way it does in a movie, my catnaps like the smooth cuts that make an hour seem like five minutes. I remember I turned around to check the kids and I thought I saw a sign for a restaurant in Saint Paul. "Forpaugh's" it said, but why would there be a sign in northern Missouri for a restaurant four hundred miles north? I did a double take, and then I heard Paula say "Oh, shit!" I turned around and saw the two lights coming right at us. Paula leaned into the horn: she was frozen to it. Her other hand was locked to the wheel. I don't know how, but I reached over and grabbed the wheel and turned it to the right. We skidded into a ditch. The semi thundered by and the car died.

We didn't say anything for a long time. Paula still had one hand fastened to the wheel. I had one hand frozen there myself.

"He came right at me," she said, and then she said she was wide awake, really she was.

I believed her. She slumped forward over the wheel, and I turned to check on the boys again. Still asleep. Snoring. Oblivious.

I was fine until I looked at them. We could have gone on home, gone on down the road, maybe even laughed about it. But I looked at my boys, and I got mad. I don't remember ever being that mad. I told Paula to turn the car around. She just looked at me. She asked me why. I told her to do it or I'd do it myself. I told her I was going to kill him. Catch the son of a bitch, kick his ass, and then kill him.

She started the car and continued south.

"You know I will," I told her. I told her I ought to make her turn the damn car around.

And I cursed that man. I cursed him with every name I knew. I was so angry I was shaking. I would have killed him, too. I still would.

Paula and I have never discussed this incident. We've avoided the subject almost superstitiously, almost as if we would be tempting fate to talk about it. I think it scared her, my anger.

But I know she feels safer, somehow, knowing I'd kill for her and our boys. I know that, like it or not, that's part of the package, part of what they have men for in the first place. Some one to stand at the mouth of the cave with a club, if you will. Something else we don't talk about is the gun I keep. She knows I have it. She can see it right there in the dresser drawer, and the first time I brought it home she fussed about it for a day or two, but that was the end of it. She knows what it's for and she knows that if somebody were to try coming in here and doing something to her or those boys, I wouldn't think twice about blowing their brains out.

Which I guess ultimately is what all this parent/family stuff comes down to, when you get right down to it, all of Walter's brooding and Paula's nail-biting. Comes down to my friend up there in the bedroom dresser drawer. He says the same things they do, and in a lot fewer words.

Paula and all them folks like her would just as soon not think about that shit.

5

*A*RM BURNS LIKE FIRE. XENOBIA, GIRL, WHAT HAVE you done? Some mess went on up in here today. Some tomato soup. The bell. That boy. Can't remember too good.

Remember as good as I wants. I got to get home. I'm comin on home, Charlie. Can't get a fix on this place. Can't seem to get my ground. This place makes me mean. Makes me ornery and weak. Makes me want to get out. Too much me here. That old me. The one I want to forget. Not enough you, Charlie. Too much of him here. Gave him over twenty years. Twenty-plus years for nothing. Got to get out. Mama, boy says. That boy, my boy, Al. You feeling better now, Mama? It's almost party time. Ain't studying no damn parties. What I got to celebrate, me locked up here. Seems all I do is sleep, I tell him. A person get tired of sleeping. You're here to rest, Mama. Get up and let me pull those sheets for you, Mama. He won't do nothing of the kind. I'll do it myself, I tell him. Won't let you shame your mama. No more than already done. You're looking better, Mama. You feel better? Talking to me like I'm simple. Boy looking like his daddy. Bunch of them old square-jawed Negroes. Can't even stand to look at him sometimes. You upset Paula today, Mama. She's trying to help you. We all are. Humph. Must have been some mess, but who knows? She the high strung kind get upset about the littlest thing. Sorry, I say. And what is he sticking his nose in it for in the first place? Must have been some mess if she gonna run to her husband bout it. I tell him, She say she'll do my hair. Paula did. OK, Mama. I'll get her for you. You come on down to the party when you're ready, hear? We love you, Mama. Boy kisses me. Must be something he learned from that girl, kissing on your mama. Never done none of that when I brought him up. Got a chunky butt, too. All them Johnson men got them chunky butts.

Paula held up a red cocktail dress. Then she draped her beige knit suit across her shoulder. She didn't love either outfit too much, or any dress for that matter. She was comfortable with loose pants and sweatshirts. She bought dresses because she could hear her mother telling her that sometimes you just needed to have one. That happened often when she went shopping. She'd be browsing in the Casual Corner, minding her own business, when there she'd be, putting her two cents in: Helen Thomas Fuller, doling out unsolicited advice, clicking her tongue at the leather pantsuits, sighing in exasperation at anything over a hundred dollars. As far as she'd run—to Columbia, to River Ridge—and as different as her life had become from the one her mother laid out for her, she could never shake that voice. "It's just common sense," the voice said. "I'm just trying to save you a little heartache." To give in meant welcoming the resentment that went with acknowledging how often the voice was right, and tonight it was once again vindicated. There seemed to be more such times as she got older. A candidate's wife was supposed to look a certain way, and the voice was telling her to wear the beige one. "That red dress is much too loud, young lady." She put it on anyway, and the red made everything about her glow: eyes, hair, skin. This was one hot dress. She allowed herself two minutes of vanity before admitting her mother was right. The color was too loud. The design too dressy. The whole effect too much for River Ridge. She put on the suit. Simple. Plain. Conservative. Like the town. Like the voice. Neither cheap looking nor ostentatious. Just a pleasant dress that a pleasant woman would wear to a pleasant event for her pleasant husband.

Just like Mother said.

I *will* wear something pretty, though, she decided. She retrieved a brightly patterned scarf from the closet and arranged it at her collar.

"Very nice," said Al, applauding from the door.

"Am I the perfect candidate's wife?"

"Is that what I expect?"

"I want you to owe me big."

"And just what have I got to pay with?"

"I'll think of something."

He came up behind her. She couldn't tell if he was admiring her or scowling at her.

"How is she doing?"

"She asked for you. Said you were doing her hair."

Paula sighed. "Into the lion's den." She grabbed a brush and some hair pins from a tray on the dresser. "Wish me luck."

She found Miss Kezee sitting on the edge of the bed, curled forward as if napping. She looked like a half moon: the exaggerated curve of her back bent painfully into a half circle. A nightgown lay in a rolled-up clump near the bed, near the faint pink stain where someone (she?) had attempted to clean up the soup. The sheets still needed changing, but the pieces of broken souvenir plate were gone.

She had gotten herself back into the blue dress, which was wrinkled and perspiration stained from the morning trip. It hung crooked across the shoulder and was unbuttoned at the back.

Paula offered to help her into something else and Miss Kezee complacently agreed. She got her standing, then began tugging the dress up over her head but soon decided with her mother-in-law's narrow hips it would be easier going down. She lowered the dress from shoulders and arms and asked her to step out of it. She wondered who did this in Saint Paul. Did Joanne Cole come over every morning to dress her? Did she return every night to get her ready for bed? Maybe Miss Kezee walked around the house half in and half out of some dirty housecoat. Maybe she walked around naked.

Paula buttoned the last button of the pink dress, the one that earlier in the day she had planned for her to wear. What a tiny dress this was, a special dress, made to order, she imagined, but what for? She had no idea. She had no idea what this old woman did with herself up there. She was silent about her life. As silent as she was this evening. Sitting there on the bed, she looked like the most forlorn person on earth.

"I'll get your hair now." Paula kneeled behind her on the bed and ran a brush through the long, yellowed hair—a surprisingly full head of strong hair—frizzled a bit at the roots and not appearing ever to have been pressed. As she brushed, the volume of the hair increased in her hands.

"Feels good," the old lady mumbled.

"Who does your hair at home, Mother?"

"Got a little girl next door comes by and brushes me out every once and a while. Mostly I just braid it up or tie a rag round it. You know how it gets."

"Yes, I sure do." Paula remembered her own bouts with the comb. "I used to hate getting my hair done. Every morning in that kitchen with that damned pressing comb. Seemed like every morning anyway. Mama and I used to fight, and I mean fight. I'd slap her hand away and she'd be pullin on my head talking about how I was gonna make her burn me." She cringed at the thought of the red hot teeth of that comb. Her mother liked to use the old-fashioned kind, which she heated up on the burners of the gas stove. She left the comb in the flame until the tines glowed red and then, slathering the hair with a palmful of grease, started the comb as close to the scalp as she dared. In the morning the Fuller kitchen smelled of oatmeal, natural gas, and singed hair. For Paula, the day the Afro came in was a day of liberation. Things were never quite the same between her and her mother after she'd gotten her first blow-out.

"Glad I didn't have me no girls. A boy just have his daddy take him to the barber and shave off all that nappy mess. Them boys of yours starting to look a little rough."

Paula laughed. "That is Al's problem."

"I know what you saying."

Miss Kezee seemed to soften under the stroke of the brush.

The girl, Paula, runs her fingers through my hair, rubs gentle at my scalp with the oil. Been so long. You forget what it's like have a person touch you this way. She ain't a bad girl. Triflin, but ain't they all? Dress the girl got on ain't nothing, but she got a scarf on that makes it something. Got all them braids and beads tied at the back of her hair in a piece of jewelry, hanging down like a napped-up ponytail. Some of the times she walk around here looking like something the cat dragged in, all sloppy and mannish. She knows better. Somebody taught this girl how to take care of herself. Her mama. She makes a nice appearance when she wants to. I want to tell her she looks pretty. Girl says, Tell me about your life in Saint Paul. First time she act like I got me a life up there. Come and take a person out of their home, away from their things. Don't know what I want to tell her. A lot of things ain't nobody's business. A person's life private. And one life is the same as another. Most everybody I know do the same things. Nothing worth talking about. Don't know what to tell you, I say. Her hands feel so good in my hair. Don't want her to ever stop. She says, You know. What do you do every day? What would you be doing right now? Persistent little wench. Surviving. Getting through another minute, another hour. I move my head to the side so she brush closer to the ear. I tell her I'd watch the Wheel of Fortune. Then I'd pick a few weeds in the yard. Sit on the porch and watch the neighbors. I got a lady up the street like to come down and sit with me. Girl puts down the comb and starts gathering hair up. That's nice, she says. She says, I bet you have a lot of friends up there dropping in. It seems like a friendly place. I don't tell her when you're my age nobody knows you anymore, don't want to know you. Sometimes nobody comes by for days. I don't tell her that some of those that do come by make you shame for what you can't do for yourself anymore, touching your nasty clothes and wiping up a mess you can't reach. They make you feel bad where your body have failed. I don't tell her how you talk to all them door-to-door preachers even though you know already what they got to say, just because sometimes you want someone to talk to. I tell her people be in and out, because she is not a stupid girl. She figure out that you get used to whatever it is life gives you. You make do with what you got. Girl gathers up all the hair and knots it at the bottom of the back of my head. I tell her, Make sure you pin it up good. She pats my hair and says "There" to let me know she's done. She starts pulling hair from the brush with a comb. You're all set for the big party, she says. She hands me a mirror. OK? she asks. Heifer got my hair all pooked out around like a shower cap. Must've been all that brushing made it stand out like that. Felt so good, though. I tell her thank you, even if it be that I look like a fool.

Paula thought Miss Kezee looked like all the turn-of-the-century photos she'd seen of old black women: worn faces, strong shiny hair spun around the head like a crown.

"You look wonderful, Mother." She went over and helped her to the closet mirror so she could look at herself. Paula liked their reflection: one tall, fair, and (if she dared think so) even a little fine, the other brown and old-fashioned looking. They were as unlikely together as the lion and the lamb.

"Aren't we a pair?" Paula giggled.

"Pair of whats," Miss Kezee mumbled. She went and sat herself back on the bed. "How long's this party lasting?"

"Maybe till nine. Be just a few people in. Some neighbors, the councilmen. You might see some old friends." Paula primped in front of the mirror some more. She was still wondering about the red dress back in the closet.

"I ain't studying no party," Miss Kezee said.

"It's sort of important to Al."

"What's that mean?"

Paula bit her lip against the hasty words. What she meant was: she hoped Miss Kezee's good mood lasted, hoped Miss Kezee would be at her best. She hoped for no more humiliations. And she decided against saying any of that.

"I hope it goes well. That's what I meant."

"Didn't mean nothing about me, huh?"

"Of course not."

"You about a lie."

"I think I have time to pull these sheets. Sit on the chair for a minute, please."

"You afraid I might show out on y'all."

Paula tossed the comforter aside and pulled at the soiled sheets and blankets. She was happy to see the mattresses had been spared the red-orange soup stain.

"I'll make a floor show if I want to."

Paula slammed a pillow down on the bed. "What is it with you, anyway? One minute you're sweet as pie and the next . . . I just don't understand. I didn't mean anything, OK?"

"Well, then."

Paula went to the linen closet. She could hear the old lady

back there mumbling about "people getting uppity" and "treating folks with respect." She thought about the long haul, about how she would survive months or even years of constant contrariness. If I'm gonna make this work, she thought, I must stand my ground. I won't stay sane if I let her swamp me every time. Especially when I'm right.

". . . forget who they're talking to. Probably never did have no manners."

She threw the sheets down on the bed. "Look, Miss Kezee, your son is throwing this party. Some people are gonna be here that could make a difference in this election and he wants to make a good impression. If you're in one of your . . . moods . . . you should think about spending the evening up here."

"Why you. You ain't nothing but a . . ."

"Don't give a damn what you call me. I'm asking you to think about your son."

Miss Kezee stood up, walked by Paula, giving her a weak shove. Paula heard the slow snap of her shoes down the steps.

I marched down them steps just as bold as you please. I walk in and sit in my old front room in my chair. My chair. This the chair I picked out that was mine. Found my chair down in Louisiana, Missouri. Got A. B.'s truck and drove down there and picked it up myself. Sat here twenty years, this chair has, and I'll sit in it all night. The rest of my life if I want to. Problem with these young girls is they know too damn much. Got an opinion on everything. Shoot. They don't know nothing. People don't know how to treat people no more. Used to be a person got respected past a certain age. Now folks say whatever they want to you. Not to me they won't. And here come the fool want to marry this triflin gal. All set for the party, Mama? boy says. Come in all dressed like a mortician. Them two boys stand back there by him looking like a pair of scarecrows. Them boys, they must favor her people, but I can see us in there. A little of my mama's side. Doesn't your grandmother look nice, boys? Can I get you something? Them boys don't say nothing. I tell him I'm fine. He stand there grinning like a chessy cat. You boys go get changed, he says. Stands there grinning some more. A man sure can be simple. Sometimes I look at that boy and see nothing but his daddy. Makes me sick. Them same eyes. That same pretty brown skin. And that smile. That smile that convinced me to come down here in the first place. Have a way of looking at you, men do, make you believe. Make you change your whole life. And the whole thing could come up to be a lie. Was a long time ago, sometime after the war. '49. '50. Whatever year that was. There I am, at home, living in Saint Paul, having me a good life. Had me a little piece of job. Some money. And here come that old A. B. Johnson. Look just like that boy here. That smile. Fool say, "Come on down the river with me. We got us a little town got nothin but Negroes. We run the whole thing. You like it down there." Talking all that kind of mess. Met him up at a little place what used to be over on Rondo Avenue. Dress like a funeral director. Just like this boy here. Talking about how down in River Ridge he own this and he own that and weren't no more important colored man in all a northern Missouri. Uh huh, is what I said. I wasn't no stupid woman. I was past thirty. Been on my own for a couple years. Provided for myself, done what I wanted to do, didn't answer to nobody. Don't know, must have been something I was looking for. A new thing. I wanted to get out a Saint Paul for awhile. Never had left. And never should have. Maybe it was the look in his eyes. That smile. Just like his boy. Whatever. I said yes. A Negro I had known two weeks and I said yes. Was living up off Lexington Avenue in Miss Ada's old house. She had a big house she rented out parts to borders. Shared a room with a gal named Mavis. I heard she passed a while back. Told her, said,

"Mavis, I'm gonna be moving down to Missouri with A. B." She couldn't believe it. None of em could. Couldn't hardly believe it myself. Mavis ask me what I want to go off and leave everybody for. I didn't know then and I still don't know. But I did it. Got married down at the courthouse. Wore me a plain white dress and some new shoes. Stood next to him in front of that judge. With Mavis and some mens I had never seen before. Said "I do, I do," and off we went. Packed up all my fine and beautiful clothes and whatever else I had into a trunk and my mama's suitcase and met Mr. A. B. Johnson Sr. at the curb. We loaded into that old Ford and hit off down Highway 61. A man I ain't said ten sentences to. Didn't know who his people was, what kind of food he ate, what he wanted with me. You're gonna love it down home, he said. Why I believe that? All I know was I was a good-lookin woman with a fine-lookin man and I was off on a road I'd never been on. Anything might happen. Doorbell ringing and the boy about to jump out his skin. Here we go, he says. I start to get up, but decide I'll just sit. Feel a little sore lately. Come on and say hello to Mama, boy says. Here he come with some people. That boy. He about the only good thing ever happened here in this house.

Circulate! the voice said. There were two dozen or so people gathered between the parlor and the living room. Paula was nervous: she didn't like to circulate and couldn't find too many places where she could keep her eye on Miss Kezee. She hung onto Al's arm and tried to keep her mother-in-law within her field of vision. The old lady had been sitting there in the balloon-back chair as if she were the queen mother. All the guests had gone over to her to pay their respects: she didn't seem to recognize any of them. She sat silent, nodding off now and then, gone back to some other world. Stay there and be good, Paula thought.

Now and again she found herself alone with Al. He'd kiss her and tell her the party was going great, and so far it had. Walter Dawkins had done his job: all the right people had shown up. There was Mayor Carlton and his wife, four of the seven town council members, two school board members, also Reverends Brown and Wilson. Couldn't have a party without the local clergy.

Tommy and Tim had been perfect gentlemen. They served snacks for a time (not eating too many themselves), politely allowing their heads to be rubbed and their cheeks to be pinched while they answered questions about ages and grades and hobbies over and over again. Tim retired early to his room to watch TV—grown-ups were no mystery to him—but Tommy sat halfway up the steps, mesmerized by the laughing, back-slapping, drinking good time. He watched, almost straining himself, it appeared, to catch a snatch of gossip or an earful of dirty joke. He would laugh, even, and roll his eyes at things Paula knew he couldn't possibly appreciate. He wanted to be down there in the center of the fun. Whenever they strolled past, Paula blew him a kiss, and he would wave back at her with that open-handed finger wave that eleven-year-old boys do when they are being shy.

Here came Berneice with Walter, and wouldn't you know no one was stopping her from wearing something loud and gorgeous. A caftan thing made from kente cloth with a matching headpiece—very African, very hip. She made Paula feel like an old maid secretary.

"You look fabulous, Berneice," Paula said.

"Yeah, I do," she answered. "Figured I'd shake these old Negroes up a little tonight."

"That ought to do it," Paula responded. She noted Berneice failed to compliment her on her outfit. Heaven forbid that woman should pass out praise she didn't mean.

One of the councilmen, Benjamin Berry, was rising from

Miss Kezee as she and Al reentered the parlor. He and his wife, Mamie, were among the last to pay their respects.

"Johnson," Mr. Berry called. "Fine party, sir. And, you're looking lovely tonight, Miss Paula."

"Thank you, Mr. Berry." Apparently it was good form for each person to tell the candidate's wife how lovely she looked. Paula felt frivolous, hanging off her husband's arm, making small talk, smiling. She'd heard that political wives drank like fish, and no wonder. She nodded at Mamie Berry, who barely responded. Mamie taught home economics at the high school. At some point, Paula figured, she must have done or said the wrong things to this woman. Whenever they met, she was cool and distant. Mamie said, "Wonderful to see Mrs. Johnson again," and Paula knew she wasn't the Mrs. Johnson being referred to.

"Mother is Miss Kezee now," Al corrected.

"Wonderful indeed," Mr. Berry continued. "Those were some days back when your daddy was mayor and your mama had this house." Benjamin Berry was in one of the generations between Al and Miss Kezee. If Al was going to win, he needed the support of those men. They were either stodgy, small-time truck farmers, or new-moneyed tyrants who'd made it big with franchise fast food or insurance offices in gullible small towns away from River Ridge. They were fairly well off and stayed around so they could flaunt their little bit of cash. Ben was the latter: a blustery robust man, tall, taken to resting his hands on his swollen belly.

"I voted for your daddy the first time he ran for mayor. Must have been in '62 or '63. He was a fine mayor. Mighty fine."

"Nice your saying that, but he didn't do a damn thing." Miss Kezee straightened her back when she began speaking. Her hands, gripping the end of the arm rests, pulsed rhythmically.

Paula squeezed tighter at Al's arm.

"How's the fried chicken business?" Paula asked.

"Always good," Berry said. "You see I'm eating . . ." His wife curled up her lip as if she smelled something. She was always giving Paula that look: at faculty meetings, at the gas station, if they ran into each other in the street. She was a fifty-year-old woman who, with the exception of her own mother, was the most fastidious person Paula had ever seen. There were a half dozen of them around town like her: middle-aged, professional women, prima donnas all, and they treated Paula the same way. She didn't know who was making her more nervous, Mamie Berry or Miss Kezee. She saw a smear on the sofa table and wished she'd done a better job dusting.

"I can't remember nothing ever changing round this damn town," Miss Kezee said. "I lived here a lot of years."

Though his wife looked disdainful, Benjamin Berry laughed a deep, hearty laugh. "Well, you know the saying, Miss Kezee: If it ain't broke, don't fix it."

"Sheeit." Miss Kezee adjusted her butt on the chair and waved her hand at the man.

Al inhaled like a bad singer getting ready to scan a long line. "We have a lot of things we'd like to see done if we're elected."

Here came one of his campaign spiels. In an attempt to orient the conversation away from her mother-in-law's range, Paula stepped back, pulling Al around with her. He just kept right on talking. "We need another playground up away from the river. I'd like us to build a small apartment building for the elderly. And a new recreation center."

Ben Berry bent forward. He listened, nodding politely, and rubbed his chin in what seemed to Paula a very stagy gesture. She could see Mamie not so subtly trying to drag him away from the conversation. She was probably afraid of contamination by lowlifes such as Paula and Miss Kezee. Janice Thompson, the other black woman teacher at Riverbluff Elementary, got invited to lunch by Mamie and company once or twice a year. The witches had a little club called Concerned Women of River Ridge, and they were grooming Janice for membership and would probably invite her once she reached respectable matronhood. Janice told Paula that the CWRR was vigilant against the common element of River Ridge that was trying to take over: people who didn't dress properly, attend church, or own full-sized American cars. People like Paula. Standing there, holding a glass between her thumb and forefinger, eyeing the undusted mantle, eyeing Paula: That these uppity crones in this nowhere place had the nerve to pass judgment on her . . .

Mamie's husband stood his ground, continuing his debate with Al. "Pretty ambitious plans," he said.

"That ain't saying nothing," Miss Kezee bullied.

"Beg pardon, ma'am."

"Boy's telling you all his big plans. What you got to say?"

"Well, one thing is: he's got a proud mama."

"Mama don't got nothing to do with this. First time in a long time I hear a politician say anything he plan to do. Tell the boy what you think."

Mamie expelled an exasperated sigh. Ben Berry pursed his lips, raised his brows. "Sounds like a lot of money to me, is what I think." Some of the light had gone out of his eyes. He shook his wife's hand from his arm, twisted his lips at the old lady in what was either resentment or admiration.

"Who would like another drink?" Paula offered.

"What you got to say about the money, boy?"

Al didn't miss a beat, he recognized his one chance to get his point made, and he sold his speech right into Berry's eyes.

"All improvements cost money," he said. "Unfortunately here in River Ridge we don't have any. We barely afford part-time police help and the fire district's fee's about to break us."

"So, the solution is to spend more money," Berry mocked.

"What I'm saying is we may be past the time when all these small towns can survive on their own. We can't make it alone." He had a voice for these political speeches that was different from his usual pitch, at least to Paula's ear it was. He spoke with a passion that had none of the edge of irony of his everyday manner. She watched for the wink and waited for the nudge, but neither came.

"You've got folks hereabouts pretty steamed up over this consolidation plan, young friend." Berry took on his "wise counselor" persona. Paula hated that.

"I've heard. Oak Grove and Cleta are communities about the same size as River Ridge. We've got a lot of the same problems. Our kids go to school together already . . ."

"Cleta and Oak Grove. Them's white towns."

"We're all aware of that, Mother." Paula said. Here came the humiliation part. She looked around for the few white guests who had shown up, politicos, Al's age all of them, people from around the area. The ones that showed up also favored consolidation.

Miss Kezee moved her lips around, mumbling at—about—Paula. "Not a lot of black towns around anywhere," Miss Kezee said. "Not in this part of the world. Shame to give up something like that."

"Your mother's right, son. We got something here worth holding onto." Ben was ebullient. He thought he had won the old lady to his side. His wife simpered at Paula, her frosty pink lips parting to reveal the sharp-looking tips of her teeth.

Al was annoyed, and Paula fought the vindictive feeling rising inside her: Let Al get a taste for a change.

He dug in. "Something you can't afford having may not be worth keeping. We're in a mess and getting deeper every year. We've got to get beyond the black/white thing."

A small crowd had gathered to listen to the political talk.

Despite Paula's effort they had formed a circle, with Miss Kezee seated at the head. She was alert, seemed to thrive on the attention.

"White folks don't want no black folks with em. That's a historical fact. I lived long enough to know." She sat back waiting for the response. Paula felt an irritation almost like an electrical surge flow through Al's body. An irritation at being set against his mother in public. Don Schwab, the councilman from Oak Grove, spoke up.

"Truth is, ma'am, we been living here together for a long time round this way. It's mostly just poor people around here, all of us struggling to . . ."

"What your mother means, Al," said Ben Berry, interrupting, "is we have a unique place here. A lot of people have strong ties. You don't just throw that away."

"Sounds like they ready to do just that," Miss Kezee said.

"Not true," Al said. Paula could hear the frustration that nibbled at the edge of his cultivated cool. "And I know how important this place is. I'm a native. Don here's a native of Oak Grove. We came back here to live because we care about this area. Drive along the river either way, you see dead or dying towns. Towns that couldn't survive in the new economy. Well, if we're not going to become one of those ghost towns, we have to do something. That's all we're saying. Consolidation is just one idea. We're open to anything that works."

Miss Kezee stood up at her chair and the room quieted. Paula thought she heard the old woman's knees popping in the silence.

"Sometimes," Miss Kezee said, "the best thing to do is not one blessed thing at all." She walked to Al, pulled his head down, and kissed him. Then she went and walked up the stairs. Paula excused herself from the silent room and followed.

Every step hurt today. Seem to hurt like hell. Who all these people they got up in here? Here this boy. Cute little old thing. Be looking like my mama. Move your butt, boy. Gotta stop to rest. Making steps steeper these days, Charlie. All the noise. All them simple-ass people down there. A person can't put up with too much foolishness. Let me help you, Mother, girl says. That girl, that Paula again. Lifts me under the arm. Seems to help. I get so tired, you know. Good night, Miss Kezee. Good night. Good night, Grandma. All these people.

Paula returned the pink dress to the hanger. Miss Kezee had gotten into the already turned-down bed fully dressed, but Paula got her up and changed her into a nightgown. She was so pliant, raising a rubbery arm on command, not uttering a sound. She could do whatever she wished with her: slap her, tie her up in the closet, drop her from the window. She had to remind herself to be fair. She hadn't behaved that badly. Not really. She hadn't behaved badly at all. She had just spoken her old mind.

"You comfortable, Mother?" She fussed with pillows and sheets. There was no response.

She knew she should be getting herself back to the party. She toyed with the idea of stationing the boys outside the room but decided, no, that was no way to live. This was not a jail. If she got up again, well . . . Whatever happened would happen.

"Anything else before I go?" She stood at the side of the bed. Miss Kezee grabbed her hand and held tight. Paula sat and waited for the familiar snore.

A bullet of silver streaking down the highway. A man with pretty brown skin. A fine-looking woman: thin, tiny-boned, older than she looks. A small suitcase packed as if for a business trip. A trunk packed with everything she owns. A warm autumn day. The hills of the river valley pulse with color. On the left the river sparkles in the sunshine.

"You're gonna like it down home," the man says.

The woman smiles.

The colors fade to gray and the river disappears. They are traveling a black tunnel, this same man and woman in his car with her belongings. A panic snatches at the woman's throat. She is suddenly lost, feels empty and terrified. She does not know this road or this man. The man's eyes shine. They are falling down a deep hole. They will never stop.

Paula lay in the dark, holding her husband's hand. They were both exhausted. After the last guests left, they had moved from room to room, rushing to stow away the evidence of the party: the half-filled cups, crushed snacks, crumpled paper debris that teetered at the edge of every mantle, table top, and windowsill. They had worked quickly, anxious to remove any sign of what had happened in their house. They acted almost as if something shameful or unpleasant had taken place. The party had gone very well. Al seemed to know what he was doing, saying all the right things to all the right people. Yet, afterwards, they had rushed around in silence, maniacally collecting ashtrays and bowls of snacks. Al hauled the garbage bags to the garage and she found herself running a damp cloth over the same surfaces she had dusted earlier.

Lying there beside her husband, she felt the same overstimulated exhaustion as after parent-teacher conferences. She had seen too many people in too little time. She had been scrutinized and cross-examined. She had made too much mindless small talk, and her brain was unable to shut itself off. She replayed conversations until the high points of the evening melded into a not-very-interesting play, one where she was the central character. The other performers drifted past, discharging lines, and she smiled and smiled. She smiled some more.

Beside her, Al too seemed restless. He'd been up a while, clacking away again on his computer. Doing so tonight hadn't expended any of his nervous energy. Though trying to be still—for her sake, she was sure—he shifted his body and scratched at himself. Every few minutes he forced air from his lungs through his nose. She squeezed his hand.

"Do you think things went OK?" he asked.

"Things went great," she answered.

He sighed. She didn't understand this insecurity, if that's what it was. For a generally competent man, often he seemed as full of doubts as she was. And, then, he could surprise her with daring aggressiveness. He was in many ways a constant surprise.

This campaign was a surprise. As long as they had been together they'd turned a cynical eye to politics and especially politicians. In his editorials he had a reputation for lambasting those public officials who struck him as ignorant or pompous. That was pretty much all of them. He'd as much as said that politics suited only the greedy and the inept. And now this.

In a queer way, this new Al—this political Al—felt like a betrayal. He was almost a repudiation of his younger self. She'd watched him all evening: conspiratorially shaking hands, glibly chit-chatting, laughing at vulgar and unfunny jokes, being the sort of person they'd both previously considered unattractive, unctuous, and self-serving.

Yet, it *was* him shaking those hands, seemingly glad to be receiving his guests, seemingly eager for their stories and opinions. She told herself he was sincere when he cocked his head forward to listen to their tales. She wanted to believe he found some true humor to spark his laughter. She reminded herself that River Ridge was a small town. That helped to keep it in perspective. It was a good way to stifle her fear that he was changing in some way that she was not. She did not want to wake up some night holding hands with a man she did not know.

"I'm worried about what Mama said about our plan," he said.

"Your mother says a lot of crazy stuff. There've been other people told you they didn't like consolidation."

"It's different when it's your mother."

"If you ask me, your mother should keep her mouth shut sometimes."

"I never asked her what she thought. Say, I never asked *you* what you thought. Tell me, am I crazy? Is messing with our town a bad idea?"

She turned to face him. True, she'd never been asked, but it was also true she'd never thought to be interested. That bothered her, but really not much.

"It's logical. I know how much you all have put into this plan. But I'm not from the area. I don't have the ties that . . ."

"What's that mean? You been here fifteen years. I thought . . ."

"What I mean is, a person whose family roots are here in River Ridge for generations will feel differently than an outsider."

He let go of her hand. "I thought you felt at home here."

She found the hand and grabbed it back. "I'm saying the wrong things. I'm tired. What I meant was I know you and I know you'll do what's right by this place. That's what I meant to say."

She hoped that was that. For her his plan was an abstraction. It was all about rearranging lines on a map—lines that were as irrelevant to her life as canals on Mars. She felt about River Ridge the way she'd felt about every other place else she had ever lived: a detached neutrality. She had long ago given up trying to make emotional connections to places. If River Ridge disappeared tomorrow . . .

There is a place on the river where from the bluffs you can see the golden corn waving in the Illinois sun. Here is the pleasant river town: a small main street with a few brick and clapboard stores. There are two church steeples and a few elegant homes. Even the poor, ill-made shacks are freshly painted and benign looking. There is a school, there are children. The people are busy and happy. The man with the pretty brown skin is beside the woman. She can see it all at once. In one look, in one view: all the people, the silos, the house. Bit by bit everything disappears, dissolves. Away goes the school, the river, the bluffs. She tries to fill in the pieces but can't. Everything is gone. All but the man. The other man. He is underwater, upside down. His lungs are filled with water, and he has been dead for quite some time.

6

PAULA HAD A GAME SHE WOULD PLAY IN THE CAR with her mother. They would drive up and down the streets of Saint Louis and make up things about the people living in all the houses. They played this when Paula was around the age of nine, and the main thing she remembered about it was the importance of the system: the game had to be played a certain way. First, her mother would catalogue the debris in the lawn and, using that as her guide, she would make a mental sketch of the occupants. There were apparently all these things you could learn just from the exterior. A perfect lawn and an elaborate garden meant retirees, people who didn't have anything better to do other than putter around in the yard. Bigwheels meant toddlers, and usually those yards were filled with other toys as well, bright, almost luridly colored things, the kinds Paula ended up buying for her own children. Ten speeds meant teens or young marrieds, and if she saw old wrecks and abandoned refrigerators, Paula knew the house was occupied by poor southern whites. After sizing them up, her mother created snap vignettes: that is where they have lost a child, and there is where they are dirt poor—have nothing, not one thing. And here they are enormously happy, and that one, this could be our home. Paula wondered what strangers guessed about her own family when they drove by the solid brick house above the river road. Could they tell this was a house where there were twins? Did they guess that blacks lived there? Were there signs a sick old woman languished in one of the rooms?

Paula played the game with herself as she drove up the drive to Oak Grove Manor. From the way it looked out here she figured it must be ultramodern inside, clean and cold: a place as scary as it was sterile. But maybe the well-groomed lawn and the orderly exterior cleverly concealed a run-down clapboard shack where, in cramped stifling wards, the residents packed together on rusting, bug-infested beds.

Actually Al had already given her the lowdown on the nursing home. He'd been out here to do news stories and more recently had been investigating senior care for his campaign. He said the place was "pleasant enough" inside and that the residents seemed well cared for. He'd told her all this the day after she returned from Saint Paul, when they had first talked about what to do with his mother. At the time Miss Kezee slept most of the day, and, when awake, seemed as fragile as a hatchling. They had taken turns keeping watch over her—feeding her broth, helping her to the toilet. They'd realized early on that the strain of full-time care might be more than they were able to manage. Paula had suggested they hire someone to sit with her, but they were both uncomfortable having a stranger in the house while they were away. Also, they didn't believe they would be able to find someone who would suit Miss Kezee. Al brought up the idea of a home.

"We have to look into finding a place for her around here," he'd said.

Paula had not responded. He'd avoided saying "a home." He knew how she felt about such places. A home is where her mother died. Without her.

Sorry, Mama.

And as she walked into the lobby of Oak Grove Manor, she

willed herself not to remember the lobby of the Chesterfield Life Care Facility. There wasn't much to remember. She'd only been there twice: once to check her mother in, and once . . . The lack of memory was a big part of her shame.

Inside, she was assaulted by a strong smell: stronger than a hospital, more sour and natural, an odor which seemed to come from everywhere around her. To her right, in a lounge papered with pale beige stripes were clusters of old people, some on sofas, some in wheelchairs. A TV blared: a golf tournament that no one seemed to be watching. The furniture faced the entry hall in a U shape in a way that made Paula feel as if she were on display. Several of the residents greeted her. A little too eagerly, she thought. A woman yelled, "Katie, Katie," to her. Paula directed her attention to a counter with a sliding glass window.

"Excuse me," she said to a girl in a blue uniform—a white girl in her twenties.

"Just a minute," the girl said. She called out, "Bill! Janet, get Bill's attention for me." Then to Paula she said, "Bill never remembers his meds. Come on over here and get your pill, guy."

Despite a constant shake, Bill looked vigorous. He sauntered to the counter and dumped down the pill from a pleated paper cup without bothering to take a drink. As he went back to the lounge area, Paula noticed a sign reminding Bill and the others in large letters of today's date and time.

"Can I help you?" the girl asked.

"I'm Paula Johnson. I talked to Ms. Collins about taking a look around."

"Make yourself at home." She offered a cup of coffee, pointed over to the lounge. "I'll find Ms. Collins for you."

Paula didn't look over at the seating area. She felt like a game-show host with hands full of money. She could feel the eager eyes at her back and dreaded getting involved in conversations about good old days she knew nothing about. She knew that probably half these people had tales of lost loved ones and neglectful children, tales of debilitating disease: enough stories back there to break a busload of hearts. She would not listen. She occupied herself with the sparse, large-lettered signage: REALITY ORIENTATION IS 24 HOURS A DAY. LOVE IS AGELESS—VISIT US. YOU ARE RESPONSIBLE FOR YOUR OWN MEDICATION. She was rescued by Jo Collins.

"Good to see you again, Paula. Come on back to my office."

Paula shook the offered hand and followed the woman a short way down a corridor.

"How are the kids?" she asked, and Jo filled her in. Her children attended Riverbluff Elementary. One, Michael, had been in the sixth-grade class across the hall from Paula's this year. She knew Jo vaguely from around town. Jo was a few years older than Al and had only moved to the area within the past two years. She was a mystery woman: no one had the full story on her: where she'd come from and why she'd relocated here to manage a small-town nursing home. Al said she had been active in the housing rights movement in Chicago and had married a Jewish lawyer. Those kids didn't look anything but black to Paula, but then she was never a good judge of that sort of thing. Another story said she was a triumphant unwed mother who had gone to school and gotten her life together, then moved to the country to leave her past behind. Paula liked that story the best. She liked the idea that someone could erase their past, choose a different life, and start over someplace new. Whatever the story, Jo wasn't talking. She admired that about her as well.

"This seems like a nice place up here."

"You have someone who'll be needing care?"

"My husband's mother is living with us now. We're thinking that we may need . . ." She choked and immediately felt foolish for doing so. She started again just as Jo began finishing the sentence for her. ". . . we think she may need more care than we can give her. You know. What with the boys and our jobs and all."

Jo nodded, and Paula thought she was trying too hard to show interest and concern. She was maybe forty-two but already looked matronly. She was fleshy, filled every crease of her blue suit. She wore her hair pressed and curled tight around her head: the way a lot of black woman her age had worn theirs for generations. She had inch-long nails, finely manicured and painted ruby red, rings on all but her thumbs.

"Don't be uncomfortable," she said. "This is not easy for anyone."

"We haven't made any decisions yet. We want to be ready in case . . ." She raised her hand to signal she'd need a minute. She was angry with herself, angry at whatever had let the tears come. She'd promised herself she would not get emotional. She felt ashamed at crying in front of this woman.

Jo handed her a tissue. "I've found over the years that by the time most people come in, things with the family member are often already at a crisis state. Round-the-clock care is very stressful. Why don't I show you around." Jo rose from her chair. "It helps to see what the facility is like. Look at some of the different kinds of residents we serve."

She walked Paula past the nursing station to where the corridor branched. Another large lounge area lay straight ahead, empty. The walls were painted the old-fashioned shades of yellow and green that to Paula were unpleasant—the colors of the appliances in her mother's kitchen in 1966. They were free of any adornment whatsoever.

"Down this wing we house our residents who are ambulatory and alert. You saw quite a few of them in the front lounge. Mostly these are people who are too frail to care for themselves alone. People who have some chronic ailment, like seizures or heart disease. People who need regular monitoring."

They stopped in an open doorway. An old man sat on his bed, leaning over on a cane and facing the window. He seemed to be looking at something on the floor.

"How's it going, Mr. Drew?" she called to the man.

He looked around, raised his cane, then went back to staring.

"Mr. Drew is ninety-one. Stays to himself. He's been with us about eight months."

Paula stepped back from the door, anxious to move on. "What's the matter with him?"

"Old age, mostly. He gets around pretty well. Feeds himself and whatnot. He has his bouts of serious illness. Pneumonia and what have you. He's sick often enough that his family couldn't manage."

A large black woman approached them on a walker.

"Hi!" she called in a cheery voice. She wore a bright housecoat and had thin, graying hair that stood up all over her head.

"Where you off to, Lou?"

"Need to stop for a while," she panted. She leaned over the walker to catch her breath. "I'm headed down to the lounge for a little visit." She extended a hand from the walker to Paula. "Hi. I'm Lou."

"Good to meet you."

"You got family here? Scuse the way I look."

Paula shook her head to let her know not to worry about her appearance. "I'm just looking around," she said.

"This is a fine place. Fine. This Jo here . . . ," Lou winked and gave the OK sign. "Can't do any better. On my way." She took off behind her walker with her mechanical thrust, step, thrust, step. She moved at a remarkable pace.

"Slow down on that thing," Jo called after her.

After she cleared the corner, Paula said, "She seems so young."

"Relatively. She's sixty-eight. The average age here is about eighty. Lou's hip joints are gone. Can't keep her house or get out to shop. She's in quite a lot of pain. If she's lucky, she'll be home in a year. After her surgery."

"Home?"

"People think of nursing homes as a place people go to die, but that's not always true. Often enough we transition people to or from the hospital. We love to see our people go home."

That idea cheered Paula. A little.

They had made an about-face and were traveling the wide, unobstructed hall into the other wing. The odors, which she had gotten used to, seemed to increase as they entered the other corridor.

"This is our acute care area. The patients here are extremely sick. Some are senile. Disoriented. Most are bedridden."

They strolled the corridor, closer to the center than in the other wing. Passing an open door, Jo would indicate a patient, list the condition, and then describe the extraordinary amount of effort that was required in giving care. Here was the postoperative cancer victim in some sort of incoherent agony, here was an apparently comatose patient, immobile except for the occasional violent shudder. From the doorway, his face was serene. Paula became aware of a sound: an incessant low moaning, a calling-out of nonsense words that rose and waned like the wail of a siren. A symphony of pain.

Jo continued her cool recitation of realities and facts. They approached a door from which came a forced sobbing—an old woman's crying.

And then it was not the same door at all.

It was the door of a different room, and inside the room a different black woman screamed in pain.

Sorry, Mama.

That door hadn't looked like this, had it? She'd been there only . . . twice?

The crying reached a pained peak. A gasp followed.

Paula excused herself and fled back down the hall. She took refuge in the empty lounge.

Thick, hot tears slid down her face. They dripped ridiculously from her jaw like rain spilling off a roof. She laughed at herself, felt like a fool, hoped the laughing didn't make her look sillier still.

Jo handed her some fresh Kleenex. She was a motherer, this Jo. Paula wondered if mothering was a habit you acquired when you reached Jo's age, the same way you acquired things like wrinkles and good serving dishes. If so, soon she would be carrying purses full of tissue and a head full of platitudes. She held up her own crumpled, sodden handkerchief: her mother'd said always to have one handy.

"I'm really sorry," she said. The words came as blubbering laughter.

"You would be surprised how often this happens. Everybody reacts a little differently, but everybody reacts. Let's go back to my office."

Where she listened to the spiel about recreational and therapeutic activities and was impressed. Then Jo handed her a fee schedule, which was impressive in its own way. Catching sight of the figures, her eyes involuntarily widened. The money thing. Her stomach clenched. She and Al would still have to get through the money thing.

"Good care is costly," Jo said. "You'll find our rates are competitive with other facilities of similar quality."

"Well, it's cheaper, actually, than where my mother was. I guess I just expected . . ." That Oak Grove Manor would be cheaper. That there might be discounts. That the people would all be well and happy. That she could be cool, neutral, and objective about the whole thing.

Paula couldn't say what she expected to happen here, how she expected she would feel. Here she was, blubbering, frightened, full of self-pity. She realized she had been totally unprepared for the visit and, more, that she had no idea how to prepare. All her mother's hard work. All the preparations to get her ready for whatever might come up in life. There were some things Mama hadn't thought of.

The façade game, that was her mother's game. It was a strategy, a technique. Paste on a face, make up a story, read someone's mind. If you wrote the story, you were in control. Those tricks just didn't work. Paula knew that. She had known for a long time. You could not make up lives for the people behind the walls—because they already had lives. Good lives and bad lives. Just a silly game of her mother's. The story you made up was always inevitably a lie. The young marrieds are lonely, the happy family has a desperate secret. Things were complex, there was never enough information.

Paula couldn't have guessed what Oak Grove Manor was like. She couldn't predict how to feel. The game was all about self-deception: a way of comforting yourself with ideas, as if you could make something true with only the power of your mind to back you up. It was her mother's way of cutting down on nasty surprises. Another of her foolproof ways of easing through life as smoothly as possible. She'd spent eighteen years trying to teach Paula all the rules. Eighteen years drilling them into Paula's head.

7

"THERE IS A RIGHT WAY TO DO THINGS AND A WRONG way to do things. You, young lady, will do things the right way."

She was always saying things like that: always giving directives, making pronouncements, pontificating.

When Paula was little more than her sons' age, she would spend long weekend afternoons with her mother learning "the right way" to do domestic tasks. She had the same sullen balkiness of all twelve-year-olds, and though many of the chores seemed absurd (starching napkins? waxing the stone floor in front of the fireplace?), she played along with a silent good humor. It wasn't hard work, just tedious and, somehow, pointless. What did she care if her bed had proper hospital corners? Who ever looked to see how the sheets were tucked in?

Her mother acted the part of high priestess, passing along the mysteries of the temple to her young acolyte. She lifted crystal from the dishwasher and held each piece to the light so Paula could learn which glasses might need an extra buff with the tea towel. They polished the silver until Paula was sure that one day it would be worn to slivers. Until she hoped it would be.

One afternoon her mother watched her lay a regulation dinner service. They had placed the extra leaves in the table and covered them with a linen cloth. The sharp, ironed creases of the linen stood erect like the spines of a mountain range. Her mother removed eight of everything from the china closet, set one place herself, and then ordered Paula to do the same seven times around. She followed behind her, bullying, lining up the butt ends of knives with the bottoms of plates. By the eighth place Paula's hands trembled and a spoon rang brightly against a glass.

"Why are we doing this, anyway?" Her frustration spilled forth in a nasal whine. Some days were especially hard, hot summer days, days when the other children up and down the block were jumping rope on the lawn or cooling their heels in an all-day matinee.

With an elegant flourish, her mother picked up and tented a pale pink napkin onto a plate. "A lady needs to know how," she'd said.

Paula knew how to do a lot of things. She knew how to tat lace, could iron a box pleat, make a béchamel sauce. She knew what clothes went with which season, made a serviceable pie crust. She lined her dresser drawers with lavender sachet, folded everything neatly before putting it away. She knew all these things by the time she was twelve, and her mother told her she was coming along nicely.

Paula's parents, Herbert and Helen Fuller, had married late in their lives. Herbert had spent his twenties and thirties peddling assorted insurance policies to the residents of north Saint Louis. He was a stolid, efficient man, full of conservative virtues. He believed if a man worked hard he could make something of himself, believed God was on his side, helping make his path easier. He shunned community affairs, thought the NAACP radical. By the age of forty he had established himself as one of the largest independent insurance agents in the city. He had an office with salesmen and secretaries and assistants, and he invested his commissions wisely. He was, if not rich, quite well off. And very lonely.

Helen Thomas graduated from the Stowe Teacher's College and began a career in the city's schools. Being the daughter of a doctor, the role of old-maid schoolteacher was neither what she wanted nor expected. She expected to marry young and marry well, but the men she met were often poorer and almost always less well educated than she. People called her striking, handsome, and full of character, but they never called her pretty. With her sharp features and her old-fashioned style, she was not the sort of girl that men chased after.

Just after her thirty-ninth birthday, she met Herbert at a church picnic. He thought she was rather snooty, and she thought him an old fuddy-duddy. They spent the day talking, found that in the small world of black middle-class Saint Louis they had spent the last twenty years just missing each other. By the end of the day, each knew they would marry the other, or so Helen had claimed.

They had a large and elaborate wedding. There was a page of coverage in the *Saint Louis American*. The yellowing and crackly clippings were kept under plastic in a large, cloth-bound album tied with blue ribbon. A gossip columnist said people had been talking about these two for weeks, that Saint Louis had been holding its breath waiting for this day. Everyone who was anyone was there. The newspaper underlined the word *everyone*, and went on to list various doctors and politicians and other people who must have been important at the time.

Helen Fuller claimed to care nothing for all the social hubbub. There was lost time to be made up for. Their peers had children entering their teens and fabulous homes near good private schools. She got to work. They bought a large old house on West Pine and set about fixing the place up. Paula arrived in about a year.

There was an urgency Paula heard in her mother's voice whenever she talked about this time. Whether her insistence was because of the lost years or because this period of her life was so short-lived, Paula never knew.

When she was five, her father died a quick and painless death in the office of the Fuller Insurance Agency. He reached up to retrieve a book from a high shelf and fell over dead from a cerebral hemorrhage.

Though she barely remembered him, nor much at all from the time before his death, she was never allowed to forget his face. Her mother had turned several rooms into shrines to her late husband. A favorite photo appeared most often: his insurance calendar photo. In the picture he was stiff and unsmiling. He looked, somehow, dependable, and there was a square of light that shone on his balding head. There were four of these pictures around the house, each in an ornate silver frame. They were dusted often and just-so, to avoid scratching. When Paula held the pictures up and tickled them with the feather duster she could never associate them with any memory. He could be any man for all she knew. When she did remember her father, she had a wispy image of a very large man with a scratchy face. It took her a long time, until after she herself was married, in fact, to realize the man her mother was remembering to her was a husband and not a father. To Helen he was wonderfully kind, patient, full of love for God, life, and for the finer things. A cautious man with elegant tastes, a genius, a saint.

Paula remembered her fascination at the day's growth of beard that scratched her face when he picked her up at the end of the work day. Oh, yes, and how tall he was. Nothing else, really.

He left them well set financially. And while their friends expected her to sell the agency and live regally off the proceeds, Helen took over the office and doggedly set about making the company more successful than ever. She shamelessly cultivated her doctor father's circle of professional friends, her own former colleagues, and anyone else she thought she could sell. She played well the role of beleaguered widow, predicting upcoming lean years, worrying over her daughter's expensive tastes. She designed new package deals for the already over-insured.

She made a killing.

She invested in speculative property—almost always selling up—and just as she was brilliant and shrewd, she was also ruthless and as hard as nails.

When she was sixteen, Paula spent the summer typing part-time in her mother's agency. The offices were in a low-rise building of tan-colored brick just north of Forest Park on Union Boulevard. The three awkwardly rectangular rooms were connected by the same corridor that connected all the other offices on the floor. Paula worked in a tunnel-like space that served as a reception area. Wilma Dixon was the secretary and bookkeeper. Wilma, as two-faced as they came, was an ally of her mother and would report back with glee who had slammed Helen so that the two women could plot the demise of the transgressor. (Unless, of course, the person was a money-maker. Helen's motto: business first.) Wilma was a prim-looking woman with a mouth that seemed permanently puckered. She always wore pink cardigan sweaters and hung her glasses around her neck on a beaded chain. She had been Herbert Fuller's secretary for ten years before Helen took over and was as much a part of the agency as the transoms over the doors. She supervised Paula that summer, handing her letters to type in a way that Paula thought smug and disrespectful. She said things such as: "When you've got time, here's a little something to do," and "Your mother would like this as soon as possible."

Paula hated her. The agents and salesmen who worked in

the large room next door gathered around Wilma's desk, whispering and drinking coffee. They talked about her mother, laughing at the things she had supposedly said and done. They used transparent codes—called her "herself" and "cow." They called her the names of other female animals as well.

Often, Paula sat hunched over her desk, shivering and numbed by the droning window air conditioner that her mother insisted run all the time. She said the customers expected a cool office. When Paula wasn't typing, she read for the summer school classes her mother had found for advanced high school students at a local college.

There was a new full-time typist that summer, a skinny dark-skinned girl who wore dirty white blouses and tight skirts. Her name was Vonda, and she and Paula ate lunch sometimes down in a musty, smoke-smelling basement room. They sat on folding chairs beside a row of ancient and neglected vending machines. Vonda belonged to an evangelical church and often brought books and pamphlets to lunch to try to convert Paula. She wouldn't talk about much else.

One day Helen came in from her office down the corridor waving a stack of letters Vonda had written. She went straight to Vonda's desk. She fanned the letters, then tossed them in the air where they drifted past Vonda like gigantic flakes of snow.

"Don't you dare send garbage like this from my office and expect to work here another day."

Each of those words, said slowly, was crisp and full of sound. They were like cold steel in Paula's ear. Her mother stomped out, muttering about shiftlessness and time-wasting.

Vonda sat quiet a moment, nodding her head and biting her lip. She gathered her purse and keys and walked to the door. She pointedly stepped over the letters on her way. Her eyes met Paula's as she passed by Paula's desk.

"That mama of yours," she said.

Wilma ran after her, leaving Paula feeling idle and foolish. They had already gone through two typists that summer.

When she thought her knees would support her, Paula gathered the scattered letters into a neat stack and lay them on Vonda's desk. The work was no better nor worse than her own. Wilma came back alone. "I guess you and I will be doubling up on the work around here," she said. Paula remembered the sarcastic tone of her voice.

The intercom on Wilma's desk buzzed.

"Your mama wants to see you."

Her mother's office was larger than the narrow rectangle the three secretaries shared. It was pleasingly more squared, still furnished exactly the same way as the day Herbert had reached for his last book of insurance tables. Old-fashioned gray-green filing cabinets gathered along the south wall. By the desk stood two silver cylinder ashtrays whose sand had to be filtered every night. The only addition was a large oil painting of her father. In the full length portrait he was posed like Napoleon with a hand tucked up by his vest pocket. He dominated the portrait, which was fortunate, because the background was disorienting and vague. He was posed in front of nothing. Behind him was muddy green receding to pale blue at the top. A brass plaque pinned to the frame read "OUR FOUNDER."

"Sit down," her mother said.

Paula's stomach clutched and bubbled. Whatever she had done—slow typing, poor spelling—she was grateful only that her mother had been kind enough to spare her embarrassment in front of that awful Wilma.

Helen sat there turned sideways at her desk, rubbing at her belly. "I tell you, girl. Some days this office . . . You have to watch those people all the time."

Paula said nothing. She sat, frozen, taking her mother in. At fifty-six she had an amazingly youthful face with bright, unlined skin. She was slightly darker than Paula—a wet-cardboard color. She'd rinsed silver and blue highlights into her hair, and, in the fashion of the day, she teased it off the crown of her head from where it fell in a stiff flip.

"Get me a glass of water, baby."

Paula filled the mug from a bubbler in the corridor. Her mother popped two aspirins into her mouth and swallowed. She rubbed at her stomach and made a moaning noise.

"Have you given any thought to that party you're invited to on Saturday?"

Paula sighed, partially in relief, partially in frustration. "We've been through this. I'm not going." Her friend, Steve— her bodyguard, her shield—was on vacation at Yellowstone. She had no intention of going without him.

"I'm thinking you should go. We'll take the afternoon off, go to Stix, and get you a new outfit."

"I'm not going."

Her mother spun and faced her. The leather chair was just higher than the one Paula sat in so her mother could look down at whoever sat across from her. She clicked her tongue. "A lovely afternoon pool party. Tell me one good reason why you shouldn't go."

"You tell me why I should."

"Aren't we full of ourself today? Why? Because I've asked you to go. Because all the best young people in the area will be there."

"I don't like any of those people."

"You don't know those people."

"I know enough."

"There's that lovely Stacy Hunter. Such a delightful young woman."

"That bitch." Paula averted her eyes from her mother's

wince. "She's the most evil person between here and Africa. She only talks to people whose daddies make as much money as hers. Or more."

"That's certainly not a problem for you."

"I do not want to go." For the first time she heard an aggressiveness in her own voice that surprised and thrilled her. There must have been something in the way she had seen her mother handle Vonda that had roused a similar current in herself. You had to be direct with people. Tell them just what you wanted.

The thrill was short lived. Her mother rose, gathered her purse and the jacket to her suit.

"Sometimes we have to do things we don't want to do," she said. She opened the door for Paula. They went to West Roads and bought Paula a dress she would wear only once.

After her husband died, as his legend grew, so grew the myth about all the great plans they had for their daughter. At some point there developed an actual list that her mother would produce with a flourish to celebrate, confirm, or reinforce: ballet class at this studio, tap instruction at another, music lessons at CASA. The Friend's School for the early grades, high school at Rosati Kane. Paula suspected the list was apocryphal: her parents had never discussed any of this before her father's death. Still, her mother followed the plan faithfully.

When Paula was eight, her mother signed her into Hansel and Gretel, a social club for the children of professionals. On Saturdays, carloads of shiny brown faces would take exotic trips to go horseback riding or hiking in the country. They rode the Admiral and went to the Art Museum, spent days at Grant's Farm. Paula remembered all of that as having been fun. She remembered being just another sticky, spoiled brat. Her mother with the other mothers would sit apart from the children. Helen was a cult figure among them: the successful widow, the competent older woman. They sat around her, heads bent and huddled. They might have been gossiping or sharing recipes, but thinking back, Paula imagined what they had been doing was making matches amongst the youngsters, planning the next generation.

When Paula was thirteen, Hansel and Gretel stopped being fun. Her first event after admission into the teenager's group was a Sunday afternoon tea. Her mother bought her a new blue dress and dropped her off at Dr. Davis's house in University Heights. She wandered the party with a girl named Cassie Thornton. They made the inane small talk they'd been taught to make, keeping their white gloves as spotless as possible. The afternoon was pleasant enough until she and Cassie were waylaid by Stacy Hunter. Since they were kindergartners, Stacy had an uncanny way of showing up wherever Paula did: same dance class, same wedding receptions. Here she was, surrounded by a group of boys with shaved oily heads and smiles that kept going crooked. Every boy's suit looked ridiculously new.

"My daddy bought him two new Cadillacs last year," one of the boys said. He made a two like a victory sign with his fingers.

"What's he do?" Stacy asked him. She touched the boy's arm and drew her hand back, fixing it just under her chin.

"He's a dentist," the boy said. "Got him a big practice." He rolled up on his heels when he said "big" as if the word itself had pulled him up.

The others all nodded in what seemed to be smug appreciation. An anemic laugh went around. Paula remembered the laughter seeming absurd to her even then. And though she had laughed with them, she had probably laughed for the wrong reasons.

"Hi. I'm Charlie Jones. Who are you?" The dentist's son spoke to her. He was about sixteen and had cute brown eyes behind black-rimmed thick glasses. He offered her his hand.

"Paula Fuller. It's nice to meet you."

"What's your daddy do?" he asked. He asked sharply, almost as a joke, she remembered.

"Her daddy's dead," Stacy Hunter said. She tilted her head to the side in mock sympathy. There seemed to be a snicker in her voice.

There might have been a sympathetic "oh" in the awkward silence that followed. Paula didn't remember. She remembered for a moment she had forgotten how to speak. And when she came back to herself she said, "My mom sells insurance." But it was already too late. The party crowd already seemed to be backing away from her, excusing themselves to join other conversations.

When she'd said "sells insurance," she felt a hot rush of shame. Her wide blue headband felt as if it were crushing her skull. Since that time she often felt that those feelings had been projected on her. All the same, the image of a tall skinny girl, dumbstruck and abandoned, still broke her heart.

She never told her mother what happened. But she made up her mind that she would not be going to any such events in the future. She knew there was no reasoning with her mother about Hansel and Gretel, so she played on her mother's predilection for overprogramming, signing herself up for every activity she could find, especially ones that met at the same time as the social club. She learned how to do a lot more things still: bookbinding, paper folding, ikibana, urban forestry. She became a walking encyclopedia of useless handicraft. This pleased her mother, a strong believer that idle hands were indeed the devil's workshop.

Occasionally her mother seemed to see through the ruse. She would cancel Paula's afternoon class in kitemaking and force her to a Hansel and Gretel outing. These wouldn't have been so bad, except the parents always left excessive time for "circulating," as her mother called it. Paula would stand there alone with a sweating glass of Coca Cola. People would wander by, always smiling and pleasant but never stopping to talk to her.

From the sidelines her mother coached her: "Go over to that group. Be more friendly. Circulate! Smile." When Paula went up to the group, the conversation always stopped. She always thought they'd been talking about her.

There were other people who seemed left out, too. There were disgusting people like Sheree Lawton, a chubby snotty girl who rudely insinuated herself into any conversation she could find. Sheree flitted from group to group, brandishing whichever fabulous piece of jewelry her daddy just bought her. Paula knew the others laughed at Sheree behind her back. They laughed right in her face, too: she didn't care. Her daddy owned a radio station and he could buy and sell all of their daddies. As far as Paula could tell she was absolutely shameless.

There was Curtis Petry. He was considered something of an idiot. He sat and bobbed his head not quite in time to the latest record. The Jackson Five was big then. He had a smile that made him look stupider than he probably was. He picked at his nose and at other parts of his body too.

There were others: a very dark-skinned girl who snapped at people, and a druggie wild girl who was almost never around. There was tall lanky Steve Granberry whose father was a surgeon. He was so painfully shy that when Paula first approached him she thought he would cry.

She first talked to him at a Christmas dance when she was fourteen. All the girls were wearing ugly short formals, and the boys looked too young for their tuxedos. To get out of her mother's line of sight Paula put a wide Grecian column between them. She found herself standing next to Steve.

"I hate this," she said.

He swallowed, loud enough for her to hear. She heard him say, almost inaudibly, "I know."

"Can I just stand here and talk to you?"

He nodded.

"My mother yells at me if I don't talk to people. Circulate! That's her thing. I hate it."

"I know," he whispered.

They stood there side by side with their backs to the column, as if prepared for sacrifice. They didn't talk. Eventually he asked her if she wouldn't like to sit down.

They sat in a row of chairs beneath the mezzanine. Before them, couples spun around and gyrated on the dance floor. Across the room, parents clustered at the food tables.

Paula sighed and then Steve sighed. Then they both sighed. They laughed, and she felt him relax beside her.

"I hate every mothafucker in this room," he said.

A deep laugh came from inside her. She had to turn and cover her mouth so as not to be seen: her mother said a lady did not laugh like a horse.

They became friends. They would arrange to be at the same events, staking out a corner, spending the evening running down the phonies and snobs they'd both come to despise. Steve knew all the good dirt. He was a sophomore at Saint Louis University High School, where many of the boys in the club went. He was something of a minor basketball star himself. He was popular and people told him things. He knew which girls were promiscuous sluts and who got drunk and wrecked the family car on a regular basis. Paula reveled in the gossip: she was the sort of person no one told anything.

Ironically, she found herself raised in stature now that she was considered part of a couple. They were invited to private parties and on double dates. Whatever scourge made her unacceptable was erased when they were together.

"Does it bother you," Steve asked her one night, "that people think we go out?"

"I don't care what people think," she told him, and she didn't.

He never did ask her out on a real date. He was a sweet, gentle person, and like Paula, he read books and seemed to care about other things beside money and popularity. He was funny, smart, and even a good-natured gossip. He never went after the little guys. Her mother told her often that she thought Steve was "a good catch."

Just before he left to go away to Georgetown to play basketball, he took Paula to get frozen custard and to tell her he thought he was gay. He cried, and then laughed, and then cried some more. She kissed him on the cheek and told him it was OK. She had no idea how it would be. She had just turned seventeen. She was happy that for the first time in her life she felt trusted, felt truly a part of another person's life.

"Everything will work out fine," she said, and for the most part things had. They had survived parents and college, marriage and, so far, AIDS. Steve and his lover visited River Ridge every now and then. He spent an afternoon teaching the twins fancy ball tricks under the backboard on the garage. But he no longer updated Paula on whatever happened to the Hansels and Gretels. She couldn't have cared less.

Paula's mother forced her to go to the pool party after all. First she made her buy a busy floral print sun dress with a pleated bodice. Thin strings tied in big bows on her shoulders.

"This is so retarded looking," she told her mother.

"We'll take it," Helen said. "I just don't know what to do about developing taste in you, young lady."

"*Your* taste, you mean."

"Don't get snappish with me. I don't like your tone lately."

Paula turned her head to the car window, hiding behind the pressed hair that fell in front of her face. She hated that hair. The seventies were here. Everyone had Afros. Everyone in *Jet* and in *Ebony* and on "Soul Train." Her mother said wild hair would never be acceptable in *her* community.

"Sullen isn't pretty," her mother said.

"I'm not being sullen. It's just . . ."

"Just what?"

"Just that everything has to be your way."

"My way." Indignation dripped from her mother's voice.

"The dress you like. The party you want me to go to."

Her mother pulled the car off Lindell Boulevard and stopped. She noisily shifted into park.

"Why do you think I spend all this time and effort on you? Tell me why?"

"Because you don't have anything else to do."

Her mother let out a loud "Hmph." "I do it because I know just how hard it is for a black woman to survive in this town. I see these Gerties out here walking up and down the street with nothing to do and I tell myself that is not going to happen to my girl. You will get every advantage. And I hope that's not a problem for you."

Though her mother insisted again and again that she answer, Paula said nothing.

"Fine," her mother said. "That's just fine. See how far that attitude gets you. Fine."

Fine usually indicated her mother was through. But not today. She was hot. She'd take the damn dress back. She'd find some other girl who could appreciate everything Paula had.

Spend a little something on herself for a change. She didn't know what became of girls like Paula, though she had a pretty good idea—you could just drive up any alley in the city of Saint Louis and see trash. She didn't know what she'd done wrong.

Paula closed herself in her bedroom against the continuous ranting. An hour later and her mother was still down there in the kitchen carrying on. She sprawled across her bed and listened to her wear herself out. It wasn't this bad usually. As long as Paula went along with the program. But she was sixteen now, and tired of the program. She was trapped, and, more importantly, there was some new kind of power taking hold.

For the rest of the week her mother spoke coolly to her, if she spoke to her at all. At the office she sent cryptic messages through Wilma, who delivered them as if they were delicious barbs.

"Your mother says she's gone to lunch with a client. You're to eat from the machines in the basement."

Paula usually went on all business lunches. Her mother thought they were excellent opportunities, an important part of her training.

"You, of course, can share a little of what I've got here," Wilma added, voice saturated with bogus sympathy.

Paula bought Fritos at a confectionery. She sat at her desk and crunched them all afternoon to annoy Wilma.

At breakfast on Saturday, Paula curled over a bowl of cereal, reading Friday's *Post Dispatch*. She avoided her mother's eye. Whatever her mother was cooking for herself was especially noisy: sizzling pans slamming against the stove, something being scraped and stirred.

"Well?"

Paula looked up. Her mother stood before her, fully made up, coifed, an apron covering her gray suit. Dressed that way, 9:35 on a Saturday morning. Paula shrugged.

"Are you doing what's expected of you today or not?" Her mother had her hands on her hips. A spatula shot out from one side.

Paula shook her head. "I don't want to go."

She turned off the stove and came and sat in a chair right in front of Paula. She took Paula's hand. "Look at me," she said.

Her eyes were stern and full of water.

"I am asking you as one adult to the other to do this for me."

Paula dropped her eyes from her mother's fierce stare.

Her mother grabbed her chin. "Look at me. Say you'll do this for me."

"All right." She cried out the words. She pulled herself away from her mother and ran up to her room. She sobbed angrily, hating herself for giving in so easily, for succumbing to such transparent manipulation. If only this time—some time—she could say no. Such a simple word: No. No, Mother, I won't. No. I'm sorry, no. I can't, no. No. No. No.

She heard her mother's voice at the door. "I'm proud of you, baby. I'll be back from the office at one. Be ready about then." She walked away and then returned. "Oh, and get the dishes for me, too, baby. Thanks."

The door closed and the car pulled away. Paula lay there on the bed, paralyzed. She rolled over and fell asleep.

When she opened her eyes the clock said "12:55." She threw herself out of bed, groggy and startled by the late hour, ripped the plastic from the dress and slid into it. She grabbed her sandals and made a run for the kitchen. If she hurried she could at least load the dishwasher before her mother came in. Halfway down the steps she faced her mother, come in the door carrying a briefcase.

"Oh. Paula. Look at you." Paula's hair was uncombed and the tags hung from the dress like party decorations. Crumbs of sleep nested at the corners of her eyes. Her mother pointed her back upstairs.

Still numbed from sleep, her mother ordered her about as if she were a toddler.

"You never learn, do you. Never learn." She followed her around, brushing at her cheeks. "You're all puffy."

"Sorry, Mother."

"Where are those panty hose. I bought you hose to wear with this."

Paula pointed at a drawer. She didn't care to argue that she'd thought to wear sandals, and why bother: her mother had already kicked the sandals back in the closet. Helen grabbed a pair of low-heeled pumps, then produced from somewhere a headband that matched the dress. She flipped Paula's hair through the restraint and said, "There," in a self-satisfied voice.

Paula gaped into the full-length mirror, appalled. "Mother. I look like Tricia Nixon."

"You are a living doll," she said, and she kissed her. "When you want to be."

With Steve absent from the party, Paula felt as if she were without a part of herself. She felt like an alien. Over the past two years they had learned enough tricks to make it appear they were being social and having a good time, even though they spent most of the time not talking to anyone. They'd even gotten brave enough to go out on solo forays to the refreshment tables and even for a spin on the dance floor now and then. She didn't want to do any of those things without him.

They were at the penthouse pool of an apartment building in Clayton. A cool day for midsummer. The sun sparkled off the pool, and some of the younger crew were in the water splashing around. The older kids would not swim. The girls would not deign to wet their pressed hair. Sharp flashes of light reflected from the water and the whole roof looked manic in the sparkly light. She parked herself near the food. Occasionally she would walk from one end of the table to the other and nibble on something. A savory cheese spread tasted good on some oddly shaped crackers.

Her mother came out from the penthouse where the parents had gathered. "Circulate! Go down there and get with the other young people." She grabbed a finger sandwich and pointed Paula to the older kids on the other side of the roof. "You look silly down here," she whispered. Then she went back inside.

Paula strolled the length of the pool to where the others were clustered under bright yellow umbrellas. She put her hands behind her back and tried to look casual.

Stacy Hunter came over to greet her. "Cute dress, Paula," she said. She was wearing an identical one in a different color, except to hers she had added a white silk blazer, which made it dressy and sophisticated. Paula was reminded of what she hated most about Stacy: she was so perfect. Barbie-doll perfect hair and figure and teeth and clothes. She thanked her for the compliment anyway. Stacy linked arms as if they were the best old girlfriends in the world. She probably did think of Paula as a friend: she called up now and then to gossip, and she always invited her to her parties, though Paula suspected that that was her mother's doing. She treated Paula, always, like the new girl in town, the poor half-orphan girl: "You know Paula, she's the shy one who won't talk to anybody. Her mother is very successful, let me tell you. They live in a fabulous house. We've been friends forever."

"Come join us," Stacy said.

Kiss my ass, Paula thought.

There was no conversation going on. A dozen or so, they sat beautifully posed as if for some painter.

"Where's Steve?" Tony Sims asked her.

"Vacation," she answered.

Tony nodded. He was a boy whom she thought was getting more handsome every time she saw him. He and Steve were classmates. Steve said Tony was so dumb his parents had to donate large sums of money to the school's endowment to keep him enrolled.

"You two are pretty tight, huh?" Tony asked her.

She giggled and raised her brows seductively.

"Yeah, I know all about you Rosati girls."

Rosati girls. CBC boys. Villa girls. SLUH boys. Paula tried to step out of herself so she could see herself in this picture, this idyllic picture of private school brats on a Saturday afternoon outing. She couldn't do it. She could see the picture all right—the fashionable clothes, the cool posture, the studied indifference—but she couldn't find herself in it. Somehow, she didn't fit. There was something she didn't get right.

They sat for what seemed like hours. Not really talking, not really doing anything. The boys would occasionally flip bottle caps at each other or get up for snacks. The girls would compliment each other on their lovely earrings and perfect nail polish.

Just then, Paula realized how different she and Steve were from this crowd. They actually liked each other. They talked to each other, enjoyed one another's company. No one had to force them to go to any ridiculous patio party. They weren't fulfilling anyone's fantasy. They had a great time, and they had been so busy with each other she'd never before heard this: this maddening stultifying silence.

She felt an unbearable tension. She felt like screaming. Yet, around her the others were calm, stiff, frozen in place. How horrible, this casual complacence. There was no need for conversation. They were doing just what Mommy and Daddy always said they should do. They were playing the roles, going along with the game. They had arrived. There was nothing more to be said.

My God, Paula thought. How happy they all seem. They have become what we were meant to become: handsome and beautiful, well-mannered, polished. The most perfect children in the world. And they really like it.

She filled with anger and resentment. Was it really this easy, this being what you were expected to be? If so, what a horror. Were this a zoo, she would rush from cage to cage and free them. "Wake up and run," she would yell. "You don't have to be here anymore." But she couldn't free them—they didn't want to be free. They liked who they were. They were happy. She was the one who didn't belong. She was the one who needed freeing.

Her anger turned to joy. She thinks now she was laughing because even then she knew she had escaped. She didn't know how she did it: to this day she still couldn't really say how, but she had. She laughed to herself until the laughter burst loose and she sat there cackling out loud, no ladylike hands over the mouth this time.

"Know any good jokes?" someone asked.

"Yeah," she laughed. "All of you. All of you suckers," she said, and she laughed some more.

She spied her mother approaching down the side of the pool, escorting a woman Paula had never seen before.

"Last one in is a rotten egg." She kicked off the shoes and threw herself into the pool.

Of course no one else jumped, though some of the boys did applaud her effort. Her mother stood at the edge of the pool barking her name.

The water was pleasantly warm. She floated on her back,

her ruined hair waving around her head, feeling light as spun sugar.

"Girl! Girl!" her mother barked.

She swam to a ladder and climbed out. She walked by the crowd, picked up her shoes, and gave her body a full shake. Water exploded from her hair and the boys gave her leering smiles. They were staring, she knew, at her nipples, which stuck through the clinging dress. Stacy Hunter was furious with shock. She glared at Paula from behind large dark glasses.

"See ya," Paula said.

"Yes, indeed," one of the boys answered.

She put an extra wiggle in her walk. She walked to her mother, who stood there with the alligator pocketbook she always carried slung over one arm. The barking was all over. There was now something stony in her expression. She wore neither a smile nor a frown, her eyes flat and vacant.

"I would like to introduce you to Mrs. Williams. Mrs. Williams, this is my daughter, Paula Fuller."

Paula took the woman's hand and nodded. She was an older woman, pale, a neat, tailored-looking person wearing a dress that looked, Paula thought, like something a missionary would wear.

"I see you're having fun," the woman said. Her tone was patronizing and belittling.

"I'm ready to go home now, Mother." She walked away to the elevator. She realized people were staring at her, but she didn't care.

On the way to the car, she steeled herself against her mother's assault. Her mother would start off on the Parkway, mumbling. By the time they reached the city limits, she would begin lecturing, and she would be on a full rampage as they pulled up to the house. Once inside she would slap her hard, knocking her to the ground. She would call her a worthless little guttersnipe and banish her to her room.

Paula decided she would not take it, she would stand up to her mother once and for all—tell her what she thought about her stupid clubs and her phony friends and their phony kids and the ugly clothes she picked out. She'd tell her about the drunken orgy Stacy Hunter and Albert Watkins threw when his parents were out of town. She'd tell which boys from "fine families" sold nickel bags in the cafeteria to support their own varied nasty habits. She'd start as soon as her mother started. She would not be beaten down. She'd say everything she had to say.

Her mother said nothing. She followed Paula to the elevator with the same icy look frozen on her face. She nodded courteously to the doorman before they walked to the car, parked a block away at a meter. Paula expected her to fuss about getting the cloth seats wet. She was still soppy, the wet dress dripping at the hem and clinging to her like a second skin. Her mother said nothing. She started the car and pulled away from the curb.

Her feelings of pride and triumph mixed with regret. She felt uncomfortable and foolish in the air-conditioned Lincoln. Her hair had sprung up into nappy, pipe-cleaner like coils, occasionally releasing streams of cold water that dripped down her exposed shoulders. She turned the air vents away from her to cut the chill.

The pride that had turned to regret turned to rage. She was angry at the fools around the pool, angry at her mother for taking her there—for taking her to all those places for all those years. Angry at her mother for bringing her to this, to where she was now: a wet and foolish person, covered in gooseflesh, in a ruined sun dress.

"I hope you're satisfied," she said.

Her mother said nothing. She drove. Same frozen look, same even breaths.

Paula began to shiver. She found she couldn't get a breath. She reached up and clicked off the air-conditioner.

"I'm freezing."

Her mother lowered halfway the power window on Paula's side of the car.

Paula's shuddering continued. Tears leaked from the corners of her eyes.

"I'm not like them. Don't you see, Mother? I'm not like them. I'm not. I'm not." She screamed the words over and over until she collapsed against the car door in a sobbing rage.

With one finger, her mother steered the car off West Pine and up the narrow drive. She let them in the back door of the house. Paula followed her like a puppy, through the mud porch, into the kitchen. Her mother scanned the room, noting the slimy plates and the greasy stove top. She added a set jaw to her cold stare. She turned to Paula.

"You shame me," she said softly.

Paula shook her head.

"Please take care of this mess before supper," her mother said. She got her purse and left.

On the following Tuesday during her lunch hour Paula walked to the Wantu Wazuri Beauty Salon on Delmar and had her hair cut and shaped into a full Afro. She walked back into the office as if nothing had happened.

Wilma did a double take, then sat staring at her. Paula looked up occasionally, giving Wilma coy smiles. Wilma stared a good five minutes before she left the office. Shortly after, her mother threw open the door. She filled the door frame, locked her eyes on Paula. Wilma stood behind her with her arms crossed. Paula straightened her back and stared her mother down. Her mother closed the door and clicked back down the hall on her high heels.

Later in the day Wilma told Paula she thought that the cut "flattered" her.

"I think it's darling," she simpered.

I just bet you do, Paula thought.

She didn't ask and her mother obstinately refused an opinion on a deed done. She expressed herself eloquently, though, through the noisy way she handled her utensils at dinner. And, there was an almost constant, probably unconscious shaking of her head.

"I suppose it will be easy to keep," she eventually mumbled.

Paula shrugged. She loved her hair and was past caring what her mother thought. She spent long hours over the next week staring at herself in the mirror, marveling at the person she had become. For the first time she realized that she might actually be pretty. She felt accomplished and wonderfully new.

Many years passed before Paula finally understood the change in dynamics that had occurred when she emerged from the pool. The difference was subtle, and to the sixteen-year-old her mother seemed as suffocating and controlling as ever. She was, in fact, quite different. Where once she had worked hard to plan each detail of Paula's life, the confrontation with the willful creature dripping on the penthouse roof had caused something inside her to go mealy. She was reduced to rules: terse prescriptions she recited in a theatrical, affected voice. Apparently there was a rule for almost any situation, and her mother knew them all: a lady never runs up the stairs, does not talk to strange men on the phone, always keeps "bread and butter" notes handy. Don't wear white before Memorial Day. Keep a sweater at the office. Never identify where you are going, even euphemistically, as the "powder room." Just say excuse me.

Her mother recited the rules, and Paula rolled her eyes. If she did anything at all. With Steve and her other friends the little homilies became a joke. Any ridiculous sight was an opening. "You know what Helen says: a gentleman never picks his nose in the right turn lane."

Mostly she just felt annoyed by the eternal counseling.

Once they were driving down Waterman Boulevard and they passed a group of neighbors clustered on lawn chairs.

"Only common people sit in the front yard," Helen said.

Paula shook her head, violently. The dangly hoop earrings she'd taken to wearing swung wildly. "Honestly, Mother, where do you get this crap?"

A smug smile spread across her mother's face.

"You make this stuff up, don't you? You say stuff like 'don't serve margarine to guests' because you don't like margarine."

Her mother stifled a laugh. Paula shook her head incredulously. "Admit it, Mama. You make this stuff up."

"I assure you, young lady," she said, "that there are indeed rules, and someday you will be thankful you had me to tell them to you." With a fist she rubbed at a place in her stomach.

Paula liked to remember how, just then, her mother had even laughed at herself.

The easy uncomfortable truce lasted the rest of her mother's life. It threatened to explode only once, when Paula brought home a boy she'd met in the Washington University library.

Near the end of her senior year in high school she met a studious football player from Soldan High School named James

Watson. He lived in an overcrowded four-family flat off of Page Avenue and he escaped to the library to get his school work done. He'd already won a full scholarship to Iowa, and Paula thought he was fine. He was well built, and he kept his hair cut short in a way that flattered his handsome head.

Helen had a fit. She had assumed that Steve and Paula were serious, that someday, after college, they would marry. Even after Paula set her straight on that account, Helen put her foot down.

"I'll not have a black gorilla like that in and out of this house. You understand me? He's nothing but trash."

"Fine. We'll get ourselves a room at the Diplomat. That'll solve your problem."

In reality there was nothing between her and the boy. Much to her dismay, he was promised to one of the cheerleaders at Soldan. He and Paula studied together, traded authors, and checked each other's math homework. She gave him rides home in her Maverick. That was the extent of their relationship. She often felt doomed to a life with men who were otherwise committed. Such a shame: they were so fine, and she kept falling in love with them.

"A motel room," her mother scolded. "I just bet you would do something like that. You're just an alley cat. I don't know where you came from. You don't know anything about those people."

Screaming, clutching at her hair, Paula fled from her mother. She decided she would bring James over as often as she could. She'd stick his gorgeous face up in her mother's until the uppity bitch accepted him or died.

But she never got the chance. James' girlfriend caught wind of her and warned him off. He obeyed. She never saw him again, but once, in an off-handed way, her mother asked about him.

"Whatever happened to that black boy?" she asked.

"I don't know who you mean," Paula said. Though they both knew she was lying, her mother dropped the subject.

It was a long time before she could admit that her mother was color struck. It made a difference to her that James' skin was so dark. Realizing this shamed Paula. Through all of the years of rules and regulations, lessons, and training, here was the real message: we are better than some people. Because they are poorer or darker skinned or less lucky.

And it wasn't true. She knew it even then. Twenty years later it seemed a miracle to have learned it. She didn't know where or how she had learned it, and, somehow, it didn't seem important. She felt blessed to have become as decent as she felt she was.

Paula spent her college years in Columbia. Though it was just over two hours in the car, she almost never went home. There were monthly businesslike calls during which Paula listed her classes and activities. Helen gave dutiful and shopworn advice: turn your mattress, get to know your professors, eat lots of roughage.

Yes, Mother. Thanks, Mother. I'll talk to you soon, Mother.

She met Al, and when they decided to marry she agreed to allow Helen to plan the wedding. There was almost nothing for Paula to do except point, pick, and raise her arms to be measured. Though at the time the wedding seemed gaudy and absurd, in hindsight her mother had done well. Everything was actually quite understated, and Paula remembered people having a good time.

Changing from her wedding gown, she found herself alone in a room with her mother for the first time in quite a long while. When she had come home from college, she had always brought friends. To act as a buffer, as protection. Helen had been in top form all day and was seeing to one final detail. She was fussing with Paula's gown, layering inside large pieces of tissue paper so the dress could be stored. Paula was changing for a flight to Miami. She would return from Saint Thomas and move with Al to his hometown and start a new life.

She noticed her mother's face had grown lined over the past four years, especially at the eyes. She'd lost some weight, yet had a bizarre swollen-looking belly.

She would see her mother a few more times before her death, but this was the picture of her she most often found in her head: a serene and efficient woman, busily fussing with a wedding gown, mouth set in disapproval.

"Any last minute thoughts?" Paula prompted. She had never known why she asked. She knew the answer. Al would be too homely, too dark, of questionable home training, not destined for success. Any of that. All of that. Whatever . . . it was OK. The deed was done. She knew the answer, but she asked anyway.

"Tell me what you think?"

"Ha," her mother said.

"It's not like you to be so quiet, Mama."

The nervousness in her stomach matched the awkwardness between them. Her mother came around in front of her, pulled her close, and gave her a gentle, dry kiss on the cheek.

8

THE BOYS AND I ARE BABY-SITTING MY MOTHER. CON-
sidering her age and how we are related, I believe a new word is
in order.

Paula is off checking out the nursing home. Let's not get
into the fact that I was just up there a few weeks ago, as well as
any number of other times before that, and the fact that I've
told Paula that if a nursing home was the route she wanted to
go, Oak Grove Manor was about the best place around here.
This is a woman who has never taken anybody's word for anything. She has to see it for herself. She subscribes to *Consumer
Reports* and even then has to go try out the products herself before she buys. Me, I figure you pay your money and you take
your chances. You buy the blender with the high rating and you
still get the one in a hundred that shorts out.

Well, if that's the way she wants to spend her time. Me and
the boys will sit here and kill ours. Tommy is laying there with
that Gameboy. He sets that thing down once, it's my turn. I told
him that. But he won't. Tim has got his nose in a book as usual.
I play with the computer, write up some shit for the campaign,
generally amuse myself. God knows what Mama is up to. She's
up in that guest room, I figure. Where she's been since Paula
brought her here.

I guess it was the right thing to do, though I know the
woman doesn't want to be here. She, in fact, swore to me she
would never set foot in this house again. She dismissed me

when I tried to ask her why, but I know how much she disliked
. . . no, hated my father toward the end of his life, and how bad
her memories must be. I don't want to keep her here a moment
longer than she needs to be.

Paula was on me because I didn't get all upset when Mother
got sick. She says I'm cold and that I shrug things off, but there's
another side of this. My mother has been out there having her
own life for years. I figure if she needs or wants our help, she'll
ask for it. No, Paula says. Sometimes people are too sick or too
prideful to ask for help. We have to intervene, and so she did.
And she's frustrated with me because I have not as actively
joined the cause. "Take her up something cool to drink," she
says to me on her way out the door. I said, sure, though I probably won't. I just don't believe it's what the woman needs or
expects from me.

Hell, I don't know what she needs or expects. She's so complicated and in many ways a mystery to me. What I actually
know about her is not much, and a lot of what I do know is contradictory or confusing.

I know she doesn't have many friends. Friends are hard for
her. Sharp-tongued, quick-tempered people always have trouble in that area, anyway, and she's got about as nasty an attitude
a person can get without a license. She will sit turtle-like and
still for hours, and then out of her mouth will pop something to
stand your hair on end. And she'll look around and dare somebody to respond. I can't remember her being close to one
person around here when I was growing up, or even knowing
who lived in the houses up and down the block. She kept to herself and minded her own business.

When she was born her name was Xenobia Mae Taylor,
and I know that happened in Jackson, Tennessee, but I don't
know when. My birth certificate says 1915, but I have seen other
documents with dates ten years either side of that one. For a

while there, she claimed 1920 was the correct date. I don't know if anyone besides her knows for sure. She told me once that her grandparents were slaves and that after emancipation they had stayed on the plantation in southwest Tennessee, right on the river above Memphis, a cotton plantation she said it was. I actually drove down there one time back in college, back during the big "Roots" craze. I found a big house on the river road with the name Taylor out front and I wondered if that was the place. Very well might have been. Always wondered if the white folks living in that house were cousins and if maybe I didn't have a share coming in some of that bottom land along the river. Didn't pursue it, and I'm not about to.

Mama never talked about the Taylors, her daddy's people. All I remember hearing about was some Pearsons, on her mother's side. They were the ones she always talked about from up around Jackson—her grandmother and her great aunt Ciel. At some point she lived in the same house with them. That's about it as far as family stuff is concerned. Not much of a family tree. Sometimes at Christmas, when I was growing up, a card would come from here or there and she would tell me that this was cousin so-and-so or Uncle J.J. I don't even remember the names, because I didn't hear them very often. Paula is always on me to tell her more about the past. As if I'm holding out on her.

I know that after World War I, sometime when she was a child, her family moved to Saint Paul. She told me her father worked for the railroad, traveling up and down the river, until he got on a Burlington Northern route that took him west, away from his family for weeks at a time. I think she said that he died on one of his trips. And that's about as much as I know about her life in Saint Paul, then or now.

She never tells and I don't ask.

She has a way of making you feel like you're prying when you ask her questions about herself. I think sometimes she would no more give you a straight answer than give you her pocketbook—and believe me she has always been tight with that. Most of what I know I deduced or heard from my father.

He didn't talk about her much either, but he was forever telling the story of how he met her. In his big and loud and blustery way. He had an extra amount of steam for this story. Took him a trip, he said, up the river to look up some friends, and he pointed north cause he was one of those who always gestured when he talked. A ham actor was all he was.

Had him a 1952 Ford, and he said it was the nicest little car he ever owned, turned heads everywhere he went. He said back in those days a lot of folks wondered how a colored gentleman came by such a car, which was probably the reason he had it, knowing him. But it didn't give him a wit of trouble—not that any of the cars in any of his stories ever gave him a wit of trouble. Back in his day there never would have been *Consumer Reports* because men like my father never bought anything that they didn't claim was top notch, even if it was a raggedy piece of shit.

He'd gone up to visit some old boy name of Roy Thomas, whom they called Skeet. They were in the war together over in Italy. He always made a point of how well the folks lived up there in Saint Paul. Clean, he said. Took care of them little houses, he said. Said he got introduced around—weren't too many of *us* up there: too cold. He always emphasized how nice the folks were and how he was going to get back up there one of these days. He was always planning to get back somewhere—to Europe, to Minnesota, to East Saint Louis. I don't think he left River Ridge once the whole time I was growing up.

He said they took him to a little VFW hall with some "old boys," as he called them. They'd arranged for him to meet a young lady. A gal named Xenobia, a name he said he had never heard before. He described her as a little skin-and-bones thing, delicate, as fine as she could be. Brown. Pretty brown, and it was love at first sight. He didn't go for them big yella gals. You could keep em as far as he was concerned. She came over and sat down with her girlfriend, and they bought em some drinks and talked. Evidently the girlfriend was the wild one, and she kept up the flirting and the jokes, but Mother was a sweet, quiet thing. Ladylike. No nasty stuff from her. She wasn't a fancy gal, and he would warn me how I had to be careful around the fancy ones. The ones who were "all dudded up and prettified. The ones that look like a doll."

"Thing is," he said, "they all looks the same underneath, and them gussied up ones think they need special treatment. Spect you to make over them like they ain't just another woman. Must be trying to hide something under all that do, anyway. You be careful round them."

Paula never got to meet my father, and I never told her his charming little piece of advice. I can just imagine it coming back around as evidence of all kinds of indiscretions of the male variety. Not that I swallowed everything that came out of the man's mouth either. But I was a good son. I said, "Yes, sir." My father needed to know you were listening to his counsel.

He stayed a few days longer because he "wanted to get to know this little gal better. See if she was the one for me." He took her out every night the better part of two weeks. They talked about everything, and evidently she couldn't hear enough about River Ridge. She wanted to know how many people lived there and what kind of houses did they live in and what did they do with themselves. And he told her. Told her about the lumberyard and the new houses going up on the ridge. She was a listener. He didn't want to stop talking. Her eyes lit up when he told her that it was black folks who ran things down here, and he could tell she liked him, too. For her, he was the complete gentleman.

More advice: "Meet one you like, you got to be a gentleman for em. Get their respect."

Apparently he'd been looking for a wife for a while to complete the picture. He had been home from the war seven years and was getting into his forties. It was time to settle down. He had a good business and a nice house. He wanted someone to take care of him. Here was the perfect woman.

He proposed. Just like that. Hadn't known her two weeks. And she said, "Yes." He had figured she would: she was getting along in years herself. Making her own way in the world. He said that a woman needs a man to look after her.

According to him, she didn't even bat an eye. They went down to the courthouse, had a wedding, packed up her stuff, set out down the river and never looked back. That was his version. Or at least one of his versions. In another there is a rival suitor he fights off, and in another my mother asks him, begs him to marry her. Most of the particulars stay the same.

Whichever edition, that story chills me. That the woman in the story doesn't much resemble my mother is part of it. But I think also his story has an inevitably about it—almost as if it was fated to happen or beyond both their controls. It is both the unlikeliness of it—the fact that two people from so far apart should get together and marry on a whim—and the way he tells it. Even in the variations, there is no sense that the story might have come out some other way. In some versions he even said that the gods willed this marriage. I know he believed that.

I find it shocking that a person could so easily surrender to fate. Neither am I a control freak, but things just don't happen to people as neatly and tidily as he explained them in his stories. Or at least I hope they don't.

Paula's mother, now there was a woman who took charge of things. She was the sort of woman who never left anything to chance, and she made Paula absolutely crazy. The few times I was with them together you could smother on the tension between them. Paula says her mother was controlling and manipulative and that she was the sort of person who couldn't deal with surprise. She says she was the sort of person who didn't just follow the rules, she preferred to make them, thank you very much, and that everything had better be just so or there was gonna be hell in West Saint Louis.

All that could be true. I never had to live with the woman, so I wouldn't know. The closest I came to the fire was when we went to tell her we were getting married.

Paula never went home. Never. We had known each other for almost two years and this was the first time I was meeting her mother. Paula was more nervous than I had ever seen her. She chewed off a thumbnail in the car and made me stop for the bathroom a half-dozen times. Before we got to Saint Louis, she had *my* stomach in knots. I was sure I was about to meet Godzilla, the big bad wolf, and the Wicked Witch of the West all rolled into one.

Helen Fuller was, in fact, a beautiful and gracious lady, or at least to me she was. She was one of those fine, old-fashioned ladies who seem to have gone out of style of late, the kind who populate the corners of E. M. Forster novels and American movies from the thirties and forties. Clearly she was a person to be dealt with on her own terms. She expected you to call her Mrs. Fuller, to say "yes, ma'am," to keep your voice down in her house, to dress for dinner. You would have to know her for many years for her to be comfortable enough to make a joke with you. I played my part just fine. Now, how I knew what that part was, I couldn't say. My mother is not exactly a formal person, and there weren't any Helen Fullers in River Ridge. I picked it up here and there, I guess—at other people's houses, in books, on TV. I impressed her, though. I think. You can never be too sure with her type, but there were hints. Her type of lady would never be rude to your face or make snide remarks. But they will look over their glasses at you funny or they will ignore you to let you know when they do not approve of the conversation or of your clothes or of you. She didn't do any of those things to me, so I knew I was at least marginally acceptable.

I have never talked to Paula about what happened while we were at her mother's house. We don't talk about her mother at all. Much. Her anger and pain—whatever the cause—are as raw now as ever, and in every marriage there are some things it is best to embargo, to draw a line around. Places where you don't want to go because you don't know what will happen there and you might not get back in the same condition you started out.

It was Sunday morning, we were getting ready to drive back to Columbia, and Helen had prepared this brunch for us. She invented a reason to send Paula to the store—claimed to need an absurd ingredient—Tabasco or water chestnuts or sesame oil, something it would take more than a minute to find. She didn't need it at all—the food had been prepared in advance: she was simply reheating it and arranging it on fancy serving dishes. Paula didn't balk. She did as she was asked, and without comment, too.

As soon as she was out of the house, Helen asked me into her study. I don't usually think of spaces as being male or female—one room is pretty much the same as another to me—but this was a masculine room. Oak paneling and large, heavy furniture. Bookcases filled with brown and green leather-spined volumes. Two red wing-back chairs. It could have been a lawyer's office, and when she motioned me to one of the wing-backs and sat behind her desk, I knew that, while it might not be court, some kind of formal proceeding had begun.

"Let's talk," she said. I nodded.

I met her eye. You have to look this kind right in the eye, else they have the advantage of you.

"Tell me about yourself," she said. A crazy question. The kind you get asked "to open you up," "to see how your mind works."

I asked her what would she like to know about me and she got a gleam in her eyes. I could tell she was enjoying the game.

"Tell me your plans. What are you doing with your life."

I told her I'd made two alternative plans. I was considering trying my hand at a big metro daily. Chicago. Dallas. Maybe St. Louis. Or, I might join my father's business. Take over his weekly.

"Ah, yes, River Ridge, isn't it?"

"It's nice country. Have you been up our way?"

"Hardly," she said.

"Well, you must come," I said, and she thanked me.

She told me that Paula had spent all of her life in the big city.

"And in Columbia," I added. I was given that point.

She asked me again what my plans were. I hedged. You never volunteer information with this type. She asked about the Johnsons. "Might I be acquainted with Johnsons here in the city?" she asked.

"We're mostly from north of there. Peoria. Springfield. My mother came from Saint Paul."

"It's lovely there," she said.

I told her I'd never been.

"And, so," she said. And, we were down to business. She was old fashioned enough to expect a formal plea for her daughter's hand, would never be crass enough to ask directly my intentions. I saw no reason to be coy.

"Well," I said. "I suppose Paula and I would like to get married. Sometime after she finishes school next spring."

She looked at me over her glasses. "You suppose? You don't know?"

"All right," I said. "We're getting married. With your approval, of course."

And then she told me that her daughter had neither requested nor required her approval for many years now.

"She will marry you if she wants to."

She rose, and I knew I was being dismissed.

"I suppose you knew that already," she said. That was the only time I heard sarcasm or bitterness in her voice.

We heard Paula's key in the door, come back from her pointless errand. We rushed to make it seem like we had not stopped in our preparations.

"May I ask you," I said. "Were it necessary, would you be inclined to give me permission to marry your daughter?"

"No," she said. "You may not ask."

She and my mother are alike that way. Deadly direct. Neither minced words. Maybe that's a privilege of age. Helen is dead and Mother lives on, bless her heart. And she's gone from direct to a lot of the time just plain rude. Mother couldn't care less what she says, who hears it, or what the consequences are. It puzzles me. It seems such a small thing to do—to be careful of people's feelings—and I, for one, don't feel that with age comes the privilege of treating people less civilly. She chooses to be ornery. She enjoys shocking people.

She's changed from when I was growing up. I remember her as a woman of very few words. She could be stern, but she never raised her voice to me. She had a way of narrowing her eyes at you and letting you know you were in deep trouble. She could get up in your face and stick a finger under your chin, lecture you, and make you feel like a dog. Her faces were worse than a spanking.

Yes, she did spank me a few times. Once for lying about something that happened at school. And once because my father told her to. It was the time I'd gotten together with a bunch of boys from town—Walter and Bubba and Joe were there. We were all around ten, it was summer, and we were bored and restless. We decided we were going to walk to Hannibal. We got our things together, told Mother, and took off. Mother, she acted as if the most normal thing in the world was walking twenty miles in the hot sun. She never stopped me from trying anything. She picked us up later in the afternoon. We hadn't gotten too far. Five or six miles. We kept getting distracted by things along the road. We had climbed a couple of billboards and explored a cliff.

By the time my father heard about it, around town the story was it had all been my idea. He had a fit. He told her I needed to be punished. He was downstairs yelling at her. I didn't hear her say anything back to him.

"Boy needs to be spanked over this kind of thing. It's the only way they learn."

He told her to get up there and take care of it. He would never spank me himself. He considered child rearing to be women's work. But he was full of opinions on the routines and procedures. If he didn't like the clothes I wore or if he thought my table manners had gotten sloppy, my mother heard about it. With little or no discussion, she bent to his will.

"Give me your belt," she said. She came upstairs. She made me lower my pants. She gave me seven sharp cracks along the bottom. I tried to get out of her way, but she grabbed me tight around the arm and finished the job. She kissed me on the head and I heard her go back down the steps. "Satisfied?" I heard her ask. There were no more spankings.

She was always there for me. When I came in from school each day, she would have a snack waiting. Before I ate, she made me tell her something I learned that day. Just one thing, and she would not let up until I did. Yes, as I think back she did all of the things that a mother is supposed to do, and she did them well.

And, as I look back from the person she is now, I wonder how much she has really changed. Maybe she is her real self now—obstreperous, self-preserving, full of venom—and the person back then was the person she imagined she ought to be. Or who he demanded she be. There was something horribly wrong with their relationship. I know that now, but it's too late to find out what it was. My father's been dead almost twenty years—something I know she feels guilty about, though it was hardly her fault. And, whatever the guilt, she has had at least one other life since then—since she ran away from the one that she hated here.

Perhaps it was her running away that changed the dynamic between us. I was grown and no longer needed a mother, and she was at last free, completely free, to get away and do what she wanted. Perhaps back then she and I were linked like a Chinese ring puzzle—held together as much by a third link as by any natural connection between ourselves.

Here she is now, upstairs, in my house. What used to be her house. Paula says we must take care of her—that she needs us—but I'm not convinced. I think that our lives—hers and mine—are completely separate. She wants to be as far away from here and from us as she can get. Her presence here is less a function of her needs than of Paula's tenacity and big blind heart, and of whatever needs of Paula's there are that she won't deal with.

A long time ago I broke from my mother's orbit and she from mine. Whatever thread connects us is as delicate as new-spun silk. We hold on casually and absent mindedly, neither giving or demanding anything from the other. It seems to be what we need.

Some—Paula—might look at us and might see some sort of . . . failure of love. That could be, but maybe it's something else.

Maybe we're just done with that part of it.

9

$\mathcal{A}$T HOME AL AND THE BOYS SPRAWLED ON THE FURN-
iture like seals on rocks in the sun. Al stretched across the sofa
writing on a pad. Tim read, his face set in stern concentration.
Tommy had fallen asleep, arms akimbo, hand-held video game
still clutched in one fist. His dramatic shuddering snore was the
only sound in the house.

She envied their leisure. It offended her, their lying there,
their oblivion. She had been through an ordeal, and here they
were, calm, contented. They should have to share. But how?
The boys: the nursing home meant nothing to them. Old age
was as remote as the Himalayas, a picture in the encyclopedia,
an image on the television tube. Responsibility? They were
barely responsible for themselves, and so be it. Al: well, he'd
been to Oak Grove Manor. He'd come back reporting on his
trip as coolly as the weatherman forecasts another average day.

It was unfair. She felt alone.

"I'm home," she said.

Al and Tim wiggled the odd limb in acknowledgment. She
nudged Tommy with the heel of her shoe: he rolled over and
adjusted his body, snorting like an old yard dog. He continued
sleeping. He was like that: he would sleep through the Second
Coming.

"You should try to keep this boy awake," she said. "He'll be
up all night."

Al picked up a shoe and threw it at him. "Get up," he said. He said it with as much emotion as a bad TV actor.

"I'm awake." A mumbled whine from Tommy. His eyes never opened. Whatever tension had been roused by the shoe left his body instantly. He resumed snoring.

She shook her head, resisted the temptation to find the whole scene endearing.

She went upstairs to attempt a rational discussion with her mother-in-law about the nursing home. She would show her the brochure, lay it out systematically. She would offer to take her up there to get a feel for the place before any decisions were made.

Maybe she'd be lucky and find the old woman at an especially lucid moment. She would be genuinely enticed by what she heard, find the activities to be just the things she liked to do. She would express eagerness to be among her peers, be appreciative for all of Paula's efforts. She would make the decision herself and Paula's hands would be clean.

Or there was the alternative. Paula steeled herself against the assault. There was never any telling what you would find up there.

What she found upstairs was that Miss Kezee was gone.

"Where is your mother?" she asked, voice calm. She stood before her husband, arms crossed, a stern smirk on her face.

"Up in her room," Al answered. He used no air, hardly opened his mouth. It was barely a response.

"No, she's not."

"In the bathroom, then," he said. He scribbled furiously at a pad.

"She's nowhere in this house. I've looked for her."

He sat up. He looked from her to the pad as if there were

some thought she had caused him to loose. "What are you saying?"

"Your mother's gone. Are you telling me you don't know where she is?"

"Don't be silly." He fumbled around for his shoes. He shook Tommy roughly, ordering him again to get up. "She's eighty-five years old. Where could she go?"

"She told me she was eighty-one. I don't know where she is. And don't call me silly."

"Tim, you see Grandma?"

Tim's look expressed the same benign concern he'd been giving the book. "Isn't she in her room?"

Paula rolled her eyes. "Jesus Christ."

"Nobody panic," Al said. He was walking around—to Paula's eye, aimlessly.

How could the three of them allow this to happen? Nobody panic, indeed. Miss Kezee was probably lying unconscious in a gutter somewhere. Or fallen in the river. Or run over up on the highway.

"How could you let this happen?" she asked.

Al gave her a look somewhere between annoyance and incredulity. He curled his lip slightly.

Tired of being cooped up in that house. Got me up and left. Nobody's business. My own business. Got to do this right. Take my time. Plan. Think. Got to be careful. Seems like if I can get down here and get me a ticket and a schedule, I can get my things and go. Walk a little bit, rest a little, stay in the shade. That's the plan. Better stop a minute. Sit on these steps. Won't nobody mind. Now seems I remember when I was living here was a bus stopped down that Shell station block up from Main. Local bus went up to Davenport, then you switch. Something like that. Always was too damn hot in this town. Gotta get me a hat. Gotta get going before they come after me. Bout five blocks, should be. Just down the hill and two over to Main.

There that yellow house. Still painted yellow I see. Gal lived up in there what had a house full of hussy girls. Couldn't tell her nothing. One time I say to her that I seen one of them gals up by the river with her skirt all hiked up. Gal tells me wasn't none of her daughters and wasn't none of my business if it was. And you best believe that's the last time I said anything to her. And didn't every one of them gals start bringing home babies by the time they was fifteen. Probably ain't caught no husbands yet either. Wouldn't know. I left before they caught any. I'd ask that Paula, but she'd say, "Oh, Mama," like I was talking what I didn't already know. That's how she is. She one of them womens think they too good to get involved in other folks' business. Like she ain't just as interested in it as everybody else be. And what she don't know and die if she did know is how these other womens up and down this street is peeping out their shades trying to get a look at her and her husband and what they wearing and what they bought and who's coming and going just so they can pick up the phone and call across town and let somebody else in on it. That's how we is. Triflin. Always has been, long as I been around, and that Paula is, too. You know she's peeking and peeping as much as the next one, though you'd never get her to admit it. Not a high soddity gal like that.

Seems like these blocks got longer. I'll rest at the corner. Right there under that big oak. Who that? Folks riding by honking. Don't even have a clue who that is. I wave and smile. If I feels like it. Most people I knowed here is dead or moved on. These folks they childrens, I guess. Grans. New folks. So hot. Couldn't be too many new folks here. Never was all the years I live here. Keep on walking. Right up there was an old woman sat with Junior when he was a baby. I heard she passed. Must have been ten years ago she passed. Sweet thing. Was old even then. Made a peach cobbler. Buttery crust would melt in your mouth. So sweet, and I remember once I took Junior up there and he was only four. First time I left him, and don't you know he pitched a fit, laying there kicking and fighting and screaming, carrying on like a heathen. And me, I was so embarrassed I liked to die. Mrs. Jane Miller, that was her name. We call her Miss Janey. Miss Janey say, "You just run along and take care of your business and I'll watch him for you." I didn't want to go. She's standing there holding on to him, and my baby was like he was gonna die if I left him. But I did. Heard him crying all the way down the block, I did. Like to broke my heart in two. So I go to take care of my business and when I come back there little Junior was snuggled up in Miss Janey's arms and she's reading him verses from the Bible. "You sure have a sweet baby, Miss Johnson." Put the charm on him until he just about don't want to leave. That's how she was, Miss Janey. Had a way with folks. After that Junior was always asking when we was going to Miss Janey's. And don't you know in this town wasn't too many reasons to go no place so I got to where I would just come down and sit with her and we'd have tea and watch the stories and study the Bible. She loved my boy. Seems like every time she scrape together a little change she down to the five-and-ten to buy him a little something and I was always saying, "Please don't spend your money on us. We got plenty." And we did too, cause A. B. was doing real good. But she said, naw, she wanted to and don't deny her what little pleasure she had since she didn't have no grans of her own. A good old soul, she was. When things got bad with A. B. . . . was always bad with A. B. . . . I could sit all day with her and talk. All she say was, "Take it to the Lord, girl." She listen when nobody else did. Make me want to cry, though, her house looking like it do now. She had it fixed up so nice, gardens all around with tiger lilies, irises, and sunflowers. Grew them peaches right out back for that melt-in-your-mouth cobbler. House standing there now looking like hell. Yard gone to seed. Needs painting. No telling who the house went to. She was like me . . . didn't have no people in the area. Ask Junior what happened to it. Sweet old thing. One of the few good things bout this place. Oh, this place. Don't know what to think about this place. Been fifteen years haven't thought too much about it at all. Junior call me up and say did you hear so and so passed or that this one's baby girl finally got married. Should have asked him how am I supposed to know since I didn't keep up with nobody here but him, and then only cause he's my son. He tell me about this one and that one and which business boarded up and it's like he's telling me about a place I never knew at all. Not like a place I spent twenty years in.

If I get up and walk one more block I be almost there. Seems like I'm tired. Too tired and weak. Get tired fast. It's the place. This damn place. Set foot in this damn place and it all came back. All of it. All the awful things and then the good things too. It's like a lie. It seems like if I never came here it would all go away. It didn't. Them memories. Wish I could find a way to make myself stop seeing them. To make myself stop. Stop. Gotta stop and rest some more. I'm not strong enough. I need to get stronger. If I'm gonna get home. Just a little stronger. But I want to go. I want to go now. One more block to where the Shell is. But that ain't it. Was it back up there? Don't get confused now. Come on. Stay with it. I can do this. I'll ask the boy. Say. Where that Shell that was owned by Casons. "You mean the convenience store? Down on the highway. You OK ma'am?" He a teenage boy. A little older than them boys at home. I ask him Well, tell me where do you get a bus around here? Used to be a bus stop here. "No bus here, ma'am," boy say. Greyhound bus, I tell him. Damn kids don't know nothing. Interstate bus. "Get those in Hannibal, ma'am.

You OK? Kinda hot to be out here walking. Can I call someone for you?" Boy talk too much. I don't say nothing to him. I go sit by myself in a little shade on a concrete step where the office used to be. All's here is some busted-off pipes where the pumps was. Grass and weeds done busted through the concrete all over. Was a time up and down here on a Saturday was so busy there was a line and you'd see everybody from around here carrying their little packages and whatnot and stopping in Blu's for a little coffee. Not much left but the feed store and tavern. That's what Paula said, and every time she needs a stick of butter she's up off in that big shoe box of a thing she's driving all the way to Hannibal. Says folks drive down to Saint Charles to shop. Don't make no sense. What I'm do now, Charlie? Can you help me? It's so hot and I'm so tired. Can you help me, Charlie? Where are you anyway ? Can't stay and can't leave. Gotta do something. Could stay for a while. Till I'm better. A month. A year. Gotta find out about them busses. At the hall. The city hall. Go on over there. It's hot today, Charlie. Too hot to fish today. We got to be careful. I can't have you comin to the house. Pick me up down by the river. People got to think you're respectable. One more block to the city hall. How you gonna cook a fish that size? Bigger than a skillet. Where you gonna cook the fish? We gonna have to throw it back. Where you been all day, Xenobia? Don't want to remember that. Don't want to remember him. You're hurting me, A. B. Don't remember that. City hall building got run down, too. Can I help you? girl says. Black girl with a funny hairdo. Don't know what I want.

They hadn't driven far when they found her sitting on the steps in front of the city hall. She was resting her head in her hands, looking like a school girl abandoned by her friends.

"Mother!" Al shouted. He jumped from the van, and Paula watched him stoop over her, checking her out, coaxing her to the car. He helped her into the backseat and then ran into the building.

Paula turned to her. She was drenched with sweat and wilted. Much of her hair had fallen from the knot she had tied on top of her head.

"How are you feeling, Miss Kezee?"

No reply. She looked exhausted and sad.

Al ran back. "Nobody saw a thing. How's she doing?"

Paula shook her head. She started the van and headed home. She was furious at Al and at the boys. They caused this through their neglect, and now, somehow, she was supposed to make things better. Cheer her up, cool her off, rehydrate her, fix up whatever was wrong. The rest would ask cautious, conciliatory questions, full of mock concern. If they were so interested, they would have been on the job in the first place. They were like the irresponsible baby-sitters, neglectful mothers, and brakemen asleep at switches all over the world. They were so sorry, gosh, if they could only get another chance they would do it right, really, they would.

Back at the house, Al escorted his mother up into the foyer, his arm draped solicitously across her back. She did not need him. "You go on up and lay down awhile, Mother," he said.

Paula feigned an exasperated sigh. "See to the boys," she ordered. She followed Miss Kezee to her bedroom, helped her out of the sodden dress and into a lightweight housecoat.

"Do you want to sleep for a while?" she asked.

"I'll just rest here on top of the covers."

"Can I get you anything?"

As if on cue, Tim appeared with a pitcher of iced tea.

"I think he read my mind," Miss Kezee said.

Tim came and went with a strange little bow, silent, oddly obsequious. Paula wondered where he had learned such poise.

"Cute little old boys," Miss Kezee said.

"Sometimes. Usually." Paula waited while Miss Kezee gulped down a large glass of tea, then got up to go.

"Sit a minute."

Paula perched on the corner of the bed while her mother-in-law sipped at her tea. She waited for her to say something, but she didn't. Apparently she just wanted her to sit. Miss Kezee put the glass back on the tray and proceeded to pull the bobby pins from her hair.

"Hand me my brush, please." She pointed to the dresser.

She worked through the limp, yellow gray strands with a slow stroke that had an insistent force behind it that Paula found surprising.

"Aren't you tired, Mother?"

"Always tired at my age." She pulled the hair over her right shoulder and ran the brush through it as if she were grooming an animal.

"Where were you going today?"

"The hell away from here. Don't look surprised. I told you I was."

"I just didn't expect . . ."

"Why didn't you expect? Because I'm an old woman? Because it's not what you wanted?"

"What were you gonna do, walk to Saint Paul?"

"Don't be a fool. Pin this hair up. Loose, but off my neck."

Paula crouched up behind her on the bed and began working in the pins.

"I went down to find out about the bus."

"You could have called."

"Got no privacy around here."

"If you want privacy, just ask."

Miss Kezee humphed. Paula tucked away the last stray strand of the hair and returned the brush to the dresser.

"There hasn't been bus service to River Ridge since the boys were born."

"I guess I'll have to make me another plan."

Paula took Miss Kezee's hand. "Mother, when you're ready to go, I'll take you."

Miss Kezee, to her surprise, stood up and started pacing angrily. "Don't know how much better I have to get. Look at me. I walked all over this damn town. In this heat. And I'm fine." She shook with rage.

Paula's heart felt like acid in her chest. The old woman seemed fine, but how could you tell, really?

"Oh, hell," Miss Kezee said. She came and sat next to Paula. She put her face into her hands and wept softly. "I know you're right, damn you. I know it."

Paula pulled her close.

"Seems I had to rest every two or three houses. I got down there and then . . . I don't know. Felt like my mind wanted to do things I didn't want it to do."

"That's to be expected."

"Expected by who? I don't expect it. I don't want it. All I know is, seems what I want I can't have."

"What is it that pains you here? Why are you so ill at ease?"

"Everything here hurts me. I'll never be comfortable here."

"Whatever bothers you, that happened a long time ago. It can't hurt you now."

"Hurts my soul just thinking on it."

"Then try and forget."

"Can't do that here. Don't you see? That's why I got to get away from here."

"What if you weren't here, but close by. Close enough so Al and me could look in on you."

Miss Kezee got up and went to stand in the window. "Bad things happen. Terrible hurtful things. Nothing you can do about that. You're just a young girl. You wouldn't know anything of what I'm talking about."

"I do know," said Paula, trying to forget her own sorrow. *Sorry, Mama.*

Here now was Miss Kezee, a face of pain and regret.

"You have to put it past you," Paula told her.

"I did that. Away from here."

"We'll get you away, then. Soon. We will."

"Promise?"

Though meaning to nod, Paula shook her head.

They are in the house. There is the dark, round man. There is the tall man with the pretty brown skin. The woman is there. She is between the men. They are in the parlor. It is her room. Her house.

"Where have you been all day, Xenobia?"

Don't want to think about this.

The tall man is accusative, rageful. "What is he doing here?"

"She's with me," the dark round man says.

The tall man is drinking. Drinking hard. His hand shakes. The ice tinkles against the glass.

"What you want this old shriveled up bitch for."

Don't think about this.

"No call for that," the dark man says. "Get your things," he says to the woman.

"Say what?" The tall man sets down his drink.

"She's coming with me."

"The hell she is."

"Listen to me please, A. B." The woman is pleading.

"Don't want to hear anything you got to say."

"Please, A. B."

"Get your things," the dark man says.

The tall man grabs the woman's arm and wrenches it behind her back.

"You're hurting me, A. B."

"Let go of her."

The man shoves the woman toward the other man.

"Get your things," the dark man says.

"If we could talk . . ." the woman starts.

The tall man raises a hand as if to slap her. The woman cowers.

"Get your things."

"Do it," the tall man orders. The smaller, rounder dark man leaves.

The woman comes down stairs. She has her one bag. One old bag.

"You don't need to worry," she says. "Don't have nothing I didn't come with."

"I ought to kill you."

"Do it!"

"Think I won't kill you. I'll kill you. I will."

"I know you will."

"Tell me one thing. Tell me why."

"Cause of me. Cause I'm doing what's best for me."

"What about me?"

"You don't want me."

"Did I say that?"

"You say it every day. The way you talk to me. The way you look at me. Don't feel like nothing around here. Almost since I came here."

"Nobody made you come here."

"My mistake. Now I'm fixing it."

"Not that easy. You can't just walk away."

"Watch me."

The man grabs her arm as she passes. "I'll make you wish you hadn't."

She snaps her answer. "Nothing you can do to me any more. Never again. Cause I promise you: I'll never set foot in this house again long as I live."

"You won't forget me. I'll see to it," the man hollers at her back as she flees down the steps to the other man who waits in a truck.

10

On the Monday before the election there was a debate between Al and his opponent in the auditorium of River Bluff School. Paula couldn't work up any excitement for it. She'd gotten sicker of the campaign as the days went by: sick of the phone calls, the posters, the gaudy hot pink-and-blue signs. She had the same feeling about politics she had when she was coming down with a cold: a distant feeling that something was wrong, something she could not quite put her finger on. The unctuous grubbing after votes—as sleazy and undignified as that was—was to be expected. But the way Al talked when he was campaigning—his passion, his sincerity—aroused in her a deep sense of uneasiness that made her want the whole thing to be over. As eager as he was to get to the debate, she searched for excuses to stay home.

"Sure you want to leave the boys here with your mother?" she asked. He was tying a striped tie into a Windsor knot.

"What I would like is to have my wife and my children at my side tonight. You know, the standard political family scene."

"Your wife and your kids, but not your mother."

"An evening out might be too much for her," he said. He gave her the sideways glance that went with all the casual lies that passed through their marriage. Less a lie than an evasion. She didn't call him on it. He knew as well as she did that Miss

Kezee was stronger, close to being her normal self. As normal as life got for her.

"OK, fine," she said, not meaning to sound as short as she did.

"For Christ's sake, what is it? What?" He sat by her on the bed. "Do you want to leave her here alone? Take her along? Do you want to stay?"

What I want, she thought, is to not have to worry about this at all. "Whatever you want to do," she simpered.

"Yeah, right." He glowered and stalked away to pout.

Fuck him, she thought. She got angrier at herself for bothering in the first place. Why did she have to think of everything? How'd she get this part? In college they had lived together on the sly for over a year, defying house mothers and parents alike. She was the one who fussed and fretted about birth control. He simply hadn't cared: he said he loved her, said he planned to marry her anyway. He told her not to worry because everything would work out. He'd never discuss what would happen should he loose control or be careless. She had been the responsible one. All the risk and all the responsibility. He, the one believing things would turn out great.

Back then his off-handed ways seemed like bravado, a kind of slack-jawed macho. If you relaxed, let things take their natural course, you would be taken care of. God would provide, and money and happiness and luck would shower from the skies. This sort of casual attitude worked for him, but not for her. She knew too many people who came up short from not being cautious. People with unplanned children, incomplete transcripts, repossessed homes. There was more to it than luck. There was knowing the right thing to do and knowing the right time to do it. You had to have your eyes open all the time; like an eagle: be alert and vigilant, watch for all the hidden trip wires of life. When the boys felt warm or behaved oddly, she was the one plotting against whatever rare disease might have infected them. She was the one with her eye to the roof, wondering whether to patch or replace. Of course, she knew women were expected to do this, that it was their lot in life, but why was that true? It wasn't biological. Why shouldn't he be just as concerned as she about the roof, about his sons, about his mother? From him it was always "Whatever you think is best," "Whatever you want to do," "I'm sure it'll be fine." And yet, turn the tables and suddenly he's trapped. Once, just after moving to River Ridge, the old Maverick she'd been driving throughout college broke down outside of town. She called him at the paper and asked him which garage she should call for help. She knew there were two, but she did not know which was honest, or if there was some protocol an outsider wouldn't know.

"Why are you calling me about this?" he'd scolded, and she said she simply wanted to know which to use.

"Pick one," he'd said.

"But which one is better? Who do you go to?"

She got an exasperated sigh as a response. They fought about it—one of their first fights, and over something so small. It wasn't an ugly fight, just a few cold sharp exchanges. She remembered being told not to be such a baby. She also remembered that later, when they were calmer and had apologized, he told her he had not expected it would be like this. Marriage, that is. He had not expected to have someone asking him what to do, and that, frankly, he didn't know what to do himself half the time. After the quarrel they had made love, and she knew then he felt like she did: vulnerable and alone, unprepared for what went with being an adult.

She had learned not to push him.

"All set?" he asked. He was in the door with his suit coat over his arm. One thing about him: he was a half-hearted sulker. And, though he carried his share of grudges, he was a big one for getting on with it.

Tim was waiting for them at the door to the living room. She knew he felt like he was the one in charge, but signs of favoritism were an invitation to civil war.

"You boys think you can handle this?" Al asked. He exaggerated the concern in his voice. He could be a terrible tease.

"Yes, sir," Tim said crisply. No response from Tommy. He was on the floor running a toy dump truck up and down stacks of newspapers.

"Hey," Al yelled to him. "Are you ready for this?"

He rolled on his back and made sputtering noises with his lips. Apparently the truck was flying. Upside down.

"I can watch both of them," Tim said.

Miss Kezee sat still and erect on the sofa, facing the TV, her eyes fixed on what appeared to be a children's program—lots of flashing lights and costumed characters. She had a prim, amused look on her face.

"You know what to do if you need us," Al said. He had devised an elaborate system where messages could be relayed to him, on stage, mid-debate if necessary.

Again only Tim responded. They simultaneously gave him an extra pat on the head. He beamed. Tommy didn't care to notice.

"We'll see you later," Al called. Miss Kezee raised her hand and dropped it as if it were leaden. She didn't take her eye off the television. Tom vroom-vroomed the truck across the rug and ran into his brother's leg. Tim shoved him away with a foot as if he were a dog.

"Have fun, you guys," he said.

"Whoop his butt," called Tommy between spits.

Al took Paula's arm as he walked her from their home. "It'll be fine," he said, with inflated casualness.

Afraid that whatever she said would come out with the wrong inflection—sarcastic, overly concerned, complacent—she chose not to say anything at all.

~ ~ ~

The adults looked awkward on the picnic table-like benches in the River Bluff cafeteria: purses and fliers lay before them on the sticky tabletops. Some sat facing the tables, looking obedient. Others straddled the benches or rode them side-saddle. Paula was thankful that folding chairs had been provided for the candidate's wives. They sat off to the right facing their husbands just in front of the audience. The candidates sat on either side of an ugly metal lectern.

Al looked nervous. He was leaning on his thighs, hunched over, his long legs gaping apart and then closing, making his body sway like a sail in a variable wind. The moderator, Reverend Brown—the Baptist minister—was making a speech that didn't seem to have a theme or a point that Paula could find. Al gave her occasional looks of confidence, looks full of swagger. There was something of a sneer on his face as well. She caught his eye.

"Sit up straight," she mouthed.

He grinned at her.

When Reverend Brown started his prayer, Paula clenched her teeth. Every two-bit event in this town seemed to start with a prayer by either Reverend Brown or Reverend Wilson. Reverend Wilson was the AME man. There was surely a law against all this public praying, though no one here seemed to mind. She and Al were only marginally religious, they went to church maybe once every year, if that often. Miss Kezee claimed to have found God recently, though Paula would have never guessed from the way she behaved sometimes. Paula knew she attended church regularly in Saint Paul, and she certainly was sanctimonious. Still, you would never describe her as a spiritual person. Paula's mother had dragged her to church on religious holidays and for the baptism of her friend's and her client's children. Helen Fuller viewed church a convenient place to make business contacts and an opportunity to show off the newest fashions. When she was a little girl Paula enjoyed getting up on Sunday mornings and dressing to the nines, and then going out afterwards for a big dinner. She didn't recall any particular religious teachings: she tuned out all of that. She and her mother were busy checking out what everyone else in the church was wearing. Heaven forbid you should wear something ugly, or—even worse—the same outfit two weeks in a row. Her mother would nudge her with her elbow and indicate with her chin some unfortunate offender. They both shook their heads and tried not to laugh out loud. The fun stopped when Paula became self-conscious—she figured out that people were doing the same thing to her. She didn't like the feeling of being scrutinized, and she decided she didn't care to be the sort of person who did such a thing. By then she was a teenager and beyond getting interested in whatever else there might be to religion. She took to sleeping late on Sunday, listening to the top-forty countdown on the radio. Her mother didn't mind this particular rebellion. She enjoyed the leisurely mornings as much as her daughter did.

While Reverend Brown prayed, Paula scanned the room, eyes wide open. She was alert, ready to drop her eyes in a flash. In a small town you could easily be branded a heathen. Tonight everyone was appropriately pious. She couldn't find any other peepers.

Next to her, Tyrone Turner's wife Mabel mumbled along with the prayer. Her face contorted, as if it were a great effort for her. Her eyes were pressed closed the same way a child's eyes did when she was told not to peek—closed so tight there was a sliver of white showing, looking as if they might pop open at any moment.

Mabel looked sweated and oily as usual. She was a good-sized woman—filled up all of a dark maroon knit dress. The dress had a lace-bordered bib that rested on her huge boxy breasts like a forgotten napkin. She wore a tiny brimless black straw hat swaddled in netting. Her lips moved along with the words of the endless prayer, and Paula wondered if this was some sort of standard prayer that she, with her heathen ways, had missed.

She had crossed paths with Mabel often. The Turners had a houseful of simple-minded bumpy-faced girls that had come through Paula's classroom—girls who shared with their mother boxy breasts and flat wide noses that filled their faces. Mabel showed up for conferences and open houses, out of breath, flustered, but always smiling. "I can't do anything with that girl," she'd say. She said the same thing about each one, and apparently it was true. They were, to Paula's estimation, too large to be sixth graders, every one of those Turner girls. They kept messy desks with wide territories around them, territories they marked with a clutter of unfinished assignments, candy wrappers, and hair implements. Their saving grace was that they left the students who stayed out of their way alone. Woe, however, to the trespasser: the Turner girls were tough street fighters. They used fingers as claws, and chests as smothering devices. Only one of the girls—Tamika, it was—did any school work. The rest of them sat posed in their desks with stupid dazed looks on their faces. "I'm afraid there's going to be a lot of trouble ahead for her," Paula would tell Mabel. "Her" being Towanda, Teresa, Tamara, and the one they called Tiny. (Tiny was huge.) "Well, I'll talk to her," Mabel promised.

Whatever she said never helped. When the Turner girls turned eighteen, Mabel packed them off to cosmetology school in Quincy. To her credit she managed to keep them all childless. Towanda, the oldest, was a whiz with a pressing comb and she corn-rowed like nobody's business. She got all the work around River Ridge; she had tightened Paula's braids just last week. Paula watched her in the beauty parlor mirror fussing with her hair, a look of deep concentration set on her face. She looked as if she were defusing a bomb. Sometimes Towanda lifted a braid, caressed it, and a look of sheer joy would cross her face.

"You sure do have pretty hair, Ms. Johnson," she simpered. Towanda's own hair was pressed into a shapeless flank and broken off into little knots around the edges by the chemicals she overused on herself. Al had a whole Towanda routine. Paula felt professionally obligated not to laugh, but he kept on until she did.

Earlier, when she walked into the cafeteria, Paula had greeted Mabel and attempted to make small-talk. She'd gotten the cold shoulder. Evidently Mabel was taking this campaign personally.

The reverend said, "Amen."

Perhaps the campaign was uglier than Paula knew. She had been busy ending the school year and looking after Miss Kezee. The politics had taken place out of her range. Al did his campaigning at luncheon meetings of local social groups, at the feed store, at the barbershop, in the lunchroom of the plastic injection mold factory. Except for the party she had no idea what had been said or done. He had mentioned a few times in the evening that there had been "heated" arguments, but in general he did not talk about the campaign and Paula did not bring it up. She watched him in the evening clicking away at the computer keyboard. That was nothing new. He was responsible for almost every word of the weekly paper, and it was not unusual for him to spend a few hours at home editing and refining his articles. The work was routine: an editorial on his choice of the most important event of the week, a page of sports news, including his analysis of the performance of the Cards or the in-season Marion County Consolidated high school team—all of them called the Hawks. There was the advice column—he made up some of the letters and all of the replies. There were gardening and car repair features he picked up from an inexpensive syndicate. She didn't even read the whole *Sentinel* anymore. Since she'd spent her adult life in the same house with him, she had a pretty good idea what the editor thought about most things.

Whatever was going on in this stupid campaign, there certainly was no cause to snub a neighbor, especially one who had made every attempt to drum a little learning into the heads of your vague, oversized daughters.

The preacher introduced Tyrone Turner. His wife lifted her head and straightened her back. The all-purpose room was stifling, as usual. She felt sorry for her students, trapped in here every day under the stanchions with their shredded rope nets, eating prepackaged lunches in the stale sweat-sock air. The mustiness tonight blended with the adult odors of perfume, after-shave, and the carried-on-the-clothes scents of various fried suppers. Paula herself had fried a chicken tonight and they had eaten every piece. The boys were getting to the point where soon she'd be frying two, and that probably wouldn't be enough. Before she left she put microwave popcorn on the counter and made an extra pitcher of juice. She only hoped things were going well back there. The boys were pretty good about staying by themselves. Sometimes they made a mess when they were home alone: a few overturned chairs, a broken lamp once. Both boys swore that lamp fell off the table all by itself. They fought sometimes, but surely no more than other siblings. Tim was a diplomat: just that much smarter than his brother, he could talk him into doing things his way. And though Tommy was aggressive, Tim was physically stronger and could subdue him in short order. When they were little and she left them with baby-sitters, Tommy was the one who fussed and cried. As he got older he continued to find ways to let them know he did not like to be left behind. He would pick fights with Tim, stop up the toilet, hide the baby-sitter's shoes. At the end of the evening he would report on himself with pride, and, while Al drove the baby-sitter home, he would eagerly accept whatever punishment she gave him, usually a lecture and a hug, and then follow up with a promise to be better forever. He was wild and as needy as a puppy and she hoped he would be cool tonight and that Miss Kezee would be cool as well. She would not think about possible disasters: that was borrowing trouble. What happened, happened. She would concentrate on the speeches instead.

Reverend Brown had just asked Tyrone Turner to briefly describe his ideas for taking River Ridge into the next century.

"Thank you, Reverend," Turner said. He adjusted the mike and scanned the room once before speaking.

"It's good to see so many of you come out tonight. Pleased to see people take an interest in our community." Tyrone spoke haltingly, but not with any sort of stammer. He chopped off each word and paused the way students with reading problems did, though in no way did he betray that he was searching after words. This was a style thing: he might be trying to show himself thoughtful and cautious, or maybe a little shy. Whatever, he had the same effect on Paula as did her slow readers: She found herself leaning up in anticipation of his next utterance. She wanted to reach inside and yank the words from his throat.

"I been in the area for forty years. Raised my girls here. I've seen a lot of changes over the years. I think we've got a good little town here."

Tyrone Turner worked in a dairy plant over in Quincy. He commuted over the US 24 bridge, preferring small-town life to the decaying river city. She saw him infrequently around town. He had showed up only a few times at his daughter's events at school. He was a tall man, rounded out in the middle like a punching bag. He had rich sepia-colored skin that his unfortunate daughters did not inherit. They had only his size and his eyes, large round eyes that naturally expressed curiosity. Or was that surprise? She was never sure. He had the strangest hairline of any man she knew, rising from a sharp point in a widow's peak—like Dracula's hair. A sculpted look: the barber had to have done something with his razor. It flattered him. He was a striking, attractive man. As long as he kept his mouth closed. Paula had trouble imagining him with good old Mabel, this plain and thick woman sitting beside her. Mabel was old-timey and Tyrone was more like what they used to call a dandy.

"I think we're in good shape around here," he continued. "Not too many complaints, I understand. Good streets, school, and sewers. Population haven't changed much in the last few years. We even had a few new businesses sprout up. The economy is looking good."

A few new businesses: right, Paula thought. There was the factory where machines melted plastic chips and then blew them into globular milk cartons. It employed two people per shift. One worker dumped the chips in the hopper and watched the temperature gauge. The other tossed the containers into a box for shipment to the dairy in Quincy. Two mentally handicapped men from a group home in Cleta worked the night shift. Then there was the hamburger stand that served traffic up on Highway 79. That franchise employed fifteen high-school students—six that Paula knew for a fact could not make change for a twenty. They were paid four-fifty an hour and all the expired hamburgers they could eat. And there was Towanda's beauty salon. A few new businesses, indeed.

Not exactly a lie. It was exactly the sort of thing that made Paula suspicious about politicians in the first place: the dishonest way they had of using facts and statistics to fit whichever circumstance presented itself: she thought of the Colorforms she played with as a little girl. You pasted the sticky plastic on your picture board to suit your fancy. The mother, the father, the dog, the car, the little girl. You could make a picture as pretty as pleased you. What you didn't like, you peeled away. Just like that. Here is a little town and look at all its wonderful features. She watched her neighbors nod in agreement as Tyrone Turner recreated his version of River Ridge.

"We have over two hundred acres in town set aside as open land. There are four tot lots in town. We have organized summer activities for our youth. The riverfront clean-up project is proceeding on schedule."

She wanted to raise her hand and say, "Wait a minute. This isn't true." But it was true, as far as it went. Just as it was also true that there were ends of streets that ran up the river bluff that had never been paved. And there were people in River Ridge who lived close to true third-world poverty—children who came to school with hungry bellies and laceless shoes, cardboard soles worn paper thin. Men lived in cars, old women burned parts of their houses in winter to stay warm. Farmers hung on by threads. Everyone drove to Quincy and Hannibal to work. Their teenaged sons and daughters drove up and down the winding roads beside the river, without aim, too often dying drunk and smashed against the guard rails. Tyrone Turner never brought up any of that. To do so was to be labeled "negative" and "pessimistic" and "unpatriotic."

Around the audience Paula recognized Tyrone Turner's peers. Benjamin Berry, tall on his bench, dignified, nodding to the speech as if to music. Maurice Jenkins, Sylvester Gray, Carl Winters. Farmers, mechanics, barbers. These were the men that Al did business with every day. He printed their fliers, put their ads in the paper. They bought his lumber and stored grain in the silo. They were veterans of Korea and of the big war. A few had been in Vietnam. Their wallets bulged with money: they seemed to carry every bill they ever earned, were fond of flourishing it. Yet, they were as tight with that money as little boys saving for their first bicycles. They sat around the VFW lodge evenings and argued over who owed whom fifty cents for the flat warm beer they guzzled by the keg. As long as the money kept coming, they were happy.

Next to them their sour-faced wives fanned themselves the same way they did in church on Sunday morning. That's what they were—church women, frittering away their time on special projects for Reverends Wilson and Brown. Paula did not judge them too harshly. Their relentless "good works" kept the hungry ill-shod children from being starved shoeless children. They were the ones who drove the old women to Hannibal so they could shop. They collected soup labels and baked cakes so that the school could have playground balls and computer equipment. They were the ones who did those things so that their husbands could sit beside them, self-satisfied and content, believing—really believing—that all was right with the world.

"Stay the course. That's what I say. Stay the course. If you elect me—and I hope you do—that's what I'll do. Thank you."

The room filled with eager applause. Tyrone Turner adjusted his trousers and sat and he raised his hand to acknowledge the applause. Next to Paula, Mabel beamed. She lead the applause—a little too aggressively, Paula thought. Paula applauded, too, of course. She knew she ought to say something to Mabel, recognize the workmanlike job her husband had done, but when she caught Mabel's eye, Mabel gave her a look that was arrogant and even a little cruel. She stopped applauding, noticed Al not applauding at all.

"Thank you Mr. Turner," Reverend Brown said, and then began introducing Al. Through the speech Al had been sitting erect, legs crossed, looking intently at Turner, yet Paula knew he was looking right through him. She recognized the glassy look in his eyes: the look that indicated that he was tuned out: the practiced, glazed-eye attentive attitude that fooled anyone who didn't know better. Sometimes, in the evening, she would be telling him a long and perhaps not-too-interesting story about what had happened at school—of, say, a fire drill or a faculty meeting—and she would find herself confronted with that same unfocused gaze. She would ask him a question about what she had just been saying and then watch the slight shift of his eyes that indicated he had come back. "Say that again. I didn't get it," he'd say, and she always said, "It was nothing." When she wanted his undivided attention, she had her little tricks— she imagined every woman did. She would make shocking pronouncements in a mincing schoolgirl voice, she'd toss off seductive cryptic hints when they made love, pinch the back of his neck hard to remind him of something she had asked him to do last week or last month or last year. When they first lived together, she threw a few tantrums because of his wanderings, times when she thought she was being ignored. She had learned a lot about him since then. She learned what a daydreamer he was and how hard it was for him to focus on anything for too long. The only movies he could sit through were loud action films with car chases and constant camera motion. Even so, when the slow parts came along—the police chief's analysis, the love scene—she would find him beside her fidgeting in his seat, or, more often, gone to get popcorn. He could not sit through symphonies or church services or P.T.A. meetings. He slumped on his seat like a twelve-year-old and sighed. He rocked his legs, he drummed his nails, he started trouble by pinching at her or at the boys. He even sometimes seemed to lose interest in his own thoughts. "I was thinking maybe we'd take the boys to Disneyworld this summer," he would begin, and Paula would respond by telling him what she knew about admissions and motels and crowds. "Well, whatever," he'd say. Disneyworld never came up again. It was infuriating. It had something to do with that part of him that believed everything eventually worked out for the best. She wasn't sure which bred what: did the inability to focus lead to his fatalism, or was it the other way around? Whichever: he didn't seem bothered. In those early days together, when she would get hysterical and wish she had a skillet to knock him back to his senses, she would find herself confronted with a face full of confusion. He never had any idea what she was carrying on about. Her years as a teacher taught her that this was a preadolescent thing. Sixth graders genuinely did not realize the thoughtlessness or stupidity of their actions or their words. They neither felt nor saw the books that their rangy elbows knocked from desk tops. "I didn't do that." "That's not what I meant." When they responded that way, they were saying that they did not yet have full control over language, didn't yet own their bodies. She had learned to be patient and forgiving with her students and with her sons. And she had learned to accept Al with a sense of wonder. She often felt envious: how nice to go through life, your mind flashing from one idea to the next, never stopping long enough to become worried or frazzled or preoccupied. Like being on an endless vacation at some isolated resort. And maybe everyone else in the world was on that same vacation. Maybe she was the only true worrywart, she and a few children she knew—children whose young faces were already lined with uneasiness.

Somewhere they had been selected. Their job: to worry about water pollution, nuclear waste, loss of the ozone layer, worldwide deforestation, the federal deficit, hunger, voter apathy, toxic waste, the deterioration of the infrastructure, inflation, urban decay, the farm crisis, racism, corrupt public officials, overpopulation, the collapse of the public school system, homelessness, pesticides in foods, violence on television, the general unfairness of everything. All the while, everyone else walked around scot-free. Who knew what went on inside other people's minds? She knew that the only time Al seemed to come to her completely was when he made love to her. He was intense and aggressive. He liked to talk about what he was doing to her. "How's that? Do you like that?" he'd ask, as he kneaded her breasts and rolled her nipples between his fingers. "Let me get the other one, too." He wanted to look in her eyes. He insisted. When they first got together, she was shy and inexperienced. She had known a few other boys, but sex with them had always had a secretive and nasty quality. It never seemed to have anything to do with her, and here was a man who wanted to look at her, wanted her to look at him. It was hard at first. He would grab her chin and order, "Look at me. Look in my eyes. Look right at me." She had succumbed. That's what it felt like —succumbing. And when she did, she felt herself subsumed, felt she had taken him in as well. She at once understood all the song lyrics about losing yourself in someone's eyes. She remembered thinking, "This is Al. I know who you are now." She still did. Whenever they made love. He always left a soft light on or burned candles so they could see each other. He no longer had to hold her chin. Often she held his head, grabbed him by his hair, pulled him, locked him in place. "Stay with me," she said, and he would, until at last he squeezed his eyes closed and was finished. Afterwards and often any time at all when their eyes met, they were shy with each other. They couldn't look at each other too long. Their secret might be revealed if their eyes lingered. They would lie together and she would feel him fading away from her. She had taken enough of him in, she hoped, to last until they came together again.

She caught his eye before he got up to speak. He had been riding his knees again toward the end of the introduction. He looked immature and distracted. She thought she saw some fear in his eyes.

". . . son of former mayor, the late, great A. B. Johnson, Senior, please welcome Al Johnson."

She blew him a one-fingered kiss and mouthed "good luck."

He sauntered to the lectern. His legs seemed stiff, and there was something contemptuous in his walk as well.

"How is everybody tonight?" He started. "Sure gets uncomfortable in this old hall, don't it? I missed a lot of baskets in this room. Ran a lot of laps." The audience murmured politely in response. His delivery was false and unnatural—a parody of a stand-up comedian.

She tried to compose herself into some sort of attitude, but was unsure what that attitude should be. She could not and would not put on the fawning adoration of Mabel Turner, so she tried to neutralize her expression, to betray nothing except her interest in her husband's words. She sat tall, her legs crossed at the knee. Her mother, she knew, would be proud of the pose, her poise. She felt eyes on her and was afraid to move. She was afraid if she tried she would find her limbs locked.

"I don't see any reason to fill y'all in on me. Most of you've known me since I was born. I see a lot of Daddy's friends out there. I'll just cut right to the heart of my message and maybe we can all get home, out of this musty gym."

Someone said "amen," and an anemic laugh circled the room.

She gave him the once over. Something—the lights, the lectern, the sharp suit and tie he almost never wore—something was making him look different. He was unfamiliar to her, the way a picture in a newspaper might be. People always apologized for such pictures. "I don't really look like that," they said. She would agree they didn't, but it was one of those contradictory things. They did look that way and they didn't, all at the same time. She had a silver-framed picture of her father on the mantle in the parlor. She once told the boys that their grandfather had looked something like that. Something like that: she had winced at the peculiar choice of words. But that's how photographs were—you only looked something like that. Al looked something like he looked right now: a tall man with a face tapering at the chin like an upside down pear. He had the sort of hair that was mostly tight kinks but was scattered here and there with stiff bristly straight hairs. He had to go to the barber shop often to keep the mess looking halfway decent. He had his mother's nose —not too broad, well-shaped, suiting his face. She could say he looked something like Miss Kezee, too.

She rarely saw him this way. She never thought of him as an accumulation of features. At the beginning she had not been attracted to his looks. She had fallen in love with the way he moved.

She had first seen Al playing football outside a fraternity house. She knew a few of the boys in the house from her Hansel and Gretel days. They seemed tamed by the big world, had lost much of their pretension and snobbery. Some had gotten serious about school. One or two had been cut off by their parents for being radical or rebellious—their tuitions getting paid by grandmas or by trust funds. These particular frat boys had a special way of treating girls from "back home." They treated them almost as if they were sisters, and Paula found it sweet. They would warn her away from certain guys, cut in on mashers and drunks at parties. She went to their parties because she felt safe there. Mizzou was a big school. A girl could get lost. Sometimes you just needed to be near people you knew.

She was sitting on the steps watching a pick-up football game. The boys of this particular house were not jocks. They were wild and the house had a bad reputation. They were taking this game seriously; they paid her no mind. The game was rough. There was constant motion: shoving, hopping around, rolling and running. They were about as graceful as drunken elephants. Except for that one. The tall boy with the wild hair. He moved sparingly, like a cat. He seemed to freeze mid-air. When he ran with the ball he couldn't be caught. At the end of the game, when the others lay panting and sweating on the lawn, this one strode amidst them, stepping among their spent bodies, ridiculing their lack of stamina. He was Achilles among the fallen Trojans, and Paula fell in love with him that instant.

She thought of having one of her friends from the fraternity introduce them, but that seemed like a desperate and trashy thing to do. And there was little hope of running into him naturally: there were thousands of students and little chance of meeting one in particular. She decided to try. She went out of her way to walk down fraternity row. She would see him sometimes ahead of her and follow him at a distance. She enjoyed the fine way his shoulders rolled and his butt snapped back and forth.

She missed classes because of him: once missed a chemistry quiz following him to a remote classroom building. She lied to get a make-up—said she was sick—and felt shamed by the whole thing. She had turned into one of those pathetic creatures who desperately haunt men. She felt helpless and out of control. And she didn't care. She needed her daily fix of the boy. He must have noticed her, and, in a way, she was afraid of that. If he turned around when she was following him she would duck behind a kiosk, dart into a doorway. If he thought she was desperate, that would ruin everything.

She confessed her obsession to her roommate Felicia.

"You've got to get a look at this boy," she told her.

So she and Felicia followed Al from Fraternity Row across the center of campus to Jesse Hall. At one point Al dropped a book and gracefully spun around, swooped to grab the text, and headed on his way. She grabbed Felicia's arm and put on a shaking swooning fit. She gasped deeply and said, "Oh, my God. Oh, my God."

"Calm down," Felicia had said.

She had sat Paula on a bench and fanned at her with a notebook. It was a cold day in February.

"I can't believe you've been chasing around after that," Felicia said.

Paula asked her was that not the finest thing she had *ever* seen, but she was not impressed. Felicia was brash, bulky, and from Kansas City. She had a lot of experience with boys and men. She was already quite jaded and there wasn't much that impressed her. She told Paula that unless he had money in one pocket and a wedding ring in another, wasn't nothing a nigger could do for her she couldn't do for herself.

"Boys are simple," she told her. "You want that simple-ass boy, you go up to him and take him."

Paula protested. She would never do anything like that. Felicia told her she might not, but that there were plenty of little bitches out there who would.

Still, she never did get introduced, nor did she introduce herself. She found out his name, of course, and whatever else she could: that he was a journalism major, a small-town boy, had a little bit of money. After six months her obsession waned, but she still found herself looking for him in the crowd. She walked his routes out of habit.

In the fall of her junior year she found herself in line with him in the bookstore. He had a stack of newspapers and a package of chewing gum. He gave her a puzzled look that made her feel she was being examined under a microscope.

"You a new student here?" he asked.

"No," she answered.

I've only been following you around for a year.

They walked from the store and talked, and he kept that perplexed look on his face. They made small talk, and his eyes wandered all around her face as if he might be looking for something.

"You're looking at me funny," she said.

"Am I?"

She nodded. He kept that look for the following several weeks as they began to see each other.

She was giving him a similar look now, staring at the strangely unfamiliar man standing at the lectern spouting political clichés.

"I'm interested in seeing us grow and prosper," he said.

Yes, you fine thing, aren't we all. For a person getting right to the point he hadn't said much at all. He was using that new voice again: the one full of passion and conviction. He had thankfully lost the comedian's cocky aloofness. He was preaching now, gesturing broadly, making eye contact with anyone he could.

"What I have to say I know many of you don't want to hear, but the reason I got involved in this race was because I feel strongly enough about our town to put myself on the line. My friends, I'm afraid that our little town is dying. Not slowly, but quite fast, and if we don't do something now, River Ridge as we know it will disappear from the map."

The whole audience inhaled deeply. They all knew Al's positions, yet they would not be denied the opportunity to audibly express their disapproval. He continued with his urgent, strident tone. Paula wanted to get his eye. She tried to signal him. Something was wrong here. This was the wrong tack.

"More than half our population is over fifty-five. Young people don't stay here because there aren't any jobs. We don't have a tax base to support even essential services. The farm economy is in ruin. . . . I could go on listing our problems, but you all know them. I know you do."

He could ignore the damn microphone. He was shouting.

He seemed a complete stranger now, never anything like this. Ready to burst into flames, it seemed.

The audience had gone rigid, turned disagreeable. They sat in defiant poses, arms crossed, mouths set in scowls. They mumbled under their breath.

"I've seen the books, and you have, too. We don't have even half the money projected to maintain the minimum of service. That includes the police force and our one-man street maintenance crew. Raising taxes won't help because we can only raise them so much, and not really enough to do what needs to get done. There is, however, a way out."

A pointed coughing cropped up in the audience. A few people sighed loudly enough to be heard. Al stormed on.

"Consolidation." And when he said the word the room exploded. A man back near an exit stood up and shouted, "No."

Paula gripped the edge of her chair to keep from shuddering. He went on, the same stern confidence on his face and in his voice.

"Consolidation with our two neighboring communities. They've got about the same number of folks, identical problems. This would accomplish several things . . . I will finish this speech. I will finish." He raised his hands against the mumbling and hissing.

She couldn't look anywhere but at him. He was like a

principal lecturing a lunchroom full of naughty school kids. He was severe but he was cool. He wasn't sweating or flustered, didn't look anywhere near as uncomfortable as she felt. Out of the corner of her eye she could see Mabel shaking her head and tsk-tsking.

"Let me finish. Consolidation may be the answer to our prayers. The new town would increase our tax base by incorporating all the productive land between three municipalities. With the combined population we would move into a new funding category, making us eligible for greater federal and state aid. And, finally, we would conserve money by eliminating the duplicate services of the three cities. The plan is more detailed than that. I won't go into it here. I have copies available for you at the door. Please take one. I'll be happy to answer all your questions. It's a good plan. It may not be the only solution, but it is one I think will serve us well. I hope I can count on your support.

"Thank you."

Paula couldn't lead the applause as boldly as Mabel had. What applause there was was soft and barely polite. Her own anemic clapping fit right in.

A question and answer session followed. Tyrone Turner got most of the questions. He was asked things such as how soon until the riverfront park might be completed and did he think it was time to buy a new squad car. Al sat there, still looking cool. He might have been listening to Turner's answers with great care, but Paula didn't think so. His evening had ended with the speech. He was probably planning what to have for lunch tomorrow.

Tyrone thought a new squad car sounded great.

Al was asked only one question: He was also asked about the new squad car. He said he didn't know where River Ridge would be getting the money for a squad car for a long time. Or for anything else, for that matter.

After the closing prayer, Paula went and stood at his side. Walter came and stood with them. He was Berneice-less tonight—apparently putting in your spousal appearance did not extend to the wives of campaign managers. He and Al tilted their heads together, whispered and chuckled. A few of the neighbors greeted them. Tyrone shook Paula's hand—held it a little too long, she thought—and gave her his million-dollar smile. Mabel dragged him away as if they were contagious.

The crowd filed out quickly. Some of the older men appeared to huddle conspiratorially as they walked to the parking lot. A bald man Paula couldn't quite place waved at them and gave them a silly grin. Al picked up the stack of position papers as they left. Not one had been taken.

"I think it went OK," she told him in the car.

"Um," he said, shrugging.

"People can be so rude. It amazes me."

"You want some ice cream?"

"Sure." The drive to Oak Grove took ten minutes, but they would still be home when expected. The so-called debate had come up short time-wise as well.

"I'm sorry they didn't respond to your plan better."

He shrugged again. "I couldn't care less."

"Say what?"

"My supporters weren't in that room tonight."

"Well, yes, but it would have been nice to win over a few votes."

"Look, I'd rather not discuss this with you. Can we talk about something else, please?"

"I beg your pardon?"

He reached up and turned on the radio. She sat for a

minute, stared at him in disbelief. She felt the way she had when she learned her mother was dead. When they called from Chesterfield Life Care and told her, she had stood there holding the phone not quite knowing what the words meant. She turned the radio off.

"What did you just say?"

He didn't answer. He hung his arm out the car window and began whistling.

"Please repeat what you just said."

"Huh? Oh, I said, change the subject." He was oblivious. He wheeled into the Dairy Queen and asked if she wanted anything.

"No, I don't. And that is not what you said."

He got her a small dipped cone anyway. She sat with it, looking childish with such a tiny item. The ice milk started melting so she threw the mess in the trash barrel. She stood at the barrel looking back at him sitting there, inhaling the banana split much the same way his boys would. He took rapid-fire bites, allowed a little to drip back in the boat every spoonful.

She got in the car and slammed the door pointedly.

"Jesus," he said, between slurps.

She thrust a handful of napkins in his face. "What you said was, 'I won't discuss this with you.' That's what you said."

He stopped the shoveling and looked at her. "So?"

She hit him in the shoulder. "I don't even know where to start with you anymore."

He leaned out the window and heaved the rest of the ice cream into the trash. "You know what you do?" he asked. "You make a federal case out of everything. That's what you do."

She looked out the passenger window. She would not let herself cry, but in case she did, he would not get the satisfaction of seeing her.

"Me," he continued. "I try to keep things in perspective."

She took in a deep breath. "I don't know what we're talking about." Though she tried to control it, her voice came out high and thin.

"We could start with privacy and space. Stuff like that. What are you talking about?"

"I . . . uh . . . what does this have to do with privacy?"

"Well, maybe that's the wrong word," he said. He started the car and drove toward home.

She let out a shuddering hiccup.

"Are you all right?" he asked her.

She couldn't answer. She was shaking too hard, couldn't seem to get any air. She felt hysterical. She hadn't been hysterical since she lived with her mother, and then she was mostly faking. Back then, for effect she would scream and tear at her hair, but this felt like the real thing.

What on earth was he talking about? She'd been blindsided by the whole thing. In the women's magazines they were always telling you that marriage was like walking through a minefield: you never knew when something was going to blow up in your face. In an instant you could be ripped to shreds. She hiccuped again.

"Excuse yourself," he laughed. He was going to gloss this over, going to try to make nice, but it was too soon for that. Or too late. There was a score to be settled. She covered her mouth with her hands, worked quickly to gather her words.

"Let's just get this straight," she said. "This is all so psychotic, and I want to be sure I've got it: As far as you're concerned, this election is off limits for me. You'll tell if there's something you think I need to know. Tell me when you need me to perform. Is that it?"

He nodded and shrugged. "You never sounded like you much cared." He reached out and rubbed her arm, gave her a seductive smile.

"So. Because you've avoided discussing this with me, and I haven't brought it up, I'm out?"

"As usual, you will overanalyze this. I guess my answer is, 'Yes.' Period."

"I'm then what's known as window dressing?"

"If you want. Interesting, huh?"

She tapped her finger against her teeth as she always did when she wanted her mind to work faster. Somewhere between fascinated and repelled, she hadn't a clue what the appropriate response was. There was the part of her that wanted to kill him. Take the kids, leave town, and start up somewhere else. There was the part that wanted in, the part that would fight till death not to be excluded, even from this stupid campaign. There was the part of her who thought it was all a joke—a bizarre, pathetic joke.

"You're playing with me, right?" she asked.

"Well, if you think so."

"Well you're just a conniving little bastard." She scooted as close to her door as she could. "Don't touch me. I need to think. Not that you care."

"You talk like a woman with options."

She laughed. "Oh, buddy. It's a dangerous game you're playing."

"Love you, baby," he said. He parked the car in the drive and offered her an arm as they walked to the house.

She took the arm; willed a force field between them. She hoped he could feel it burning up his arm.

It's not that easy, smart boy. You met your match, and you should have learned that long before now.

Opening the door they found bitter thick smoke swirling through the house. Alarms buzzed steadily on both floors. Tim was at the phone dialing and hanging up, and someone was pounding on a door.

"What the hell?" Al said.

"Come quick," Tim said. His eyes were tearing from the smoke. In the kitchen Miss Kezee bent over the smoking oven and removed a tray of black rocks. Four similar trays cooled on the counters around the room.

"What's going on here?" Al shouted to his mother. Paula opened windows and doors to release the smoke.

"Baking me some cookies. What you think?"

Al grabbed the tray from his mother and burned his hand. He dropped the hot metal and cursed.

"I told her she was burning them, but she wouldn't listen."

"I like a crisp cookie," Miss Kezee said. "Most folks don't cook em through. Nothing worse than raw cookies."

The pounding continued. "What the . . ." Al turned a key that Paula had never seen and opened the cellar door. Tommy burst from the basement like any trapped animal would. He was flushed and sweaty from pounding. He ran to Paula and threw his arms around her. He was crying.

"She locked me in the basement. She said I got smart with her."

"Little foul mouth heathen. I want that boy's ass beat and I want it beat good."

"I didn't say nothing to her. She's crazy. Crazy old witch."

"I'll tear your black ass up myself. Bring that little bastard over here."

Tommy hugged Paula tighter. She extracted herself from his tentacles. The old bat couldn't hurt him. He went and cowered behind his father.

Paula walked away shaking her head. It was like a silly dream.

Al caught up with her at the steps. He was coughing because of the smoke. "Help me out here. What's your problem?"

My problem is my husband wants to play games and my

mother-in-law is old and sick and almost burnt down my house with my son trapped in the basement.

"I don't want to discuss this," she said. She opened every window upstairs and decided that in the morning she would arrange for Miss Kezee the next available room at Oak Grove Manor.

11

I THOUGHT THIS ELECTION DAY WOULD NEVER ARRIVE. I have been, I'm afraid, rather like a rich kid anticipating the Christmas haul, to the point I've caught myself watching clocks and calendars as if somehow that might speed the time. And I sleep the way those eager greedy little ones do—not at all, and then falling into a tingling semiconsciousness.

Out here on the patio it is steamy as a sauna. We have left spring and entered hard summer although it's still early June. Like a dome, the heated air will be fixed over town the next several months.

I left Paula asleep. The boys, well, the one you have to drag out of bed, and Tim will just hole up somewhere with a book until the others make their presences known. Like me he gets sick of the hubbub. The pot's always on the boil in this house. The hornets are in constant swarm. And there is never any sense of perspective on the crisis: a roach in the kitchen is the same as a bloody nose is the same as a flat tire is the same as a nuclear war.

When I was growing up here I do not recall that we had such crises. Things went slow and, if the road got a little bumpy, my mother and father took it in stride. I recall how the glass liner on the water heater ruptured one time and how the three of us went down in the basement and looked at the water seeping across the floor.

"I guess we'll have to get someone in tomorrow," my father said. We went upstairs and probably went to bed.

Nowadays around here there would be much wringing of hands, and Paula would do a lot of sighing and the boys would fuss about how they wouldn't be showering in any cold water. I would get so wound up with calming them all down that I would get hysterical myself and say a few choice words to each one of them. Then we would check into a motel for the duration.

It isn't Paula so much. She is a calm woman, optimistic and brave even, though neither would I say she takes the bumps and bruises of everyday life in stride. She gets sullen, down in the mouth about the littlest of things, tends to see a ding in the windshield as a personal affront. Might I add humorless as well, something I learned the time I laughed at her dejection over a little car trouble with an old Maverick she had in college.

The boys, on the other hand, could use a couple of years in a boot camp somewhere—hard cots and abusive drill sergeants included. Like all these kids nowadays they are under the impression the world was created with air-conditioning, Nintendo, and V-6 engines. Not that I didn't have a comfortable childhood myself, but I don't think I had the . . . expectations of comfort these gentlemen do. I don't think I was ever that blasé. They wear their regalness in a different way, those two: one, in the form of privilege—hands that assume that everything within reach must be his; and the other with his smoldering superiority, a belief on his part that people can talk all they want because after all the talking is through, his opinion will emerge as the correct one. More often than not he is right.

That's what keeps it stirred up around here. Mr. Grabbyhands and his brother Prince Timothy. Walter says it will get worse. He says wait till they get another year or two on them and the hormones start popping and the phone starts ringing and there starts to be all kindsa folks in and out of your house you never seen before. He says I won't know what the hell is going on.

I can't wait.

Paula, she thrives on the madness, revels in the chaos. She knows who is supposed to be where, when, and doing what, and she gets them there, too, and on time. I have no idea how she keeps track of it. She has this calendar hanging up by the phone in the kitchen with these cryptic little notes scribbled on it, which I suppose tell her something, but could be in Russian as far as I'm concerned. (*T* dnts hbl 12. You tell me.) Some of the items are crossed out three and four times, some stuck on top with Post-it notes. She says it's just like down at the paper. She says things have to happen in a certain order and at certain times or the paper doesn't publish. You have to have your materials in stock and your jobs complete and on time.

So she thinks. It's hardly the same thing. Down there you lay out the work on a big flow chart and it never changes, and if somebody doesn't get their job done they're out on their ass.

Here, every day is some different crap going on—this birthday party over here, and that orthodontist over there. And then with Mother here there is another whole set of items.

I know Paula thinks I don't pull my weight, and I don't. But if it was me in charge of this crazy shit, people would be lucky if they got fed. I'm a person that likes a routine. If the same thing happens everyday, that's just fine with me. A lot of people would criticize that, say it's boring or lame, but it works for me. It's what I grew up with. No, the Johnsons weren't the most exciting family in town, but we were consistent. I knew what I could count on: meals at the same time, a regular time for homework, the same chores every day.

So every now and then I try to have this discussion with Paula. I suggest we simply put up a schedule of some kind so that certain people around here know what's expected of them and when. She rolls her eyes and asks me if by certain people I mean me. She knows very well whom I mean, but far be it from her to miss the opportunity to get a little jab in.

My point: I think the boys could benefit from some more structure. But I will never be able to make that point. Why? Because Paula turns any kind of suggestion into a criticism of her.

Or worse, she turns it back on me. She says that if I took more of an interest around here, there wouldn't be a problem. Or that if I want the boys on a schedule why don't I put them on a schedule myself?

And why I don't do that gets us down to the real shit, which is that if I did—if I sat down and did something up that I thought made sense to me and that I thought would work for the boys—she would just do it over again until it suited her. And in the end—because she enjoys a certain amount of drama and chaos (one wouldn't want to get bored, after all)—when she got through with it, the two of them would be back to their old tricks in no time.

So if the choices are to be the villain and stick your hands in it or to be the villain and keep your hands out, I'm keeping my hands out. Which makes her crazy, I know, but it works for me.

I don't get it: she wants me in the middle of this shit, but then only up to a certain point. When she wanted to add the patio, for instance, she started out completely helpless. (As usual.) Oh, sure, she'd done her homework: she'd gotten out the *House Beautiful* and *Better Homes and Gardens* and had some ideas of what she wanted, but she didn't have a clue as to where to begin. Just being helpful, I called some contractors in the area and got a few rough estimates. All the while she's getting crankier and crankier because "I'm not showing much interest in the thing."

IT WASN'T ME WANTED A PATIO IN THE FIRST PLACE.

I said "fine." I got a builder in to sit down—with the two of us—to go over the plan. Which is when I made my real mistake. A fool, I suggested landscaping the whole back yard at the same time. It made sense to me to tie the project together, somehow, and I made some sketches on a placemat.

So the guy leaves. And then I get this pouting and sulking. She doesn't say anything, but I can tell she's upset. This was *her* project, after all. I had a lot of nerve putting my two cents in.

Of course, in the end she gets right behind the landscaping, and now the yard looks about like what I'd sketched—oh, sure, she'd moved a bench from here to there, and enlarged the flower bed behind the garage. But she loves it.

Go figure. I give up.

Seems to me that when you sit down to sign the marriage certificate there should be some pathetic mousy-looking lawyer type with a big magnifying glass standing by who will go over the fine print with you. A lot of this shit a person just doesn't count on.

Which is not to say it is bad or unbearable or something I want to walk away from. Maybe it's that at some place along the line a person needs to be able to sit down and . . . renegotiate. You should be able to say "this part and this part we keep, and this part, I'm sorry, baby, but I don't play that no more."

Maybe at some point we do that, Paula and I, though I wouldn't know how to even begin such a discussion. Best I can do right now is to carve out of this family stuff some pieces that just belong to me.

And so I decide—unilaterally, I admit—that I will claim my own space in this life, and that it doesn't have to be one of those nasty secret deals—like some sort of hidden perversion—

or, like hunting, some sort of male-bonding thing where I go away with a bunch of guys and do . . . whatever it is they do. I decide that I will draw a line around something that is right here: my political life, and I break it to her on the run the other week after the debate.

And she thinks it's a game. Ha!

This election: This was my idea. Mine and Walter's. She's got nothing to do with it, and I like it that way. And it makes her crazy, too, and I knew it would—like I said: she's got to have her hands in every damn thing. But not this. Not this time.

And I'd like to see what she's gonna do about it, too. Not too much, I don't think. Oh, she'll pout and scream and tear her hair out maybe, but—and I know this sounds cold—what choice does she have. Leave? Over something this petty. Get her own private thing? More power to her.

And if I lose the damn election, well that's that, I guess. She's got nothing to complain about.

Until the next thing, at least.

12

Once the decision to put Miss Kezee in the nursing home was made, Paula felt relieved, less rushed to take action. Still, something didn't feel right. Something had been ruined. The little-girl Paula adhered strictly to the lines in her coloring books. Her mother hadn't taught her that: it was something that was her own. If in her zeal she colored over the line of the queen's dress—scratched a red streak across the green grass—she would quit that page and never return to it again. It was ruined. She had the same feeling now. Things would never be the same: she wanted off this page, wanted this chunk of her life behind her forever.

She had decided about the nursing home a week ago and, further, she had decided to wait until after the election to make Al sit down and face the facts: his mother was out of here.

The past week he had been as vague as a distant radio signal, walking around the house, bumping into furniture, and mumbling to himself. His face was fixed in contemplation, creased brows and squinched eyes. Now and then he seemed to reach some kind of realization. He would snap his fingers and wave his hand in the air at nothing. "That's it," he would say.

Sometimes he brooded, sullenly, slumped in a chair, arms folded across his chest. He looked mad and hurt.

She didn't ask what was wrong and he didn't offer to tell her.

Most often he was just gone. He spent the week on a flurry of last-minute campaigning. Or that is where she imagined he was. He would come home after midnight smelling of smoke and beer. She would be in bed, reading—it helped to get lost in a book. He would come in and chat at her aimlessly about the weather and the headlines and about how tired he was. He didn't notice that she didn't respond: he would just keep rambling. He would be too tired to make love, and she kept her hands away from him. She wasn't sure how she would respond if he attempted and was relieved he didn't try.

Today was election day, and at least one part of this would be over with. She'd spent the past week willing herself not to think about it. It: Al, the election, his repugnant new attitude.

Over the week in her own way she had become as distractible as he was. It was a new experience for her: pleasant and frightening at the same time. Sometimes she found from one minute to the next she was unable to remember what she had been thinking. On Friday she drove all the way to Hannibal before realizing she had brought no money or purse. She had had to borrow from the boys to get a few groceries, and then forgot what she had come for in the first place. She went back later for the laundry detergent.

She wondered if this was how Al lived, but he rarely seemed flustered, embarrassed, or frustrated—the way it felt to her. Either he was used to being lost, or more likely his vagueness was a put-on, a way to avoid ever being responsible for anything. Whichever, he would not get off easy this time. When the ballots were counted she would sit him down and make him deal with *his* mother problem. She would put the issue in the affirmative so as to avoid the trap of seeming to ask his permission. She would tell him the facts: that his mother was more than she was able to or cared to handle. And then she would tell him she had decided to get Miss Kezee a room at the Oak Grove Manor until she could go back to Minnesota and care for herself. Then, after allowing him his say (she'd pretend to listen, but he could recite the "I Have a Dream Speech" for all she cared: her mind was made up) she'd drop the big one: he was the one who would be telling his mother. He would not worm his way out of that. And if he decided he could not, then the ball was in his court. Her days as nursemaid were over.

The week had been hellish in other ways, too. Miss Kezee had taken every opportunity to wander away. She sneaked out on Thursday when Paula was in the basement doing the wash. Paula wouldn't have known she was gone at all if she hadn't toddled into the kitchen covered with sweat demanding a glass of iced tea.

"Mother, where have you been?"

The old scoundrel gave her a crooked smile. "I'm not sure that's anybody's business, baby. Will I have to get that tea myself?"

Saturday morning she had walked away from the breakfast table and right out the front door. Just like that. She'd gotten bald-faced about her wandering, couldn't have cared less what Paula thought. Apparently she had been taking off since the day they found her sitting outside the city hall.

Paula asked the boys to stand watch, but they were no help. There was something wrong with those two as well, and she hoped whatever was going on would keep until Miss Kezee was packed off. Tim—her sweet Tim—had lost all patience with his brother. A nasty streak had emerged in him that she didn't care for one bit. He no longer tolerated Tommy's constant rough-house and silliness, not for even a moment. He barked at him angrily the same way a dog barks at the postman. It was a reflex. On Saturday, Tommy came in from breakfast and changed channels on a show Tim was watching. It was an old attention-getter for Tommy: there were plenty of televisions in the house. He just wanted to wrestle. Tim got up without a word and changed it back. On the way back to his seat he slapped his brother, hard, right across the face. Paula could hear the smack of skin on skin from the kitchen, and she came out to investigate. Tommy was shocked and there was a moment before what had happened to him registered. His jaw dropped open and she wasn't sure if he would laugh or cry.

She had been shocked, too. The handprint on his face looked hot and out of place. He looked at her in a helpless rage. She remembered thinking that there was some sort of test going on and not having a clue what the correct response should be. Sure, she had dealt with unprovoked violence at school, and as the mother of boys there had been plenty of tussles around here, but she was drawing a blank.

Tommy had screamed, not in pain, but out of frustration. She'd taken too long to react and he'd decided she was on his brother's side. He ran to his room and slammed the door.

Tim kept his eyes on the TV, calm, as if nothing had happened. She was furious with him—furious at the coldness of the whole scene and furious at his pretended casualness. He was being Al. She was furious because he had turned into his daddy. She grabbed the remote and turned off the set.

"Go to your room," she ordered.

He didn't move.

"You heard me, boy. I said get going."

"I'm not going up there with him." He made "him" sound like a dirty word.

She was so angry that tears filled her eyes. The anger shook her voice. "Your brother," she'd seethed. "Who do you think you are? You know what's good for you, you'll do what I say."

"I'll sit in the parlor, but I'm not going up there." He strolled from the room but walked a wide arc around her as if afraid she would hit him.

She might have, too. She felt like she would: hit him or

curse him. She sat on the couch, hugged a pillow to herself and breathed deeply. Everything was coming apart. They were on a spaceship that had been blown apart. Everyone was flying in opposite directions. If she didn't do something they would stay apart forever.

That was Saturday, and by Tuesday, election day, she knew what needed to be done. Somehow, Miss Kezee had been the catalyst for all this. Miss Kezee and the stupid election. She knew what to do about her mother-in-law, and then, in the same thought, she knew what to do about the election. There was no doubt which way she would vote.

Sometimes stuff gets away from you. That's what I told that gal, but it's like she didn't even hear me. A little bit of smoke ain't hurt nothing, and the cookies wouldn't have burnt if I hadn't had to trick that little heathen into the basement to keep him out of my cookie dough. Eatin right up in my face like I'm not even there. Saying "That old woman don't even know what day it is." I showed his narrow little behind something. Child got me so upset I put some cookies in and let em fall off the tray. A heathen. A little smoke but that ain't no cause to get fractious. She been walking around here for a week with a chip on her shoulder. Face all pulled down and sour, giving these short little answers like it's a big strain for her to speak civil. All the same she's trying to act like nothing's the matter. Come in here trying to do stuff for me she been doing all along. Lord knows I appreciate it, but I got back my strength now. Most of it. And I don't need all that fussing and seeing to that I used to. I know I'm better, but she can't seem to figure that out. Sunday I'm here on my bed, have combed my own hair out, and here she come, gonna hop up on the bed behind me like she does, saying, "Here, Mother, let me get that for you." I'm fully able to pin up my own hair. Been doing so my whole life. I say to her, I say "I got it," but she's grabbing at the comb and doing it her way. Not that I mind the way she does it, but a person has to do for herself. That's one thing I've learned in this life. A person's got to do for herself. I say to her, "You seem to got something troubling you lately." She don't say nothing. I say, "You got some troubles, you know you can bring them to me." She lets out some air and says, "I'm fine." She pins the last hair and leaves, saying, "Let me know if you need anything else," but the way she says it is like she was a nurse or something. Like she's gonna come and do something for you only because that's her job. Not because she wants to. I want to tell her, "Look, you might as well not offer. Don't nobody like that. Don't nobody want somebody doing something for them because that's supposed to be their job. I know. I done it. I done it for twenty-five years." Cook, clean, live with a man cause that's my job. It's what caused A. B. to hate me so. I know that. I know a lot of things to tell that girl. I do. I know that look on her face. I know that whatever she got she's not the first woman got it. We get all kinds of blues. The lowdown man blues. The not enough men blues. The no money, the lowdown man walked off with my money, the damn kids, the too many eggs to fry, too damn hot, too cold, don't love me no more, when's my man comin. All them blues. And she got some kind of em. Though she never admit that. She one of them soddity gals. She pretend like she not, but she is. Had all kindsa money. Lived in a big house down in Saint Louis. Full of everything you'd ever want. Every new gadget in the store, everything brand new, and I know cause I was in that house and I looked around and I seen all that stuff. Her mama, that Helen, she didn't even try to hide it. She weren't shame. She made most of that money herself and she should've been proud. She had a reason to have her nose up in the air. Sat me down at that wedding to tell me how her daughter have had the finest of everything. Said everything twice to let me know she meant it. Have had every single thing, and only if I was blind wouldn't I have know that because right there in front of me all of it was. Every little thing, and this gal is sitting there sipping on her tea with her little finger all stuck out. I'm drinking her bitter tea, too. I don't even drink no hot tea. I sit there saying, "Yes, ma'am," to her, while she's telling me how lucky my son is to be getting a girl like this. I don't tell her how Al's daddy had him quite a wad stuck away in the bank in Hannibal himself, but see if that tight Negro would spend a quarter on someone else. Didn't have his money displayed all over some house. That was a big house, too, that Helen had. Put the Rockerfellas to shame. And meanwhile, there that gal was, at her own wedding, sulking around, pouting, like she was ashamed of all that stuff. Here her mama have got vases of fresh flowers on every table in the house. Her mama had bought for me a basket full of beautiful soaps and lotions just cause I come to stay at her house for the wedding. Had a seven tier wedding cake, and one that had a bride and groom on top that was even a colored bride and groom, too. Tell me how much she had to pay to find something like that. Had some mens playing fancy music. Live. Three of em. And that gal got the nerve to apologize to me cause her mama have spent a fortune on the wedding. "Mrs. Johnson, I have to apologize for my mother. She goes overboard." I wanted to tell her right then, girl, if I had all that stuff I sure nuff would flash it around. "You got it honey, you flaunt it," was what Miss Pearl Bailey always said, and don't you know she's right. I didn't never have none myself. No money. None of my own. So I never myself had the chance this Paula gal had to start feeling guilty. There she was apologizing to me like I was the one who felt bad cause her mama knocked herself out. Me, I was walking around that house thinking I sure would like to have me one of these nice cut glass bowls just to put fruit in. Helen, her mama, caught me, too. Caught me walking around her house touching her things, admiring them. Her eyes kinda lit up cause she saw I was appreciating them. Cause I knew that's why she had them. Why all women have all their nice things. Cause they like em and want to see other people like em too. That Helen, after she saw me admiring her stuff, she took me around that house and showed me all her nice things. Seemed she had a beautiful thing tucked away behind every door. In every drawer. Saying, "This is a piece of Irish lace my husband bought in Dublin. Lovely, isn't it? Here is a decanter I picked up on a business trip to New York." Bacarat? Bacharach? Whatever she said it was, she was proud of it, too, and should have been. I have never seen finer things. Girl say "Stop it, Mother. You're boring people." But not me. I could have looked at that mess all day long. I just said, "You sure have lovely things, Miss Fuller." Not much else I could say, cause I couldn't believe one person would have much. And, also, she was so busy making over her own things herself that didn't nobody else have a chance to get a word in. She'd picked up one of her pretty little glass animals and hold it up to the light for me to see. "Go ahead," she said, "Touch it," and I was afraid to touch it cause it was such a fine and delicate thing. But Helen insisted. She practically forced the thing into my hands and made me hold it. That was her attitude. Wasn't nothing but a thing. Cause she had her plenty of money and could go out and buy her a case of glass toys if she wanted. Didn't have to ask no one or give no explanations. Wasn't nothing but a thing. That Paula got an attitude somehow that there was something wrong with her mother and her things. Or her mother being proud of her things. Or her mother showing off her things. Cause when she finally had enough she blew her stacks. Her mama was showing me her jewelry, and believe me it was fabulous stuff. Paula come in, start fussing, saying, "Just shut up about all that, will you Mother. It's so embarrassing." I felt so sorry for that Helen, but she was what you called a lady. She knew not to throw no scene in front of company. She didn't say nothing, but I could see her eyes were full of hurt. I didn't say nothing either, and I guess that Paula felt shame cause she just went away and didn't say too much more to her mama the whole weekend. Still with Helen it was "my baby this" and "my baby that" the whole time I was there, and if I saw another scrapbook or photo album with pictures of that girl I would have died. After the floor show, Helen picked up a pair of pretty jade earrings. Tiny little things. Gorgeous. "I want you to have these. They will look perfect on you," she said. "They are not the sort of thing I wear." I told her, no, I could not take them. They were so nice, but I told her that she didn't need to be giving me nothing at all. She insisted. She said she wanted me to remember her, and she pressed them into my hand and closed it. She held my hand and closed her eyes like she was praying. I kept those earrings. I wear them all the time. They are perfect for me. And here I am now in Paula and Al's house. And, don't you know they have as many nice things as they want to. I see that Paula looking at her own things. Touching them, rubbing on them as if they had some kind of magic. She's moping around here like she needs some magic. I can hear her out there now. She can't seem to do nothing right. The towels aren't folded. She balls up the sheets. When she's not looking, I pull them out and do them over. She don't seem to even notice. She can be a strange little wench, but sometimes you just need somebody to show they care for you. When I go out later I'm gonna buy her something nice. She will be real surprised.

Al had left early in the morning to be at the polling place when it opened and Paula had frittered away most of the morning. She fixed Miss Kezee's hair, did a load of laundry, she watched Phil. All of that felt like frittering. She was angry now that she had decided not to teach summer school, but when the jobs were available she thought she would be taking care of her mother-in-law. Now the thought of wasting a whole summer was depressing. She would call the school district office tomorrow. Maybe someone had quit or had a baby. Otherwise, she would have to take up a hobby. Just like the old days. She could learn Arabic. French Cuisine. Belly Dancing. She could get her closets organized for once. Plan a real family vacation. Things might work out after all.

Al came in the door, and, though soaked with perspiration, he looked good in his white polo shirt. She wanted to tell him that his phony political smile had frozen to his face. She heard that could happen to you, and here was living proof.

He saluted her. "What's the story, chief?"

She laughed at him, a surge of lust rushing through her. He was hard to stay angry with.

"Things look pretty good out there. You seen some brochures?" He was rummaging around the desk.

"No."

"I thought I left them right here. A whole stack of pink ones."

"Only pink thing around here is my tongue," she said. She stuck it out at him and made kissy lips. Forget some brochures. The stupid things could be anywhere. At his office. On the roof of his car.

"And you haven't seen them?"

She started to tell him what he could do with his damn brochures. Instead, she said, "The pink ones, you say. I gave those out. All of them. Around the block. I did."

He gave her an incredulous look. Then he shrugged. He was as easy to bluff as a sixth grader. "We all set for the victory party?"

"Beg your pardon?"

"Victory party. Friends and supporters. Sit around waiting for the call from city hall."

"And how was I supposed to know about that?"

"Just assumed . . ."

"How stupid of me. You don't just want window dressing, you want clairvoyant window dressing. Isn't the campaign manager supposed to throw the victory party? Walter and Berneice have a lovely home."

"Forget it. It's no big deal." He rearranged the papers on his desk one more time.

"God, I hate that look."

"What look? What are you on about now?"

"You come in here at two o'clock and ask me if I'm ready for some party I know nothing about. Then you look at me as if I'm the one being unreasonable."

"I said forget it, OK?"

"Oh, no. See, that's what you do. Make me the bad person, and then say "let's forget it" so I get left holding your shit. Uh, uh. I'm not forgetting it. Not any more." She rubbed her hands together, circling him like a cat while she talked. He balled his hands into fists, but she didn't fear them. She didn't think he would ever hit anything. He couldn't even spank the boys when they were naughty.

"Don't do this today, please," he said. He threw up his

hands, and started for the door. "I got to get back out there."

She grabbed his arm. "Nothing is settled. You can walk away, but don't think this is over."

"I'm sorry." He shrugged.

"Sorry." She smacked him across the shoulder. "Sorry don't solve nothing. You better get real. Are we having this party? Am I included in this or am I not? What do you want to do about your mother? You want chicken or fish for supper? Come on. Let's go."

He shrugged again and headed for the door. "What's up with you?"

"Answer a question for a change. Pick one. Go ahead."

"If that'll shut you up. How about: Let's have a party."

"Fine," she said. His sheepishness raised the contempt in her voice. He walked away. He didn't seem to know whether to wave or even if he should look at her.

"Look," he began. "I could pick up some . . ."

"Just go," she interrupted. "But tonight when this damn election is over you better be ready with answers for all of it. Good answers, too."

She opened a cupboard to see what there might be to make a party with. Not one blessed thing. She snatched opened all the cabinet doors, left them gaping open, their not-so-neatly ordered cereals and canned goods a silent witness to her frustration. She thought, this is what it's like to be in one of those mad housewife movies. You wake up and find someone has changed the rules on you. The people you thought you knew have become strangers, and no one speaks your language. You tear through the house like a fool. No wonder you saw the headlines on the tabloids: Crazed Woman Goes on Rampage: Kills Husband, Self. Mother Trades Baby for Bottle of Beer. Behind those headlines was a person just like her. A nice normal woman who had reached her limit. This was not a comforting thought: Paula had never believed there was anything glamorous about being crazy. Neurosis was another indulgence for rich white folks. Further, she was stronger than that. She knew she was. She was a survivor. It was her curse. She would be the one to crawl away from the flaming wreckage, the one whose body was thrown clear. How ironic that getting through, surviving, having things work out the way you wanted, should in the end seem, somehow, unfair. But sometimes survival was unfair, and you just had to keep going.

Despite a quick, trashy fantasy, she couldn't imagine sabotaging the damn party: putting hot pepper flakes in the Chex mix, freezing flies in the ice cubes, placing whoopee cushions on the chairs. It would be immature and tacky, and, worse, people around here might actually enjoy it. She'd once again have sent the wrong message.

She could leave, just walk away from the whole damn mess, but that would mean writing off everything she worked for, saying it had been wrong, a mistake. That wasn't true. This man, these boys, this house. The whole thing was right. Was. Is. Worth fighting for. I'm like the driver who got off the interstate at the wrong exit and got lost. I just have to find the correct ramp. Then things will be fine.

If she worked fast she could get to the grocery store, vote, and get the house picked up a little before the polls closed. Tomorrow they would arrange a place for Miss Kezee at Oak Grove Manor. Then she could sit down with Al and start to work on the rest of it.

She heard things clattering against each other in the next room. There was a scream.

In the living room she found her sons wrapped around each other, legs intertwined, arms swinging wildly at each other and everything else. They made throaty, high-pitched animal-like noises. They grunted. One of them bit into the other one. She could not tell which piece of the bundle belonged to whom: they were rolling back and forth, wildly, blurred together.

"Stop it!" she yelled. "Stop it right now."

They showed no sign of stopping.

"Tommy. Timothy. I mean it. Right now." Her fierce teacher voice was failing her. One of the boys connected with a blow that produced a loud crack. Against her better judgment she reached in to break it up.

"Separate!" she ordered. She got a hand between them. It was hot and damp, like reaching into a dryer full of half-wet clothes. They rolled, taking her wedged arm with them. She tumbled over them, slamming her shoulder against the corner of the coffee table.

"Shit. Damn you," she said. A sharp pain wrenched her arm. They pulled apart and looked at her, astonished. She sat there crying, rubbing at her shoulder. For just a moment she forgot who the little monsters were.

"See what you did," one of them said. Tim. He again swung out at his brother.

"Just stop," she wailed. Her voice sounded childish and out of control. "Just stop. Please."

Tommy crawled over by her. He was cowering again, she knew. He had probably taken the worst of it. "He started it," he cried.

"I don't want to hear it now. I can't. There's too much to do." Her shoulder started a dull ache and she continued rubbing it. Everyone had tears on their faces.

"Are you all right, mom?" Tim asked.

"No. No, I'm not all right. You hurt me."

Both boys said they were sorry. Sheepishly Tim swatted at his brother. "See what you did," he said.

"No more," she said. A flat cool voice she used. "I mean it. No more. Ever. I'll take you to an orphanage in Mississippi. I'll sell you to gypsies. I swear."

"You wouldn't do that, would you?" Tommy sniffed. He was pathetic.

"I need your help. We've got a lot to do, and fast. You," she pointed at Tim, "Get your grandma down here. Tell her we've got to go shopping. Now. You, get this room picked up."

She stood up, swung her arm to see if she had full motion. It didn't seem to be broken, but hurt like hell to touch. There would be a nasty bruise.

Tommy gathered together the magazines and whatnots that had been strewn around the room. The brass apple her students bought her for Christmas had rolled under a chair. He was still at the end of his gasping and crying fit.

"Stop your sniveling," she told him. She rubbed his head. "You're going to live."

He managed to gasp out an "OK" and nod. He carried the self-righteous, oddly optimistic countenance of all victims. He would milk his martyrdom for all it was worth.

"I mean that about the gypsies," she said. "I'm not having this in my house. Do you understand?"

"Yes, ma'am," Tommy said, "But I didn't . . ."

"I don't want to hear about this right now. Later. Maybe."

Tim stood in the doorway. Cool. Except for his slightly mussed hair, he seemed no worse for wear. He had none of the welts or scratches that his brother had.

"Well," Paula said.

"She's not there." He had his arms behind his back, a smug look on his face.

"Don't tell me this. How can she not be there?"

"Ask fathead over there."

"You kiss my . . ."

Her look stopped Tommy mid-sentence. He made a lot of meaningless angry gestures.

"Perfect. Just perfect. Just what I need today." She grabbed Tommy's arm. "Come with me." His body was still hot from the fight or from anger or both. She gave Tim's ear a pinch on the way out the door.

"Ouch," he said.

"We'll be having a long talk," she said to him. "Start cleaning this house. Clean like your life depended on it. It just may."

She took Tommy and went to search for Miss Kezee.

Too hot to be out here today. Don't remember it being this hot. Sun about to fry my head. Got to get me a hat. Got a lot of things to do. What I got to do? Get a hat. Get that girl a present. Something else? Don't know what else. Don't know what to get that girl. Don't know what she likes. Seems like she got everything she wants. She smart. She got her own money. Learned that from her mama. God bless the child what's got her own. That's what they say. Got to get her something. Personal. Something she wouldn't buy for herself. Something to remember me to her. Charlie give me them dinosaurs. Them damn dinosaurs. Every time he give me a gift he give me a dinosaur too. Said I was like an old dinosaur. That I would never die. I give each one a name. A name for when he gave them to me. The big pink one, Christmas '80. A yellow one, Birthday '78. Love each one. Miss em. Going home to see em. Going home soon. Too hot here. Hot by the river.

Flashes of river. Bright sky. Fish. A big fish.

Paula never did cast her vote. She drove around with Tommy searching for Miss Kezee. They found her collapsed on the riverfront at the foot of Wharf Street, unconscious and trembling. They carried her to the van, drove her to the small clinic out on the highway, and sat with her while Dr. Nagashi examined her. He said she had suffered a heat stroke and was dehydrated, severely so. She was admitted for observation and would be sent home in the morning if she was better.

Paula and Tommy spent the evening sitting by her bed. They forgot all about the party, which was just as well, because when the votes were counted the election was a tie.

13

*T*HE MAN AND THE WOMAN ARE IN A TRUCK DRIVING north along the river. The man is dark skinned. Around the middle he is round, and around his head he has various patches of white woolly hair like cotton balls. He is a friendly looking man, always smiling. But he is not always happy. This day he is happy but anxious. The woman is anxious, too. They make small talk, rambling and vague. He asks does she like Dixieland music. She answers that she has never been to New Orleans. She is happy and anxious and relieved and uneasy. She turns around often to check to see if it is true that River Ridge is at last behind them, but all she sees is Highway 61 rolling away, the hypnotic pulse of the white dashes as they speed away in the truck. She feels they are being followed. She has made this trip before, only in reverse. She feels she is living her life in reverse. Like a salmon destined to go back the way she came. That is true and it is not true. This is not the same trip. This is not the same man. That other man is dead. He was driving his car and he was swallowed by the river. The other man said he would make her pay. He said she would never forget him.

The woman eyes the man beside her. The new man who is an old man. He is the man she chose and he is returning her home. If she can return she can forget. She faces front and she wills herself never to look back again.

Paula pulled the sheet up to Miss Kezee's shoulders and then tucked it in. She still didn't act like she really knew where she was. She had been silent since they found her, a week ago. When she woke at the hospital the day after the collapse she did not respond to the doctor's questions. She stared dully ahead, and though she took food and drink and rose to relieve herself, she showed no other signs of being part of this world. After two days, Dr. Nagashi decided she no longer needed hospitalization.

"Her vital signs are good, and she's had plenty of fluids."

"But she's withdrawn," Paula said. "What about that?"

The doctor shrugged. Another shrugger. Just what Paula needed. At least he was an honest shrugger. He really didn't know. He offered to refer her to a gerontologist who might be able to determine the problem.

"The tests alone could cost you a good deal of money. And I guarantee they won't be able to offer you any fast cures."

She had listened, distracted, annoyed at his ramblings—about senility and about the vagaries of old age. She was sure he thought he was being kind and treating her with respect by telling her that doctors didn't work miracles. He came off sounding helpless and cold. Paula gathered her mother-in-law and her things and pushed her wheelchair to the van.

There was an endearing sweetness in the way Miss Kezee had allowed herself to be led around. When you took her arm what you hung onto felt dead. She could have lead her any-where: to the nursing home, to the edge of the bluff.

Paula took her home.

She knew that her decision was crazy, just begging for more trouble. It was contrary to everything she had decided. She would never have predicted it, had a hard time understanding why. Yet she did it: she took the old woman home.

At the clinic she had lingered at Miss Kezee's bedside. She neither paced nor preoccupied herself with busy work, but sat silent, watching her mother-in-law shudder her way through exhaustion. She sat even after Dr. Nagashi announced Miss Kezee would survive, perhaps even thrive. Sat until Tommy reminded her that it was getting late, and that no one knew where they were.

She'd been reluctant to leave, felt as if, in some way, it was important that she be there, not for this old woman, but for herself.

She'd spent most of the two days in the stiff-backed chair in the drab clinic room. Sat and stared and tried to figure out just what it was she felt about this woman.

Here was a woman who had disrupted her life: with her divisiveness, her contrariness, by her mere presence. A woman who represented attitudes and ideas that Paula disdained. A woman who made her, in a fundamental way, question what it meant to be a black woman.

To be a black woman: she'd spent her whole life puzzling that out. What was the right way to be? Who had the secret formula?

There was her mother: strong-willed, hard-working, respectable bourgeois. Paula had repudiated that image years ago. There had to be some other choices, just had to be, but where? On television? There all you got were mammies and whores and showgirls and superwoman housewives who were just white women painted black. Television women never seemed ordinary enough. They were too beautiful, too aggressive, and too loud. They had big bosoms, practically oozed motherhood. They had guns. Who were they supposed to be anyway? She had never met any women like that.

The women she knew through her college years talked a good game—were full of plans for how they were going to get ahead and change the world and have it all. Still, so many of those girls seemed to define themselves only in terms of men: which ones they wanted and what was the best way to go about getting them. They spent much of their time primping and preparing themselves for one date after another, spent their evenings gossiping about boys and exchanging beauty tips. Whatever else they wanted seemed incidental, to be addended to their lives. As maddening as it was, she understood. She did the same: spent a year following Al like a madwoman. But she had never felt like he was her whole reason for existing. And she was lucky: he didn't treat her that way. He never defined her only in terms of her looks or her sexuality. She caught up with some of those college women now and then. When she shopped in Saint Louis, or sometimes she'd see them on the business page. She couldn't get a fix on who they were, on what kind of people they had become. Mostly they seemed like her, playing at adulthood, keeping their five-hundred-dollar briefcase in front of them to hide the run in their dollar-forty-nine panty hose.

And still, just as carpenters check the craft of every house they see, she checked out her sisters everywhere: to see which of them was the woman she was, should be, might become.

And, after all, didn't it all come down to this, come down to this feisty frail creature trembling on the bed? She knew one thing: this old woman had better not be her future.

How could she abandon her? Paula wiped her brow and offered her sips of water, and when she got up close she looked at her face, trying to see deep inside. Trying to see if she could discover what it was, if anything, that bound her to this woman. The best she could figure, it was curiosity: she wanted to know who it was that was hiding inside this failing body. She wanted to find the soft places she was sure were there. She wanted to see her soul.

When Dr. Nagashi released Miss Kezee, for Paula it was less a decision to take her home than a compulsion to do so.

They had entered their summer routine: the boys with their day camps and baseball, Al with his tinkering and typing and wandering. This summer's new features: the unfinished election, whatever was wrong with the boys, whatever was wrong with Al.

Paula detached. Let someone else deal with all that. She spent her days in and around Miss Kezee's bedroom. She'd never intended it, but that's where she ended up. She would bring up a tray of ice water or a bundle of clean towels. Something would catch her eye on the TV, or she would notice a drawer that demanded cleaning and sorting. Before she was aware, several hours had passed. It became her routine, and as she became conscious of it—of the unlikeliness of spending so much time with her mother-in-law—she did nothing to change it.

She talked to her, talked about anything and everything. Miss Kezee never replied.

Paula would fuss with a basket of mending and blabber about what was in the news and what was on the soaps. She kept the set tuned to the ABC stories that she knew Miss Kezee liked. Miss Kezee stared at them dispassionately. The closest Paula got to a response from her was once during a love scene on "One Life to Live." Paula was complaining about nudity and promiscuity on television when Miss Kezee shot her a nasty look. Paula learned to talk only during the commercials.

"Are you comfortable, Mother?"

Like an old hound she would indicate her needs through her actions. She'd be found sitting in her chair when she wanted the sheets pulled. She'd set the TV tray next to the bed when she wanted some lunch. Though no words passed between them, they had reached a brilliant compromise: Paula did her duties without pressing or prodding, and Miss Kezee kept all opinions to herself.

On Saturday Paula ironed while Miss Kezee spread a game of solitaire on the quilt with a deck of cards Paula had left on the dresser.

"It's hot out there today," Paula said. "Must be ninety-five. I could hardly stand to bring in these clothes."

No reply as usual. She knew she'd been heard, figured the old woman was just playing possum. Or maybe just being her old stubborn self.

"I see you found the cards I left you. I like a good game of solitaire myself. When I'm feeling frazzled. Occupies your mind. Keeps you busy."

Paula kept her own hands busy spending too much time ironing Al's dress shirts. She sprayed each panel with a blast of starch and then ran the iron until the shirt looked store-bought crisp. If Paula wasn't satisfied, she'd ball it up in the damp clothes bag and do it over later. She worked on one of his dress whites for twenty minutes. Miss Kezee spread game after game of one-handed cards.

She sat the iron on its base and looked at her mother-in-law. She was a little shocked at what she was planning to do. She was going to break the truce. She was going to push a little.

"Would you rather I did this somewhere else?"

Miss Kezee played a nine of clubs from her hand, rather dramatically, Paula thought. She said nothing.

"I can always go to the living room. If I'm bothering you, that is."

Miss Kezee looked around her spread for a play.

"Maybe I should do that. I'll be out of your way in a second." Paula made a half-hearted effort to pack together the laundry, watching to see if she could get any kind of response. There wasn't any.

"I guess I could stay a while longer," she said. She said it as if it were a big sacrifice to do so, as if she had been begged. "But you must let me know if I'm in your way. I know you will." Paula smiled at her, felt relieved, the way a show-off feels after making it to the other side of a narrow rope. She'd tempted fate and had lived to walk again. Miss Kezee had her big chance to get rid of her but had not. That must mean something.

She ironed a few shirts in silence. She looked up now and then to see if she could catch Miss Kezee's eye. Miss Kezee watched the cards closely, as if she were afraid that they might move around on their own if she looked away. She was still fragile; her hands trembled as she lifted and turned the cards. When she took a deep breath it seemed to exhaust her.

"You OK, Mother?"

She met Paula's eye and Paula felt victorious.

"I was just teasing before when I said I was going to leave. You know that, don't you? I like sitting here with you. I guess so, or I wouldn't be up under you all the time.

"Seems like housework never gets done. I hate it. When I married Al, we had a deal. He was gonna do his share. You can imagine how long that lasted. I'm the one who couldn't stick to it. I always get behind. What I say is that everybody should just take care of his own. That would be the easiest, but leave it to Al, and he'd be out there in the street looking like a rumpled bed sheet, and then there'd be all these folks around here talking about how I don't take care of my man. That's what they think, you know—never think that maybe he's the one too lazy to pick up an iron. I feel like I'm the maid around here sometimes, but I only do so much. Those boys and that son of yours: as long as they keep the outside clean and make a fairly decent appearance, I figure I did my part.

"Listen to me rambling on. It's nice to talk to you, though.

"I used to tease my mama the way I was teasing you before. Only different. I'd take her keys and move them around so she'd think she was getting forgetful. That kind of thing. Not too much, though. You know how she was. She didn't go in for too much teasing. Not too much teasing at all. She didn't really get the joke. I think she thought laughing was undignified. She always said 'A lady does not go around guffawing like a horse. People will think you are common.' If you didn't know her you'd think she had no sense of humor at all.

"She was too serious. She didn't relax. I don't know what she thought would happen if you relaxed and tried to have a good time. Maybe she thought something bad would happen to her if she let down her guard.

"I used to try and get her to tell me about herself and about her family. I wanted her to tell me what she was like when she was growing up, because I really couldn't imagine. I always had this picture in my head of this very stiff little girl dressed in old-lady clothes and carrying a giant purse. She wasn't the sort of person you could picture as being playful or carefree.

"We didn't have a lot of family around. She had some cousins on her side, I think, but she didn't have much to do with them except at weddings or funerals. And her brother moved off to D.C. long before I came along. I get a card from his wife at Christmas. My father's side, well I think there must have been some bad blood about the business when he died, because it's like those people disappeared from the earth.

"I get jealous when I hear about people having these huge family reunions with all these aunts and uncles and cousins. It was always just me and Mama. Of course, she knew everybody in the city of Saint Louis. What she called friends, I would call acquaintances, or maybe less. These were mostly just the people she did business with or was in clubs with. She never seemed to know them very well or for very long, either. Sometimes it seemed like every year there was a fresh crop of them. Like she'd worn out one set and had to replace them. What I missed was there was never anyone around she had any history with. No one who knew her when she wasn't my mother. You know what I mean?

"Another fantasy I had was she had been this very wild

teenager—the kind who stayed in trouble at home and at school. Maybe she'd been sent off for a year someplace to have a secret baby. If you knew Mama you'd know just how far out that particular fantasy was, but for all I know it could have been the absolute truth.

"When I was seventeen, just before I went away to school, I tried to get her to talk about herself. Literally all I knew about her was that her father was a doctor and that he practiced up off of Franklin Avenue. I knew her brother, Mark, was a doctor also. Grandmother stayed home.

"But you know the sort of thing I wanted to know: I wanted some stories about her, some adventures she had, some silly things she did. I'd badger her and badger her and always get the same response. 'That's a long time ago,' she'd say.

"In her library, that big ugly room with the leather chairs in it, she kept a photo album on one of the bookcases. Get this: every picture in that album is posed. All studio shots. Everybody's scrubbed and dressed and perfectly placed for the camera. I guess back in those days people didn't take candid pictures, so now I have this record—I've got it downstairs, I'll show it to you—which tells me nothing except what people looked like when they were at their best. That, and that they could afford to go to photo studios.

"When I went through her things after she died, I looked at every piece of paper. I kept hoping I'd find a diary or something. There wasn't one personal item in all the stuff I dug through. Not one letter or note or anything. If there was anything, she'd probably destroyed it.

"Should I starch this shirt? No? I'm probably the only person on earth who still uses starch, thank you, Mama, for that, at least.

"Maybe folks are more private than I think. Are you?

Maybe not. I have exactly two stories I know about her. One was one of the routines she did. Mama was one of those who, when you'd be at a party, at some point she'd have everybody gathered around her and then she'd go into one of her routines. She had about a half dozen she'd cycle through. Let's see: there was 'My late husband Herbert used to say,' and 'That raggedy old car I had to get rid of.' 'Paula was a fussy baby,' was another one and I've forgotten a couple of them. And then there was the always popular 'When I was a little girl we would go to Martha's Vineyard' story. This was the one she'd pull out whenever the talk turned to vacations. Now, Mother and I never went on vacation. Never—in fact, I didn't know what a vacation was until I went on one with your son. So you'd be standing around at some wedding reception or cocktail party, and the talk would turn to summer plans. My mother, standing there with her purse hanging off one arm and a glass of something fizzy in the other, would announce the beginning of her story. I could never do justice to her presentation—which was the main thing. The story itself was the same three-point outline: 1. Her father knew a gentleman with property on Martha's Vineyard. 2. They took the ferry over from . . . Oh, damn, I can't remember the name of that place. Something head, I think. Whatever it was, it was a critical detail—it was very important to say this place's name at least four times. The third detail: we had the most delicious fresh seafood one ever tasted. I'm trying to capture all the hoity-toitiness in her voice, and she'd get this ecstatic look on her face when she'd talk about the lobsters or what have you.

"I must have seen her perform that story a thousand times, and you know, there was never more to it than that. I never knew how they got to Massachusetts, how many times they went there, who these people with the property were. She might have had a fond memory in there of some kind, but the story was pure theater, that's all.

"The other story I got through persistence. I told you I'd been nagging her to tell me about herself. I'd figured out that general nagging wasn't getting us anywhere, so I'd give her prompts. I'd say 'Did you and your girlfriends ever get in any big fights?' or 'Did you ever stay out after curfew and get into trouble?' That sort of thing. A lot of times, and particularly if she was upset with me about something, she'd use these little prompts as an excuse to get one of her little shots in, saying something like 'We were much better behaved back when I was coming up.' I'd mumble something back to her and go on about my business.

"Let me get to this other story, cause in so many ways it is so out of character for her. There was this boy she thought I was interested in, but we were just friends, and I wasn't his type, if you know what I mean. She pushed and pushed until we got into a thing over it. She was always looking for that perfect man for me, and as far as she was concerned, he was it—good looking, college man, from the right family. Little did she know. We went around and finally I told her to give it up and asked her didn't she ever have any men she was just friends with. She starts telling me this story. She and her girlfriend were on the streetcar coming back from doing some shopping and her girlfriend started to talking with this man. Of course in Mama's version of the story she wouldn't be the one so brazen as to start up with some strange man. She said this was the most unusual-looking man she had ever seen. Reddish brown skin and straight jet-black hair cut close to his scalp. Evidently he was more interested in her than in her friend and he moved to where they could carry on a conversation. He was part Indian, he told her, and he worked in a garage on the south side. She said he stayed on the car until they got off and followed them to where they lived. She talked about how flattered she was that he had paid attention to her instead of her girlfriend, whom she described as being very beautiful. Evidently he kept coming around. He'd meet her on her way up to school, or walk her home in the evenings. This was happening at the same time she was about to be presented. You know how in Saint Louis they have all that social mess. Well, Mama was going to be presented at one of the black cotillions. When it came time to select an escort, she wanted to choose this fellow. I think she said his name was Henry. She said her parents threw a fit, put their feet down, etcetera, and then the story went into its moral instruction part—far be it from Helen Fuller to miss an opportunity. 'I had to,' she said bravely, 'let the young man know that any future contact on our part was pointless. That it was best we go our separate ways.' Sometimes, she told me, a woman just had to bite the bullet and put practical issues first.

"I remember sitting there with my mouth open listening to this story. Seems pretty tame, but for her to put out that much information about herself—even if she does get to be what in her mind is the heroine—was a big deal. She didn't tell me any more about it. Every once in a while after that I would tease her and mention Henry's name, but she let me know that it wasn't to be joked about and she didn't appreciate my even trying to do so. She didn't let anybody get too personal with her.

"Sometimes I don't think I knew the woman at all." Paula mumbled. Her hand was hot and sweaty around the iron handle. She'd been holding it upright and tight through most of the story.

Miss Kezee sat, holding the deck of cards, looking in Paula's direction, but not at her.

"Do you need anything? Can I get you something, Mother?"

Miss Kezee lowered her head and spread another game of solitaire.

Another house. A different place. It is a large and elegant house. A person with money and taste lives here. There are two women. Both of them well kept. Both woman are older than they look. One is plainly dressed with long hair wound at the back of her head in a bun. She is slightly built, and the other woman is slight, too, but for her swollen belly. She could be pregnant, but she is too old for that. She has silver-gray hair, a touch of blue to it. The elegant house belongs to her. She shows it off to the plain woman. Here is crystal from England. Here are ivory napkin rings. Here is my girl. Here is my girl. Here is my girl. The girl is different ages everywhere. Here is a gap-toothed smile with braids. Here is a graduation picture. Here is my girl. Here is my girl. Here is my girl, again.

The fancy woman takes pride in her things. The plain woman admires them. It would be nice to have nice things.

"It's hard for me alone. To raise my girl," the woman says.

"Hard even if you got someone," is the reply.

"Your son seems like a fine young man."

"Yes, ma'am. He's been a good boy."

"I think you know what I mean when I say he's got his hands full now."

Both women laugh.

"That girl of yours seem like she knows what she wants."

The elegant woman tosses her head. "If I could only tell you."

"They'll be just fine, I think."

"I hope you're right, Miss Johnson."

The woman of the house opens the drawer of a highboy. She removes a tiny blue velvet box. "I have something for you. I feel so bad. I know the groom's mother should receive a gift. But I got so busy . . ."

"You don't have to trouble yourself."

"I want you to have these. Please. They're not at all the sort of thing I ever wear. Just not right for my complexion or style, but I think they're perfect for you."

"I couldn't . . ."

"I insist." She places the box in the plain woman's palm and folds her hands around it.

"Thank you so kindly."

They hug.

"I just . . ." The elegant woman dabs at tears. She does not want to smear her makeup. "I've got good feelings about this. And I'm not easy about these things. Let's pray and hope."

The plain woman patted the other woman's hand. She had good feelings, too. There was one man, now another. One place, then back home. You could go forward and you could go back. Things could work out. You could forget. This woman knew that.

14

$\mathcal{M}$ISS KEZEE IMPROVED STEADILY. A VITALITY RE-
turned that Paula hadn't seen in quite a while. There was new
speed in her movements and a glint in her eye. She busied her
hands with the cards while Paula talked and ironed and sorted
and folded. She had not been this robust since they had visited
her in Saint Paul, back before her husband Charlie died.

On an impulse Al had closed the newspaper over spring vacation and they had driven up to Saint Paul. When they arrived,
the streets were clotted with slush from a spring snowstorm.
They had to stop for directions at a gas station by the freeway.
Even though they had been there before, the streets were
arranged in some kind of cryptic pattern that defied mastery,
and they had to ask the station attendant to sketch the directions on the back of an envelope.

Miss Kezee greeted them with spicy chili, cornbread, and
orange soda. Charlie held court. He sat at the head of the table
and quizzed the then seven-year-old twins about what they
thought about President Reagan, and whether or not the
Cardinals had a chance. He quizzed them with a wide, open-
mouthed grin that charmed them completely. They galloped at
his side, hung on the crooks of his elbows. He charmed Paula,
too. He called her 'little lady,' though she was taller than he, by
two inches, at least.

He seemed to be one of those people who was genuinely interested in whatever trivia about Paula's life there was: how

many students she taught, what she had studied in school, what roads they had driven to Saint Paul. Only Al had failed to be amused. He didn't seem to know what to make of the man who had taken his father's place, didn't even know where to look when his stepfather was around. When he answered Charlie's questions he was polite but cool. He didn't call him Charlie or Mr. Kezee. In fact, Paula never heard Al address the man directly in any way. Still, Charlie was as gracious and as dignified as a diplomat. If he was bothered by his son-in-law's snub, he never let on. He was too kind and too much a gentleman.

Miss Kezee didn't notice any of this. Paula had never seen any woman so completely in love with a man. She followed her man with her eyes and a silent communication passed between them. She anticipated his needs: Before his coffee cup emptied, she was there with a refill. She massaged his shoulders and laughed at his jokes before he finished. Paula was touched but still thought there was something inappropriate about them. They shocked her, and she was upset with herself for feeling that way. A person didn't usually think of older people as lovers. Not openly and passionately the way this was. She'd certainly never known any. Charlie was openly affectionate. Attentive, and full of energy. Miss Kezee doted and was coquettish and shy, the way some teenage girls were around their aggressive and cocksure boyfriends.

One evening during their visit, after she had put the boys to bed and left Al curled up in a guest room checking out the local papers, she had wandered downstairs to get something to wash down a pill. The house was quiet so she assumed she was the only one up. To her surprised she came across Charlie and Miss Kezee, close up against each other, sitting at the kitchen dinette, sipping something from mugs and whispering and giggling. Charlie was in a sleeveless undershirt and his wife wore a long flannel gown.

"Caught us!" Charlie laughed. Paula had covered her mouth, partly in delight, partly in shock. She remembered excusing herself, as if she had walked in on something shameful, instead of finding two people enjoying a quiet moment together after a long noisy day.

Miss Kezee said nothing to her. Not then, and hardly the whole stay. To Al either. Charlie dominated: set the tone for the day, organized outings, led the conversation. She was not the woman Al had described. When she had asked him what his mother was like, he had said she could be as sweet as honey— that she usually was—but that she also had an ornery streak through which you could steer a barge. When they were in college he told her about the time his mother had gotten angry with his fourth-grade teacher because she made him sit out of lunch and eat by himself. "I was being a little jerk," he said. "Mumbling under my breath or something. So this teacher, old Miss White, she said 'Young man, if that is your attitude, you can just eat by yourself today.'" Paula remembered Al making a high-pitched, ridiculous voice for Miss White. "And that's what she did, the old witch. Made me get a tray from the cafeteria and eat all alone. I knew I had it coming, but I decided to fix the old bat. On the way home I ran real hard so I was out of breath and had some color in my face. Then I put on my best hurt puppy dog look and went in crying to Mama. She had a fit. See, I was never one to cry wolf. She figured if her baby was that upset, must really be something wrong. She grabbed me all up under my arm. Like this." He had stopped telling and wrenched Paula's arm behind her back. "And I was supposed to be the innocent one. She marched me right up to that school, right up in Miss White's face and she showed out. She said all kinds of stuff. Said she 'didn't know what kind of school they was running up in here,' and since her baby had started school, 'hadn't nothing like this ever happened,' and how Miss White 'didn't have no right,' and on and on. I could tell pretty quick that Mama had stopped believing my story. Miss White knew it, too. Miss White acted real cool, and I knew that as soon as Mama ran out of steam, which was coming quickly, she'd hear the truth, and then my ass was done for. That's how Mama was. Fiery. Like gasoline. She could sit around forever, but when the right spark came along, you better watch out. You bet I never did pull a stunt like that one again."

Paula's image of Miss Kezee came from Al's stories, and from the stories of other people around the town. Some neighbors in River Ridge told of an impulsive tyrant. Others remembered a sweet, even-tempered soul who never had an unkind word for anyone. The woman Paula had been nursing somehow ought to give her some insight and help her solve the puzzle, yet she was having trouble getting to the truth. Here, barely a week after hospitalization, Miss Kezee seemed most like the woman they had visited in Saint Paul. Nobi, Charlie had called her. Though she remained silent, much else about her seemed new. Her skin, which had often been ashy, now surged with color. Muscles that once trembled and creaked, now seemed to move fluidly and almost with a bit of grace. The eyes were clear and Paula even thought they twinkled a bit.

"You're looking so much better today, Mother," she said. She got a smile as a reply.

To discuss the tied election, a city council meeting was planned for that night, and Al wandered the house sighing, half-heartedly piddling at everything. He moved the encyclopedias from one shelf to the next and then back again. He resprung a window shade in the kitchen. He told Paula he was frustrated, but the way he acted was dejected, as if he were lost in a maze.

Late, after the meeting, she ventured to talk about it. She fixed a midnight snack and he sat down to join her.

"So," she began tentatively.

He shrugged and she shrugged back at him and smirked coyly. She loved mocking him when he was being ridiculous.

He shook his head. "I just always expect things are going to be simple."

"You're a simple guy." She winked at him. She put her hands over her heart and said with a voice full of false magnanimity, "If you deign to talk, I would be honored to listen."

He looked away. He was too distracted for sarcasm to register.

"My daddy always used to call it Amos 'n' Andy stuff. You know: the way *we* do things. I can't believe . . . you know it took them two days to figure out they needed to call a special city council meeting. Then two more days to get everyone together to call one."

"Well I would just give up if I were you." She slapped a palm on the table.

He shook his head again, a short defiant motion. "Are you serious? No way."

She wasn't surprised. Behind the confusion was rigid determination. He leaned in close to her. "Why should I give up? It was a tie. Means there are as many people want me as want him. Means if one more person—just one more person—voted for me, I'd be in."

She lowered her eyes from his intensity. He brought his sockless foot up and began rubbing around her knee with it.

"And so," she said. She rolled one hand over the other, prompting a conclusion to the rambling. She kept her eye on the foot. She was curious what it would do next.

"So while Kingfish and Lightnin played find-the-city-council, Walter and I dug up a law."

"A law! Really!" If her false enthusiasm didn't start the

fight, she didn't know what would. Apparently, unfortunately, he was ignoring her.

"Simple, really," he continued, oblivious. "The statute says that after all ballots are accounted for, ties are broken by a coin flipped by the highest ranking outgoing official." He fondled her wrist while he said that.

"Feeling lucky?" she prompted. The foot was massaging the muscle on her inner thigh.

"Think about it: You work your ass off to get elected. The time, the money. It ends up turning on the toss of a goddamn quarter."

"We aren't bitter, are we?"

He waved that off. "I'm pissed off. You know how we try to tell the boys to keep on trying and never give up. How hard work breeds success and all that . . . bullshit. Lose the election the usual way—I could live with that. But to lose over something so . . . capricious. A fucking coin toss? Uh uh. No." He got up and paced the room for his tirade. He filled his voice with the same passion he had used for his campaign speeches, the same passion that had surprised and bewildered her. He sat down and put his foot on the seat of her chair up by her crotch.

She raised her eyebrows seductively. "And so when's the big flip?"

He gave her a look that combined hurt and disgust. She had him now. He rubbed at his chin, once again the dejected little boy. He sneered. He was feeling up and down her legs. "Do you want to do something, or what?" he asked. He gave her a wet kiss on the knee.

She laughed. There never had been anything subtle about his propositions. "Something. And 'or what,' too," she said.

When in bed he tried to ease himself on top of her, she tickled at his sides where she knew he was the most helpless. She kept tickling until he gently pinned her hands up by her ears. He loomed above her, on his knees, panting and sweating, still giggling from being tickled. She felt like a crazy woman.

"Come on, big man. Show me what you can do." He slid into her, scooped her up by the shoulders, releasing her arms. He stared into her eyes, staying still a long time.

"Want me to scream?" she asked. He could not answer.

He always fell asleep quickly after such times. She lay beside him, tried to forget about the guilt that was there: she had used him. She had wanted so much to be close to him and, at this point sex seemed like the only way. She didn't care about Amos 'n' Andy, coin tosses, which ones voted which way. She didn't care a whit for the Al that had invested in all that. Still, she felt the need to possess him again. Deep inside she knew that if they were to survive, she would have to find her way back to him, to every part of him. She was thrilled, felt selfish and devilish.

He snored. She put her hand on his back above his heart. "Lucky for you I didn't make it to the polls last week," she whispered.

She left the bed feeling reckless: she felt like setting the house on fire, like turning on all the lights all over the world, like running around town naked. She put on her robe and started down the stairs. Her eye caught the nightlight that glowed dimly beside Miss Kezee's bed, a pink clamshell lamp that gave the room a fragile translucence. The door was barely open. She crept in and sat near the bed in the rocking chair. She wrapped her robe tighter and tucked her feet up beneath her so she could warm them under the afghan. The room was chill, cool and dry as a winter morning. Miss Kezee huddled under a blanket and a comforter. She looked peaceful. Now and then she mumbled something Paula could not understand.

"Where are you?" she asked softly. "I hope it's nice. You deserve a nice place. We all do.

"You are such a mystery to me. I bring you here to my home and you completely mess my life around. You don't even like me—that's the funny thing. I know you don't. But I just couldn't stand to think of you up there by yourself. I could imagine what it would be like, and it broke my heart. I made that mistake before.

"I don't know. I shouldn't be telling you this. But I did. I made a mistake and I guess I need to deal with it. It's so hard.

"My mama and me, we were just different kinds of people. Like you and I are different. Maybe even more so. I needed to have my own life, so I just left. I went away and I thought that was that. I didn't feel guilty about it or anything. I had my life and she had hers.

"I hope you don't think this has anything to do with love, because it doesn't. I loved her . . . I still love her. It's about the way people treat each other. If you're not careful, you can destroy another person. Do terrible damage. I loved my mother. Nothing will ever change that. But I couldn't live with her, and I went away. Everything would have been fine, except she got sick. She was much sicker than you. Pancreatic cancer. She was in a lot of pain.

"I didn't count on that happening. I mean, how can you? You don't think about your parents dying. Cancer, this particular cancer, is a fast worker. She called me. Called and said she needed me to help her. She needed me to take care of her, just for a little while, she said. She asked could I come down. I didn't believe that she really needed me. She never needed me.

"No. That isn't true. I believed she needed me, but I didn't want to hear that. That would have meant changing my life because of her. So I made up a lot of excuses. They weren't excuses really. They were real. I told her that Al and I needed to be together—we'd only been married a few years—and that the twins were so small—which they were. I didn't even talk to Al.

"She asked couldn't she come up and stay with me. Until she got better, at least. I didn't say anything. She got the message.

"She called a few days later and asked me to come down and help her check into a clinic. I said I would.

"When I saw her . . . it was . . . horrible. She was wasted to nothing. Her skin was a dead color, like old tree bark. She had painted on all this make up. Trying to fool me, I guess.

"She had all her papers in order, telling me where everything was and what to do about it. The refrigerator was already empty.

"I knew. Right then I knew. She was dead. I asked her if she really didn't want to come home with me after all. I said she was welcome. More than welcome. She said 'no.' She'd decided on the . . . clinic, she called it. She said they had some treatments for her there.

"I know she was saving her pride. It had been hard for her to ask in the first place. She was trying to maintain a little dignity.

"I drove her out to this place. Out to the Chesterfield Life Care Facility. A nursing home. I don't care what she called it, that's what it was. Oh, it was very beautiful. Gorgeous lawns. Fountains. There was a television in every room, and a kitchenette in mother's. But it was a nursing home. I knew that right away.

"Before we left the house, Mother went down a checklist she made of things she wanted to take with her. A picture of my father. One of me. Her wedding album. Her big make-up kit. Cosmetics were a new thing for her. She was never a woman who wore a lot. I bet you never did, either. She would sometimes put a little rouge on her cheeks, and then sometimes a little lipstick. Always the lightest tones so maybe you'd think it was her real coloring. So you wouldn't notice at all. And now here she was with this . . . suitcase full of the stuff. She didn't even know how to put it on. She looked like a clown. I was sorry for her. But she was a proud woman. She was going out looking good or she wasn't going.

"And then there was this other, smaller bag. It was filled with pills. All kinds of pills. She saw me looking at it and took it. She didn't exactly snatch it away, but that was the message. I was not to see it and it was not to be discussed.

"I got her settled into her room. Listened to her fuss at the staff because things weren't just the way she had ordered. We put her pictures up, got her designer sheets on the bed. And then we sat. It was so awkward. I tried to make small talk, but she wasn't interested. She wouldn't even look up from her magazine.

"I didn't know what I was supposed to do. I didn't know what she wanted from me. I think I was being dismissed, but Mother is much more direct than that. If she wanted you to go, she told you and you went. I know she was hurt. But she couldn't let me go.

"I excused myself. Finally. We didn't have any sort of big emotional good-bye. I told her to call me if she needed anything, and she said she would. She told me to come back and see her, and I said I would. Soon. Very businesslike, as always. She was so brave and composed. I was really fooled. Almost. I drove straight back here. I felt numb . . . like a zombie. I didn't want to think about her, so I didn't think about anything. Was cold like my heart was dead.

"I couldn't think about it because I knew even then what the right thing to do was.

"I should have gone back for her. I should have brought her

home. To her home or my home—it didn't matter. If I thought about it I would have done it. But I chose not to think. That's the worst thing I did . . . not leaving her there—that was bad enough—but worse, I pretended like if I didn't think about it, it didn't matter. As if it would just go away. And it did. She did. She left me.

"They called me to tell me she was gone . . . so fast. Less than a month. Mother refused any kind of treatment. When they called me I remember that I had acted genuinely shocked at the news. How could my mother be dead? I performed so well, I convinced myself. I played a good grieving daughter. Al, he was the perfect accomplice. You know how men are about this stuff. They stop up emotions better than a champagne cork. He held my hand while the doctor assured me she hadn't suffered too much. Evidently they kept her drugged.

"I arranged the funeral. There wasn't much to do actually. Mother had left detailed instructions on whom to notify and what she would wear—on everything. All I had to do was sit there and cry. Which I did. For a week I cried. Without really knowing why. I know now. I remember feeling ridiculous for crying, like a blubbering idiot. All of Mother's friends making a big fuss over me—the poor orphaned girl. I didn't even pretend to be brave.

"I was crying for myself. I know that now. Crying because I knew I was going to have to live with my choice. With believing I could just walk away and forget. But you never can, can you? You have to live with everything you do. It becomes part of your life. All the little lies we tell wait for us, and then they come back and get us when we least expect them to.

"I'm sorry, Mama. I'm sorry I was so selfish. What you wanted was so simple. You just didn't want to die alone. It would have been so easy. Sorry, Mama."

Paula let the chair rock to the rhythm of Miss Kezee's breathing and send her into a deep sleep.

She woke to Miss Kezee's touch on her shoulder.

"You OK?" Miss Kezee asked.

She started, unsure where she was. Her knees were stiff from being turned to the side, and during the night someone had wrapped her in the afghan. "What time is it?" she mumbled.

"Morning."

"Must have fallen asleep here." She was too knotted up and sore to move.

"Made some coffee." Miss Kezee handed her a cup. It was burn-your-tongue hot and bitter: she had boiled up the stale coffee from yesterday. Paula sipped at the mug and tried to hide her displeasure at the taste.

"You work yourself to death, girl. You should take it easy." Miss Kezee halfway made up her bed. "My own mama worked herself to death. A lot of womens do."

"Tell me about her."

Miss Kezee shrugged. "Not much to tell."

"Do you remember her?"

"I think about her all the time." Miss Kezee sat at the edge of the bed. It was as messy as before she'd attempted to make it. She brushed her hair briefly, and then began braiding. "Can't say I remember too much."

"Did she die when you were young?"

"Well, I was around thirty. That was many a year ago. Many years gone by." She set the brush on the night stand and settled back against the headboard. "As you go through life, you struggle to keep holding on. To the memories. It's a shame. You lose the special things. The good things. Remember the ordinary stuff, cause that's what you seen over and over again. And the bad things."

"What do you remember?"

"I remember her working. Mama with her purse going off on the streetcar to her job. Mama digging in her little garden to grow a few vegetables so we could eat. Mama standing at the basin cutting potatoes for dinner. I remember me, standing next to her helping, cause I was the only girl and that was my job."

"Your father?"

"Working. Gone. On the Burlington Northern. He'd be home every now and again. But, he worked, too. Everybody did back then. If you could get a job, you worked. If you couldn't get a job, you made a job. Sold apples, picked up scraps and sold them. Unless you was a rich white woman, you worked. Everybody worked. You worked till you died."

"What did your mama do?"

"You name it, she done it. Laundry, ironing, scrubbing floors, maid work, picking vegetables. She done it all. Worked two, sometimes three jobs. Got my brothers through school."

"Al never talks about any uncles."

"He only ever met two of them, I think. Big Ben and Mike. I lost two in the wars. Family gets scattered, you know. Boys moved here and there. We send cards now and then. Eugene, he just passed I heard. Out in Boston. It's a shame. You tell them boys of yours they got cousins out there. Cousins all over. Taylors. Tennessee Taylors. When they get older you tell em to look em up."

"I will. I promise."

"I see a little Mama sometimes in those boys of yours. Ain't that something. It's the cast of an eye, or a cheekbone. I don't know what, but I see it. Something that skipped over me and Al and showed up here. I see it and I think of Mama. There's a picture of her downstairs. She was a big square woman. And

Daddy was a big man, too. He worked as a porter. I don't know where they got me. He called me 'Little Bit,' and Mama and the boys called me Cissy. I want my picture back."

"It's yours, and so is anything else . . . "

"My picture of Mama I was talking about. I think she made that picture down in Tennessee before her and Daddy moved up with the railroad. What I like about it is her face. Back then you had to sit for days when they made your picture. And she looks like she's coming right out of that frame and grabbing you. Like she was mad bout something. You know that picture, don't you?"

"I figured that was her. I asked Al, and he said he didn't know for sure."

"He about a lie. Ever since he was a baby I showed him my pictures and told him who they was and what little I knew about each one. Now, I didn't know a whole lot cause Mama never told me much. I know that she and Daddy come north after World War I. Come with the railroad. I was a little thing, I guess, but I don't remember moving. Mama had some schooling, and so did Daddy. I didn't think to ask how much. Mama stayed too busy to bother with a lot of questions. Always a pot or an iron or a needle in her hand. She would hum to herself them old-time spirituals. She seemed like she was happy, but I can't imagine working that hard and being happy about it, can you? I think about her all the time, but I can't say I really knew her. I never knew what she was feeling or whether she liked any of them jobs. I tell you something terrible. Sometimes I felt like I was working for her. I had my routine, too. Come home, get the water boiling for washing and chores, do some ironing, do some dishes. She come in and we'd go on about our work. She'd say 'Get some onions from the cellar,' and I'd say yes ma'am. Or she'd say 'Make two pie crusts,' and I'd do that. I had a lot of things I would do just to make her life easier. I would have some cold lemonade waiting everyday in the summer when she came in. I would be the one that got her clothes organized for work, whatever she needed. She didn't even have to ask. I just remember it was what I always did for her as long as I lived with her. Since I was a very little girl I did it. We didn't talk much, though."

"And when you did, it was about the pictures, right?"

Miss Kezee nodded. She sat straight-backed and tall against the headboard, arms folded, head bent forward as she spoke. She punctuated her statements with exaggerated finger gestures.

"By the time I was a young woman, we got more personal. Mama was working over at the seminary then. This was just around the time of the second war. I guess the brothers would talk to her and try to draw her out. She was a big old thing. Walked around huffing and puffing. But she kept moving. Kept working. She did their shopping and cooking. Some light cleaning for them. She told me them priests would come and sit with her when she was working in the kitchen. They would talk with her about God and religion and what all she felt about it. She would come home and tell me. She never did that before. Mama never talked about her jobs till she worked with them priests. I don't know if it was because I was grown that she started, or if she was just changing herself."

"Could be both," Paula said. "I already see how I'm treating Tim and Tom different as they grow along."

"Mama would come in and say 'Cissy, I didn't get all my work done today. That Brother Willie liked to talk my ear off.' I couldn't believe Mama not getting her work done. She talked *my* ear off. Saying 'Listen to what he said to me today.' She'd set her spoon down and look at me and wait till I set mine down, too. 'He said that since he was a priest, God worked through him to offer forgiveness of sin to those who repented.' Something like that she said he'd said. She asked me, 'What do you make of it?' She stood there looking just like I'm looking now." Miss Kezee put her hands on her hips and puckered her lips out.

"I didn't know what to say. I think that was the first time Mama'd asked me something other than what had I done in school today or where have I been."

"What did you say?"

"I told her it sounded suspect. We was AME. When we was anything. Mama liked to lie in Sunday morning if she could. Mama thought it sounded suspect, too. 'Let me get my Bible,' she said. We dropped what we were doing and got down and started through the scriptures looking for . . . I don't know what for. Some evidence?"

"She was gonna set those Catholics straight."

"Yes, ma'am. She came in every day ready for the next battle. Some days we didn't get nothing done, what with her questioning me and searching her scriptures."

"Your mother was turning into a philosopher."

"Mama did their wash and cleaned their toilets. She wasn't having no special favors from God for someone whose dirty drawers she seen."

Paula heard Miss Kezee's laugh for the first time since Saint Paul, since back at Charlie's table. She had a high cackle that sounded derisive if you didn't know better.

"It was that way until she died. I was the one working hard at the end. Downtown, at the War Department. So when I'd come in there would be Mama with the lemonade and the Bible and the stories about what the priests done today. They treated her good. Christmas, she come home loaded up with gifts. Always a gift for me, too. I think those last years were happy for her."

"How? When?"

"In forty-three. She was working. Sat down for a little rest. Never got up. Worked herself to death. Priest came by and told me. They helped me make the arrangements. Daddy had already passed. Left it to me to round up those boys."

"Must have been hard on you."

"Always is. For everyone. But you know, Paula, in a lot of ways I was happy for her. She had a full life. She seemed to enjoy it at the end. At last she could get some rest."

Paula closed her eyes and tried to suppress a shudder.

"She's been gone a long time. Many a year. I look at them boys of yours and I see her and I remember. That feels good."

"That's funny. I do the same thing. In my boys I see my mother, too."

"That's the way things be."

What is this? June 12th? 13th? How many days I'm sitting around this house? Sitting around this room. Just look at this room. What kind of person would make a room like this? Now if you was an adult you would never make such a room. Not for a child because you would be afraid a child would mess it up. And, if you was a child you wouldn't pick out all these little flower prints and old-lady white-painted furniture. And no adult I know like this kind of thing, really. It is a doll's house in here—everything pink, to my eyes almost the same shade. After a while it all looks like nothing. Even the row of rag dolls on the dresser are wearing pink dresses. This room is like what a grown-up thinks a little girl wants. A grown-up who never asked no little girl's opinion. And it all looks real fine, but truthfully all them lace frou-frous and porcelain dogs is just dust catchers. Put some of my dinosaurs up here. Shake some of this mess up.

That Paula.

She up in here dusting and ironing and folding and vacuuming. All day long it seems. Girl can't even iron. Can't do no housework. I know how to iron. My mama taught me. I bet her mama didn't. They had people in to do everything, most likely, and if they didn't, her mama wasn't about to have her lift a finger. Not her precious baby. I sit and watch her as she irons the back of one of Junior's shirts. She got the sleeves all dragging on the floor and the collar turned every which way, and when she done, the shirt got more wrinkles on it than when it come out of the drier in the first place. I'm not saying anything to her, though. You can never say nothing to her. She's got skin thin as tissue paper. You say something to her and her eyes get all teared-up and she gets testy with you. You go around people like her. Got towels all mashed up in the linen closet looking like hell. When I go by, I fold up one or two the right way. She don't notice. Must think them towels folding themselves. Naw. She thinks she done it right the first time. She don't even notice. That's how she is.

This being up and down is a mess, this . . . tiredness that come over me. Seems like I lost a few days in there, but since I come around this time, I been mostly up. Up here in this room. Girl keeps bringing me my meals and sitting with me. Seems like she sits with me most of the day. Yes, it's some kind of sickness the girl's got. I never had it, but then I am not a sickly person. I been healthy my whole life. I don't know how to be sick. When you sick I guess you supposed to lay and let folks do for you. I never done that. Not even when Junior was born. Why, I was up and about my business like I had a case of the sniffles. And how did I get the sickness I got now? Going along doing what I do and the next thing I'm laying in bed all day. Ain't got no energy. Can't think straight.

I'm coming back now. I can tell. Feeling better every day. Wasn't getting nowhere fighting her on this. Decided I better do whatever the girl says. Lay here and rest. Every time I tried something seems I took two steps back. So she's feeding me and pampering me. Getting so I kinda like it. She must be liking it, too, because all day long she's up in here like she ain't got nowhere else to go. She's up in here and just running her mouth about anything and everything. For a while she was just talking to the wall, too, cause I wasn't saying nothing to her. First, it was just too much work. Then I didn't have nothing to say. Then when I did, I realized she's not needing to hear it. What she needs to do is talk. I don't nearly know what it's about, but I know enough. I lived in this town. I know it can drive you crazy. Crazy from the loneliness. I know that sometimes a man don't listen or won't listen or don't understand. Even a good man like Charlie. It's hard to find someone who will. I know sometimes you just got to talk.

So I lay here and listen to her. It's comfortable. She got me some playing cards. And the TV stories are getting good again. Had a couple of shoot-em-ups the other day. She keeps the air the way I like it in here . . . cool.

I'm thinking ahead to when I get better. I'll be up in my own house again. Me and Charlie's house. The house we made.

First thing we got up there was a brand new place that was just ours. Not his before or mine before, but ours, new. We got us some paint and paper and fixed it up just the way we wanted, with beautiful things and my dinosaurs too. When we finished we made ourselves at home—settled in like we had been there our whole lives. I would cook us good foods, and we would sit and watch our TV, or sometimes Charlie would read me the headlines and I would massage his feets just the way he liked it. Sometimes we would just sit.

When the weather was good we'd take to our screen porch and watch the comings and goings. This one or that one from the street would come by and sit with us and we'd talk about the various ones we'd remember. And if you didn't remember them sometimes you'd say you did. The sky would get that lavender color of a long summer evening and the ice cream man would come by and ring his bell. We'd sit under that yellow porch bulb a while. Charlie or me would wander back inside, and the peoples would all know that it was time for them to go.

I hope I'll be there before the leaves turn. I think about the street lined with sugar maples planted when they cut down my beautiful old elms. How their fine colors make up for that hurt. How a purple cloud in October tells of the first snow coming, and how the other old ladies and me play like we've got dread of it, but, really, we're thrilled, as excited as babies when those first snow flakes fly.

Right now, at home, it is as hot as it is here. The sun makes the attic burn like the devil's oven, and upstairs it smells of all the old things that are baking in those suitcases and trunks. I can smell the mildewed covers of the 78s from back in the old days, and the mothballs holed-up in Charlie's old suits. Dear sweet Charlie. So many years missing from my attic. Only a few years of things that we saved. Those years are here in this house, I guess. In this basement, in these rooms. I don't want none of that. Not Junior's report cards, nor them scratched blue-and-red plastic plates. None of it. I want to hold onto the memories, is all, and they aren't of things, they are of people. Got to hold on to the people. That's what I need to tell the girl. Hold on tight, and don't let go of the memories. Of this time or these folks. Hold on.

I'm gonna tell her and she will do it. I know. She is not a bad girl. She is triflin, like all them her age is. But she is not a bad one. She may be simple and have soddity ways, but her heart is as big as the moon. She tries to cover it, but I can see through her. She bruises easy as a peach. I'm gonna treat her good, Charlie. Treat her better. I swear by you I will. She done right by me. Despite it all, she done right. That means something. I am an old woman now. I will tell her to hold on, and she will because she is my girl. She is my girl.

15

WALTER SAID THIS WAS SUPPOSED TO BE EASY—QUICK and dirty—but here we are and the whole thing drags on. I should have known better than to listen to his fat butt about anything. This, the same man who tried to convince me to invest in a Yugo franchise. Said folks around here would snap up a four-thousand-dollar car. I didn't bite on that one, and probably should have passed on this one, too.

Boy's always looking for a scam someplace. Looking for that fast buck. He's a natural for this political shit, I guess. Seems the biggest part of it is looking for that opening, searching for that vulnerable spot.

I always turned my nose up at politics, particularly the shaking hands and smiling part of it. Running for office was something you did in high school to see who was the most popular, and the sort of people who did that were always these real insecure pretty boys, like Steve Randle, who just had to have some sort of public confirmation that they were better liked than the others. And as far as adult politics is concerned, I always figured it was pretty much the same thing, except that, in addition to the popularity contest, you got your basic graft and corruption. I keep waiting for somebody to slip some cash into my back pocket.

Walter says that's a stereotype, that there is such a thing as sincere public service and that there are more honest politicos out there than people think. He says it's just the bad apples that get the attention, and I'd like to believe him, but I remind my-self that in his business floating ugly rumors is all in a days work, as also is what he likes to refer to as "mutual backscratch-ing." He has freely and with open eyes already chosen a position a little further down the moral slope than makes me completely comfortable.

Walter says politics is more like gambling than anything else. He's always talking about crap shoots and putting all the money on the wheel. The only parallel I see is that, like gam-bling, you know you are doing something dumb, and you know that you probably won't win, and you know you might as well be flushing the damn money down the toilet, but still you keep dropping those quarters in. Walter says you got to roll the dice, Walter says you got to go for broke. Thing is, it's mostly my money out there—none of his—and here we sit, when it should all be over one way or another, in limbo. Which is nowhere. Winning is fine, and I could deal with straight up losing, too. But this tie shit is too unreal. I guess one vote really does make a difference.

That's how the system works, Walter says—it's a majority rules kind of thing. It's who comes up on top, and it doesn't matter if it's by one or by a hundred and one.

I guess it could have been worse. It could have been a land-slide the other way. It could have been nobody bothered to vote at all.

Paula, she acts like she couldn't give a good goddamn. All day long she's up there with my mother, doing God knows what, and you'd think there never had been an election. Here she should be dying to know what's going on, and from her I get nothing. OK, so I had it coming, I guess, but that's the thing about women: they fight dirty. When there is a crisis, people are supposed to rally around. She knows this election is important. But she's gonna hold me to my word, make me come crawling to her, make me the one to eat some crow. She wants to play, we'll play.

And then she says that shit the night of the party of not being from here. That's another thing. She is like a tumbleweed—she has grown and grown without getting attached to any one place. It's abnormal. She may not like it here—though she has never said that—but the truth is, she doesn't much like it anywhere. Here is just another place to be bored with.

A person might not think there'd be much to a place like River Ridge—couldn't be too much important going on—but in its way what goes on here is just as important as what goes on down in Jeff City or out in Washington, even if we are just a bunch of poor black folks. Take that issue right there—about this being a black place. Me, I'd never given that fact much thought. You take things for granted. But my mother is right. There are not a lot of towns that can claim that for themselves. Not out of the black belt in the south.

I like a small town. To me the city just looks strange and wrong. All those people and all that hustle and bustle. It's like looking through the other end of a telescope. Things are distorted. You recognize shapes here and there, but you don't know quite what they are. You don't have any perspective. Me, I like the smallness.

And I like the people.

One of these days I ought to write up the history of this place. What I know I've picked up because every once and a while one of the old-timers gets to spinning out his tales of this place. That and the drawer down at city hall. Down at the city hall there is a file cabinet marked "History." No one seems to know what it's for or who started it, and all it contains is a stack of paper. I don't know how deep it is. One time while checking a fact on an obit I was digging around and came across it. It's a bottom drawer of an ancient file, out of the way, and the whole thing looks like it hasn't been touched in decades. Apparently somebody decided to collect notes and clippings and receipts—anything might tell somebody something about the town. Best I can tell the last person to leave anything in the file did so in the mid-sixties—a clipping from the *Post Dispatch* about an area boy who led the state championship basketball team in scoring. The item underneath that was a recipe for pineapple upside-down cake.

I remember asking our part-time clerk about the drawer and getting a shrug as a response. She said "didn't nobody go in there" in a way that indicated she didn't much care about it and hoped nobody would assign her to do something to or about it. I dug down to see if I could find out anything about the war service of old Willie Simms when he passed. (There was a contradiction about whether he had served in Europe or Asia. According to any number of men who swore they had served right next to him, he had been all over the world and helped win every major engagement of the war.) Some of the papers in that drawer crumbled in my fingers, and I had this sense of actually having my hands on the real history of this town. It made me sick: it was so fragile. And I closed it up pretty quick and left it, and I haven't said anything to anyone about it being there.

Anytime I have reason to be in that office I check to make sure it's still there, and as of March it still was. I'd be more worried that some overzealous secretary might clean it all out so she could have a place to store her bag lunch, except I know how bureaucracy (literally) works: it's highly unlikely anyone will touch any file down there unless they have a court order. Still, I feel this need to protect that drawer—to put a big sign on it says "Very Valuable and Very Fragile. Do Not Touch or Discard." But I'm afraid to draw attention to it. Don't you know around here there would be some big battle over who it belonged to and who had the right to look through it. A few of these old Negroes would assume there was something in there they might be able to take some place and get some money for—from a museum, a rare documents collector, who knows?

The historical society couldn't care what went on down here with all us black folks, so there's no point in telling them. Knowing their type they'd box it up, stick it in that big house they restored over in Oak Grove and let it continue its decay— same process, only in a little classier environment.

Part of me wants to sneak in there sometime and steal it. Or brazen right in there and take it. Who better to have it but me? My people been in this town most of this century. And there at the paper I have the best record of the last forty-five years or so. That'll be my first act as mayor—go in and rescue our town's treasures. Turn it over to some graduate student along with the back issues of the newspaper and let him pull together a history of River Ridge. Who knows? Maybe there's some folks out there that do care about this kind of place.

Might be someone who cares that this fine old house—my house—is an exact replica of an 1880s house down in Louisiana, Missouri, that my grandfather admired. He copied it to the last detail, from the balustrade on the front staircase to the wain-scoting in the dining room. He threw an open house when it was finished so that everybody in town could see what a big man he was.

Might be somebody cares that back in the twenties there was a black man around who had the kind of money he could do that sort of thing. Maybe. And, there's a lot of other stories like that up and down this ridge.

If you look in the River Ridge phone directory today and compare the listings from 1950, not much has changed. All those people born back in the '20s and '30s are still here. Getting up in the years now, they can tell you when the sewer was put in, when the phone came, the first cable TV, the municipal well.

They remember when Main Street had a dozen or so shops, and when every family had four or five kids. When the future seemed bright. They talk about River Ridge the same way that immigrants talk about the old country—tell you how nice it was back there and how much you would have liked it. A lot of those folks will be gone soon, and they will take all those stories with them. It's a shame.

There are also a lot of people around here like Paula. The woman's been here fifteen years and she is oblivious. All the same to her we live here or in Alaska, and if River Ridge dies, it will be as much the fault of people like her as it is of the economy or the lure of the big city.

As it is we die by attrition. My father's generation was the last to stay here. Of the twenty-two Ridge Runners (as we call ourselves) in my high school class, only thirteen of us are still around. Mostly those of us who joined a family business, or married someone who did. We are holding our own, I think. 1,532 souls, half as many as the all-time high. We go up or down one or two people per year. We could go on this way for a long time, forever, even. And so be it. I'm not one of those naive people who believe things should never change, and I know that for the most part the mainstream of American life is elsewhere.

But I like River Ridge. I like knowing everyone who lives ten miles in any direction. I like the way the air smells and the trees surround you and the animals are not caged but are a natural part of everything. I like the way the news of the world sort of drifts in like a fog, has an ethereal other-worldly quality, how we soak up that news eagerly like the parched earth soaks up rain. Our satellite dishes reach out for Chicago, Atlanta, New York, afraid we will miss something. Even so, the news seems to drift in.

In the cities they think we are hayseeds out here. They send their news crews with their remote uplinks to find the oddball, the quaint, the traditional. They think we are ignorant, uninformed, that we fuck our daughters and cousins, and that we talk like country music stars. And some of us do. And so do some of them. It's a strange thing being stereotyped. While you know that what they believe about you is a lie, at the same time you are always on the watch for things that confirm what they say—folks in overalls and hats advertising seeds, big backwards country boys chewing on stalks of hay. They're here, too.

Still, we know who we are. We laugh at those big city folks and their caricatures of us as hard as they do. If we're still that way, well maybe that's because we are basically content. No crime there.

And more than anything that's what I like about being out here—the limited horizons and all. I like the diminished expectations. I like the fact that, when you get right down to it, there are only so many things you can do, and only so many places to go. Things are distilled. Every time a baby is born, every wedding, every feast, every lost dog, every graduation, every open house, reception, "for sale" sign, parking ticket, two-inch rainfall—all of that is important out here. I put it all in the paper, and people eat it up. Which in a way proves the opposite. Nothing is, in fact, really diminished. In River Ridge, everything, simply everything, is important.

I like River Ridge for all those reasons, but I stayed here only because it was the easiest thing to do. There I was, after college, deciding where to go and what to do, and my father died and left the business and something had to be done, and here I am, doing it still. It was a non-decision. For the most part, it has worked out. So we're comfortable—prospering, to be honest. We have a beautiful home and do not want for anything. I sometimes wonder how things would be different had I chosen to go to Chicago or Kansas City, but those kinds of thoughts are just a part of your life when you live in a small town.

And so here I am: I may be the mayor of this little place, and maybe I won't be. Just like staying here in the first place, I guess I sort of stumbled into this political shit, too. Walter and me, we spent all this time coming up with these position papers and sound bites and what have you. He gets into that mess, the boy does, and he's good at it, too. He tells me to memorize my parts and to smile real big and pretty. Somehow I think he misses the point.

I listen to these political guys and they have this high-minded crap they sell you about making the world a better place for children and putting their dreams into action, but I never really believe them. I don't believe there is one of them who lives with his people or really cares one way or another. Hypocrites.

I must win this election. That is the first point. I want to win. I want to be number one. I want to make the rules and I want people to do what I tell them. I think politicians are lying if they aren't forthright about it. It's what the game is all about, after all.

But it's more than that, too. It's about a place—this place—which, with a little more neglect, just might not be here any-more. I can do something about that. If it's worth saving—and I say it is—then these people need to be made to do whatever it takes to do that. If that means joining up with the white towns down the road, if that means we change our name to South Oak Bluff or Podunk or Smithereens, if that means a lot of people will wish I'd stayed away and never come back, it's worth doing.

This town is special.

And, I want to win.

It's a childish chant, but politics is a childish business.

I've spent a week or so playing mind games: sluffing it off, trying to pretend it doesn't matter. I tried to tell myself I really don't care who wins, convince myself that any enthusiasm I muster is false enthusiasm: I pretend I'm too cool to care. What a lie.

This *is* important. As important as almost anything I've done.

16

$\mathcal{P}$AULA STOOD A SPRIG OF FRESH MINT FROM THE YARD in each glass, filled them with ice cubes, and set them beside the pitcher on the tray. Miss Kezee told her where to find the wild mint growing along a rock fence on the far side of the yard. She had doubted her: after fifteen years, landscaping, and two boys daily scouring the ground for arrowheads, snakes, and other treasures. But there it was, soft, fragrant, just waiting to be found. She gave the pitcher a final pointless stir. The sediment of undissolved sugar spun around sluggishly at the bottom along with a few stray lemon seeds. Despite her better instincts, she was learning to enjoy her tea sickeningly sweet.

"You're not dressed," Al said, coming up behind her. He sounded exasperated, as if he were her parent and had asked her half-a-dozen times to get ready.

"Is your X-ray vision on? Are these not clothes?"

"The city council meets in twenty minutes. We need to get a move on."

"Your mother and I are having a tea party."

"Great. Just great." He came and stood in front of her so she could tie his tie. "Did it occur to you I might need you tonight?"

She pulled the knot unnecessarily tight. "Why darling, how insensitive of me. Here I am spending time with your mother, who happens to be sick." She gave a mocking sigh. "No, I'm afraid you'll have to take one of the boys in my place."

"I don't want to take one of the boys. I want to take my . . ."

"Your window dressing? Ah ha! the worm turns."

"Jesus," he said. He dropped his arms to his side like a frustrated schoolboy. "Please."

"Uh uh."

He made the pathetic puppy-dog eyes that usually worked. "Pretty please."

"You might as well give up. You are looking at a retired doormat. One who is instead devoting her life to good works, gossip, and dessert." She arranged a plate of Pepperidge Farm cookies and set those on the tray. He came up behind her and planted soft kisses up and down her neck and shoulder.

"Please, baby."

"This has some potential." She turned around into him, exaggerated her passion, opening her mouth wide as he kissed her, running her hands wildly around his back. "More. More. No, stop, stop. To think I almost gave in to your transparent deviousness. But, once again, virtue wins over vice. I stick with my original plan."

"Fine. To hell with you, then. Boys!" He grabbed after his keys and jacket.

She covered her cheeks with her hands, feigning shock.

"Boys! Let's go. One of these days you'll need . . ."

"One of these days I'll need: hmm, let me see, a cashmere coat, that diamond-and-ruby bracelet at Saks, a new husband." She picked up the tray and sashayed out. She passed her sons on the way up the steps. They were sweaty and disheveled. The perfect companions for a government meeting.

"Hurry up," she said. "Your father needs a baby-sitter."

She set the tray on the chest of drawers and immediately filled the glasses. "Here," she said, handing one to Miss Kezee. She sat down in the rocker, drank half her tea, and then let out a long exhale over her bottom lip.

"I see you found my mint."

"Right where you said. I had no idea."

"You have to be careful with mint. Pick just enough so that there is plenty to get through the hot season. You take care of it and it'll take care of you."

Sounded like b.s. to Paula. There were maybe two sprigs of that weed left out there. It had survived by some cosmic accident only, and nothing she did or didn't do would make a bit of difference. . . .

"What's the matter with you?" Miss Kezee asked. "You seem all hot and bothered."

"Nothing. What are we watching?"

"This one of them old Bette Davis movies. Watch this. Before she through, bitch'll have killed a couple of these white men and taken all they money too."

"They probably have it coming."

"Amen to that. Pass me some of them cookies over here. You get fat eating them all yourself."

Paula plucked off two of the chocolate-filled kind before handing them over. On the TV Bette was ordering servants around with a toss of her head. Paula crunched the cookies, put her feet up, and sighed again.

"You gonna talk about it or you gonna sit here and make noise all through my movie."

"It's just . . . Al."

"I figured that much. When a woman gets to sighing, it's usually a man up in it somewhere."

"I don't know. I can't discuss your son with you."

"Nothing too much you say could surprise me. I know my boy. He's not just my son, he's a man. For the most part, a man is a man."

That idea gave Paula the shivers. Not the callousness of lumping men together, but the idea that there might be some truth to it. That in some way Al had something in common with all the other men out there. The men she had been pinched by, propositioned by, men who attracted her, repelled her, impressed her. Men who sickened her.

"Tell me about it," Miss Kezee prompted. "Might be I could help you."

"I don't know how to explain it. We're at some funny place. Al said something to me the other day and it was like someone changed the rules on us."

Miss Kezee laughed her evil-sounding cackle. "Ain't laughing at you. I was married a lot of years. This shit happens every now and again."

"Never happened before."

"You was arguing?"

"Oh, no ma'am, nothing like that. We argue sometimes. No, it was just he said something . . . thoughtless."

"Look: the boy don't think. Or he thinks too much. He's always been that way. Was he being mean?"

"I don't know. What he said was, 'I don't wish to discuss it with you.' Those exact words. We were talking about that silly election. I don't know if he was joking or serious or trying to provoke me."

"He said that, huh?"

"He did. Maybe I should just forget it."

"Don't know what to tell you. I know every person's got their private things. You got to let him have his place."

"I know that. I know you can't own a person 100 percent, but this is different. He's drawn a line around part of his life. An important part. It's supposed to be off-limits to me. That's not right."

"Men have always done that. Always had their little things they went off and did on their own and acted like they was too important to share with you. I always figured to hell with them."

"It's never been that way with us. We talk about everything.

He tells me everything that goes on with the businesses—even when I don't want to hear it. I bore him to death with school stories. I'm not naive: I know we both have secrets. But here, out of the blue, he draws a line. This much and no more. All of the sudden I've got questions and doubts I never had before, and I don't like it." She poured the dregs of her tea down her throat and considered her mother-in-law. "I don't expect you to have any answers for me."

"You feel a little lost, don't you? Like you was out in the desert. It was that way with me and Junior's daddy, A. B. He had me in a pen much smaller than you in. He didn't tell me nothing at all."

"Did you know that was what it would be like?"

"I didn't know the man at all. Never did know him. Isn't that something? Married over twenty years and I didn't even know him."

"But you loved . . ."

"Well, love, huh? Back in them days was other things to worry about besides love. First of all, a woman didn't have no husband, well she was just nothing. And you didn't just go around with different men. You dated a man, you was looking to see about marrying him. I'd been sharing with another gal in this boarding house. After Mama died. Thought I was gonna be one of those women that folks felt sorry for. But, you know, I had grown up in a house full of boys, and, for one thing, I wasn't too eager to immediately get me another man to look after. Mens were no mystery to me. I knew their nasty habits and ornery ways."

She took a long sip from the iced tea glass. The sound caused an involuntary shudder from Paula.

"And anyway, I was a scrawny homely thing."

"I've seen your pictures. You were pretty."

"That's very kind of you. Too bad you wasn't back there

looking for a wife. Seems men in Saint Paul was looking out for them light-skinned gals. Liked em big, too. With big titties and big butts. Little round-shouldered brown gal like me wasn't nothing."

"I bet you got asked out a lot."

"Every now and then, yes, but wasn't too many places to catch a man. I didn't go to church regular or hang out in taverns. Yeah, every once in a while a man would invite me, but like I said, they was looking for a wife, and I was supposed to be looking for a husband. And, if you wasn't interested from the get go, wasn't much point to going around with them.

"I liked my life. I had me a good job with the War Department. I'd get up, put on my uniform and go to the office. You worked a full day back then, and you worked hard. After work, I'd fix me a nice supper and settle in with the radio. Had my own money. Bought myself nice things. It wasn't bad, especially when I thought back to Mama. By my age, Mama had me and four more babies besides. And was working, too."

Paula closed her eyes and tried to get a picture of those times. A picture with Miss Kezee in it. She could not quite put it together. She could see the woman in the uniform, in padded-shouldered coats, in high-waisted dresses. She liked hats, as well. Robin Hood green hats, with feathers. Tall spike heels to match. She could see the clapboard bungalows and could imagine what they looked like when they were new. She could remove the sky-scrapers from the skyline and replace them with the old brick block warehouses of the downtowns of the forties—they must have seemed old and dreary even then, their ornate cornices dripping pigeon waste and soot. She could not, however, make the picture come together. In fact, she was never able to imagine living in any other time. Life must have had a different texture, as different as a blouse made of satin would feel from a blouse made of burlap. They were different, but unless you touched them you had no idea, really, how different they were. Of course, you could see the texture, see the coarse hairs of jute unwinding themselves, see the shiny smooth richness of the satin, and she knew that a woman came of age differently in the forties, but she could not feel in any sensuous way what that was like. There was too much to learn. And unlearn.

"How did you meet Al's father?"

"I went to a tavern with this girl I shared a place with: Mavis. That girl was a hell-raiser from the get go. She was always in them taverns. She was what you call a party gal. When Mama was alive, she didn't allow Mavis to come around the house. Mama said she wasn't nothing but a tramp. I guess she was. But she had fun, and all the mens knew her. All of em. She knew I didn't go in for too much of that stuff. You could go out with her and no telling where you might end up. She weren't choosy, and most them old dogs she knew, well first of all you knew they wasn't up to no good with they heads all slicked back and their fancy clothes. And they wasn't interested in but one thing besides. I had to be careful because back in those days a reputation meant something. But I liked Mavis. She was fun."

"What happened to her?"

"You know I don't know. Lost track of her somewhere when I was living down here. I never thought much on her. What does happen to women like her?"

Paula thought about her college roommate Felicia. She remembered the parade of different men who went through that bed. She remembered how remorseless Felicia was, remembered how that lack of guilt was the thing she admired most about her.

"I had a roommate like Mavis once. In Columbia. She loved men. All kinds of men."

"No good come of her, huh?"

"Well, actually she's become a lawyer and married another

lawyer and is living happily ever after. Or so they tell me."

"Hot damn. If that don't beat all. I guess it just goes to show you. You can't go too much on any of them rules. You gotta make your own way."

"I don't believe that. You get punished later—that's what I think."

"You get punished anyway, more like it. Now hush up and watch this show a while."

They finished the pitcher of tea and watched Bette Davis scheme and manipulate. Her character seemed so evil, and when she'd say something particularly hateful, Miss Kezee would shriek madly and call out, "Tell her, girl," or "Go on now."

"I love these old shows," she said.

"I like the tearjerkers myself. You know, like *Dark Victory*. You see that one?"

Miss Kezee waved her hand. "Ain't studying any that silly old mess. Wanna be depressed, watch the news."

"Finish telling me about A. B."

"Well," she started. She scratched her head and rubbed her chin as if she couldn't quite find the story. "It's not too much to it. Mavis said she wanted me to meet a man from out of town. Said he was good looking. Had his own car and a lot of money."

Paula waited for the story to continue. She felt as if she were being asked to beg for it. "So," she prompted. The same prompt she used in college when she and Felicia exchanged stories of their dates.

"So. I met him."

"And."

"And he was in town for a few weeks. And we went out a few nights."

"Did you like him?"

Miss Kezee shrugged.

"I don't understand."

"Don't think I do either." She shifted her weight. "Life is like that sometimes. Sometimes stuff just happens. You go along like it don't got nothing to do with you."

"I wouldn't want to live like that."

"Oh, but you might. Sometimes a chance comes and you go on it."

"So you just married? This stranger."

"Yes, ma'am. Went out with him five or six times. He asked and I said yes."

Paula shook her head.

"Oh, lots of women did that kind of stuff back then. Around war time and them years after." She looked at Paula and cracked a sly smile. "Believe me?"

Paula shook her head again.

"No, I guess you wouldn't." Miss Kezee stared at the television and Paula could see something—a chuckle or a shiver—pass through her like a ripple on a pond.

"Why'd you do it?" she asked.

Miss Kezee shrugged again. "Seemed like something to do, I guess. Didn't give it too much thought. I had never been out of Minnesota. A. B. told me about a place called River Ridge. A place on the river where the rainbow ended and where the pot of gold overflowed. He said was nothing but colored people down here and they was the finest folks you'd ever want to know. Said they all lived in grand houses and his was the grandest house of all and I would be his queen. The queen of it all. I believed him. Not him, but I believed that there was such a place. My world was so small and I just didn't know. River Ridge could be just what a person was looking for. I came here after this place."

"Wanted it bad enough to marry a man you didn't love."

"A man I didn't know. I took a gamble, girl. Figured, hey, if it works, I'm riding high, and if it don't, well it just don't. Wasn't too much happening in Saint Paul. Wasn't like I was giving up much."

"I could never do that."

"No. Not you. You like it safe and easy."

"Well, that's not true."

"Yes, you do. No shame in it."

She did feel shamed, though. That back over her life of safe choices she had never come close to doing anything nearly so adventurous. Her shame was not in having avoided adventure, but that she had never considered it an alternative.

"I admire your courage," Paula said.

"Seems a waste now. A quarter of my life, wasted."

"You never loved him, did you? Did he love you?"

"He loved money. Loved making money. Loved this town. This house. This part of the world. Me, I was a thing. A piece of furniture. A wristwatch. I was just . . . here. A quarter of my life I was prisoner in River Ridge. In this house. Listen: here is what my life was like. In the morning I'd do A. B.'s books. Count his money. Then I'd clean his big old house and fix his supper. And at night I'd listen to the radio or watch TV. Sometimes if I was lucky I'd go sit in someone else's house for a while."

"That's horrible."

"No, no, no." She shook her head violently. "That ain't a bad life at all. Some people'd be happy to have what I had. It just wasn't for me. None of it. I kept hoping something would happen to me, but it never did."

"Well, there was Al."

"My little Junior. He was a good thing. I held on to him to keep me going."

"And just think if you hadn't come here, you'd never have had him and everything would be different. For both of us."

"Where you think you'd be, girl?"

Paula sat back in the rocker and thought. "You know, now that you mention it, I have no idea. I had my dreams. Of being famous and successful, but they never felt real. The scary thing is it seems like so much of my life just happened to me."

"A. B. loved his little boy, yes Lord. He treated me like I was the mammy. The old bastard." She laughed. "If I'd buy strained peaches he'd make me get pears. If I bought a blue dress shirt for the boy he wanted white. There was no pleasing that Negro."

"Why didn't you leave?"

"I should have. I thought about it a lot. I couldn't decide where to go or what was best for my son. It could have been worse somewhere else. I think almost a dozen years went by in there that didn't one word come out of A. B.'s mouth to me that wasn't 'Do this for Junior,' or 'Do that for Junior.'"

"How did you survive?"

"You just do. You find little things that make you happy. The river, the garden, your child. You know about that. Hang on to them boys."

"I am." Paula said. Her boys, her wild boys. Some days they were easier to hang on to than others. There'd been a truce lately, or as far as she could tell there was. They stayed so busy they didn't have time to fight.

On television, Bette had a gun. That meant the picture was almost over. Miss Kezee shook her head with disgust.

"Sillyass mess," she said.

"You didn't finish your story," Paula prompted.

"Where was I?"

"And then Charlie came along . . ."

Miss Kezee smiled, "Like a bolt out of the blue."

"And you didn't look back."

"And I didn't look back. And I won't."

"Regrets?"

"Not allowed."

"Always good times with Charlie?"

"Didn't matter."

"Why not?"

"You ask too many questions, girl."

"You never talk about Charlie."

"We all got our private things. You said so yourself."

"I know you loved him very much."

"What else you need to know?"

The man and the woman are in bed together. The woman has brown skin and is older than she looks. The man is darker. His head is surrounded by white puffs of cotton-like hair.

"I feel cheated," the woman says. She is holding onto the man.

"Why so?" he asks her.

"I'm an old woman." She rolls away from the man.

"Come back here," he says. "You're not old at all. You're healthy and you're beautiful. To me you're fine."

"Ain't thinking about you," she says. "Worrying about myself."

"Is you, now?" The man smoothes her long gray hair.

"All them years. All them lost years. I want to die when I think of it."

"This is now, Nobi. Forget that. We got to hold on to now."

"It ain't fair. All them years."

"Hold on." The man embraces her.

"I know one thing," the woman says.

"What's that?"

"They can have the rest of it, but this part of my life is gonna be mine. I'm keeping it. Here." She touches her head. "And here," and her heart.

"Won't tell nobody, huh?"

"No. Nobody. Never."

17

$\mathcal{A}$ SIMPLE REQUEST. JUST COME AND BE WITH ME AT THE damn city council meeting. That's all.

And not that I ask much, cause I don't.

I'm not like Walter, who can't get himself dressed in the morning if Berneice ain't there to lay things out for him and tell him which order to put things on. Seriously. She says, "I pulled out those blue pants and make sure you wear that clean shirt hanging in front there." Thank God the woman has good taste. Some days you would think Berneice was his mama or something, and frankly, for a man who is generally competent he can be pretty simple sometimes. Every once and a while Berneice blows her stacks and starts hollering and screaming about "his simple ass," as she calls it. Then for a few days you see Walter around town looking like he slept in his clothes for a week. The man is a dentist and a campaign consultant and all kinds of other shit, too, and he can't even dress himself. What's that about?

Me, I make a simple request, and can Paula do it? No, of course not. She's got important things to do with Mother all day. Like gossiping and watching TV. Knowing my mother, they ran out of anything substantial to talk about weeks ago. I know my name comes up: I go up there the other day to get a phone number from Paula—one of those ones that isn't written down anywhere in the universe and exists only in that secret file in her head. "See," she says to my mother, and they start giggling. Not that I care.

Paula Denise Fuller. The woman drives me crazy. Has driven me crazy since the first time I saw her in that bookstore back in Columbia. I saw the girl, and those alarm bells and whistles and warnings went off, and I ain't been the same since. I honestly can't say I've had a clear-headed day in going on twenty years. I am a victim of that chemistry shit they talk about, though I don't even know what they mean. For me it's like all the time in my head I've got something I forgot or need to worry about, but I can't quite put my finger on it. It's like some sort of microscopic scratch on the finish of a new car— one of those ones that only you can see, and then only if you are really looking for it. Still, you know it's there and you can't keep yourself from thinking about it. Try not to think of an elephant. A pink elephant. It's an obsession.

And she plays head games. I'm sitting at my desk the other night with a stack of journals to review, looking for some different stuff to fill up the paper. Now the truth is, most of these folks around here couldn't care less about anything but who died and when the bake sale is and what's the going price for soybeans. Still, I'm always looking to pick up something new— a cartoon or a series or even a poem if I find one I like. Now it ought to have been clear to anyone that I was very busy, and here she comes—"La, la, la, la, la," pretending to sing and reaching across me and sticking herself in my face and all kinds of transparent shit.

"Something I can do for you?" I say, and she makes one of those Marilyn Monroe cooing noises in the back of her throat.

"I'm working," I said. She plops herself down in my lap.

"Don't mind me," she says and starts licking around my ears.

So there went another evening. What was I supposed to do? One of these days my dick is gonna fall off.

Obsessed with the damn woman, and I remember every moment I've been with her. I remember on the day we met the trees had just begun to leaf out and the weather was warm enough for T-shirts and shorts. She was wearing a dark blue top with gray baggies. She was buying gum. I remember all that.

I remember we strolled along the wide sidewalk across the common and that I forgot I was supposed to be going back to my room and pulling together some research about how different papers around the country were covering the end of the war. We walked and talked all afternoon. About what? Who knows. It was so trivial the words faded as soon as they passed our lips: where you live, what classes you're in, do you know this one or that one. Paula is the queen of small talk. That's the truth. That girl can and will talk to anyone about any sort of foolishness. You'll be walking through the grocery store minding your own business and the next thing you know she'll have struck up a conversation with somebody. Me, I assume it's some old friend from school or from the city, but it turns out it's nobody she's ever seen before and she's just talking away to whoever about whatever.

She sure talked my ear off that day. Wasted my whole day, and I loved it. And I remember I didn't want to be done with her, and I asked her if she wouldn't like to go to a movie some time. She said, "Of course," and I remember being shocked how direct she was. She's not coy. Didn't mess around. She still doesn't. When she makes up her mind that she wants something she goes after it and gets it. You wouldn't want to get in her way, either.

A lot of those girls back in college, you had to play games all the time. You had to beg them for a date, and they treated you like it was a big favor if they said yes. Not that I knew a whole lot of girls before, that is.

Before and after. I think of it that way.

Before, I went with a girl named Deborah, though when I think back on it I can't imagine why. She was a solid, strong thing, with medium brown skin and wore her hair in one of those close-cut, curled-around-the-head styles. She had those gray-green eyes, too—we used to call her Cat Eyes.

Deborah was one of those girls complained constantly: she didn't like Mizzou, there was never anything on the menu for her to eat, she didn't like that movie (she'd never seen that movie), it was too hot, too cold, the sun was out or it wasn't. She hated the way I dressed and I bored her. She said so to my face.

The bitch got on my nerves, and she knew it. We went out the spring of my sophomore year. Seems a lot longer than that when I think about it. Sometimes you get into things and you stay there out of inertia. We were done when the school year ended. There were no big scenes. We took our finals, packed our bags, and said see you around. Painless and simple.

I took out other girls off and on. Dating was a chore. You had to beg them to see you, get dressed up, pick out something to do, and pretend like you were interested in their little small talk. And you had to get them some food. Black women expect to be fed, and fed good.

Then you had to decide whether or not to ask yourself in. Paula, she'd like to imagine my life began the day I met her. As far as she's concerned I'm her first and she mine, though we both know that isn't true. It's like she regrets all those other experiences—like she thinks they were sinful or some kind of mistake. That makes her sound prudish, and she's not. It's just more of the truckload of garbage she hauls around with her—

David Haynes   265

garbage of her mother's. And though it makes her crazy and as much as she'd like to cut it loose, every once in a while she unloads some on me or on the boys.

The other day she announces that if her children are going to be spending the night over someone's house, then she and I are going over there to meet their parents first.

"OK," I said.

"You see," she continued as if I'd objected, "you just can't be too careful with some of these . . ." And then she started laughing and I nodded.

"I sound like her, don't I," she said. The older we get, the more that happens. And while I know she'd like to be the model of progressive parenthood, the first time she finds one of these boys wrapped up on her couch with some honey, she will freak. She'll trot out some speech about saving it for marriage and expect me to take the little stud upstairs and put him back on the straight and narrow.

Like I'd ever heard such a speech.

I'd tell him, I suppose, to use a condom. Maybe I'd try to find some way to convince him not to spread it around too much—for . . . decorum's sake? (Is that why we don't want to spread it around too much—for decorum's sake?)

Just our luck one of these two will turn out to be like old Keith, my college roommate. That boy was a dog. He couldn't keep the thing zipped in. Sex was his hobby, and he would practice it with anyone at any time. They would line up at the door to get them some Keith—it was like he gave off some sort of a scent, and he didn't have any qualms about who or what time of the day. Keith believed it was his role in life to spread a little happiness around, and sex was his ministry, as it were.

I have to say I was shocked. And it's not like I had all this moralistic training. We never set foot in a church when I was growing up. My mother and father let you know what was wrong and right by who they turned their noses up at. Used to be a woman on our street let her daughters run wild. Mother barely acknowledged her presence, wouldn't even answer the door if it was her. So I was bothered by Keith. Even if it seemed like everyone was enjoying themselves.

I was closer to the other end of the spectrum. I dated, but a lot of these women . . . People have this idea that dating is a casual activity, like taking a walk or going fishing. No way: It was serious business back at school. The girls I went out with were looking for mates. If they'd wanted to see a movie, they would have gone with a girlfriend. Most nights I was being auditioned for the role of husband. That's the truth. Some nights I got the part. I could see that some Sharon or Sandra thought she'd reeled in a keeper. That was scary—sitting there with a girl I felt nothing for, and she's looking at me and I can see the wedding album reflected in her eyes. I know a lot of fellows back then took advantage of these girls, especially if they were pretty. Hustle them up, give em some sort of vague promise, fuck em a few times, and adios. I went out with some who'd been down that road. They carried this trace of desperation and fear.

And, yes, I knew my share of those party girls, too. You called them up if you wanted to laugh, let go, dance, party. Off and on my junior year I went out with this Teresa—a brown-skin girl, thin, wore skin-tight dresses in primary colors. She was a wild one. She expected gifts, expected to be told your troubles. She was demanding in bed. She barked out orders, and, then, wanted you gone before sunrise.

Even those girls—even Teresa—were shopping for something out there. It was as if the whole thing were some kind of commercial enterprise.

Then came Paula.

I met her and kept thinking about what she looked like. She had this hair that intrigued me. Those other girls either wore big full-headed afros or hair that was pressed-out straight and shiny. Paula gathered hers, kinky, unpressed, into a knot at the back of her head. I wanted to get my hands in it, and I thought that if I touched it it would feel like silk thread. I wanted to loosen that knot—see if it stood around her head like a crown or fell around her shoulders like a waterfall.

"Don't pet me," she says. I am always trying to put my hands on that hair. I am a dog, she says, always rutting around and feeling on her. It's her fault. She is one of those wily women—one of those has ways of keeping a man under her spell. I try not to think about her sometimes, but my mind goes back, just like she's trained it to do.

She teases me. She says she knows everything I'm thinking, says she can read my mind. One of her many superpowers.

She sits around and figures the one thing that will drive me the most crazy—the brownies with nuts, the maroon nail polish. She does them, and then sometimes she doesn't. But you know she's keeping those options open.

She puts her toes on the muscles on the inside of my thighs, touches the thatch of hair between my shoulder blades. She shamelessly succumbs to baby talk and goes along with whatever I tell her.

She is calling me now.

18

$\mathcal{P}$AULA WAS WASHING OUT THE PITCHER WHEN AL RE-
turned with the twins. They went straight to the refrigerator
and got into a shoving match, bottles slapping and cracking together as Tim pushed Tommy into the door.

"You know what's in there. Get it and get out," Paula said.

"Nothing good anyway," Tommy whined.

"You had your ice cream," Al scolded. "Scram. Git." He
scooted them along with his foot. "What's with those two?" he
said to Paula. "They act like animals all of the sudden."

"Growing pains," she said, standing the glasses in the drain.

"I don't know about you, but I'm not gonna put up with
that crap around my house."

"And what are you gonna do about it?"

"One day we got two normal boys and the next day a couple
of heathens. Knocking each other around. Calling names. I
don't like it." He was standing next to the table absentmindedly
getting undressed. She looked back and forth from him to the
pile of clothes gathering on a chair.

"And, so? What you're gonna do about it is . . . ? And for
God's sake put your clothes back on."

He shrugged. "Something. I guess. Don't you think things
are getting weird around here?" He stepped back into his
khakis, fumbled with the rest of the clothes as if unsure what to
do with them. She took the bundle and tossed it down the basement stairs.

"You noticed, did you?" she said right in his face. "So do I get to hear what happened at the meeting, or have I been a bad girl and it's a big secret?"

He looked for a minute as if she'd just spoken in another language. "Well, we get to this meeting and Brother Berry and Brother Wilson and the rest of them have decided that since the people couldn't decide, it was up to them to settle things. They come in there with this speech all prepared as to how they have met in special session and taken into consideration this and that and so on and so forth. Them old Negroes was up there about to announce who the next mayor was, and I could tell it wasn't gonna be me."

"What did you do?" she sighed, struggling to show enough interest. He looked ridiculous standing there, telling his story, barefoot, shirtless, suspenders strapped over his naked shoulders.

"Walter jumps up and reads from the old county ordinance book he found. Left them old boys harrumping and snorting and chewing on their nasty old cigars." He punched into his hand triumphantly.

"And . . . so . . ."

"They toss a coin on Monday. That's what the law says."

"Just like that?"

He stuck his thumb up. "I'm feeling lucky."

Upstairs there was a loud thump and a door slammed.

"What the hell?"

They met Tommy at the bottom of the steps holding a blood-smeared hand over his nose.

"He hit me," Tommy cried, and then he collapsed into his father. The blood leaked from his nose and dripped down his father's naked stomach.

Al cringed, pushed him toward Paula and started up the stairs.

"No," she said. "You take care of this. I'll go up there."

He walked Tommy to the downstairs bathroom, handling him the way someone might handle a sick stray cat.

Miss Kezee leaned against the guest room door, robe gathered around her slight body. Paula rolled her eyes. From inside the boy's room she heard furniture scraping across the floor. The door was locked.

"Tim. Timothy. Open this door. Tim . . ."

"Go away."

"I need to talk to you. Please. Let me in."

"Boy ain't studying you." Miss Kezee cackled her laugh. "Tell him you gonna beat his ass he don't open that door in five seconds."

She ignored her. "Tim. Please."

"Open that damn door," Miss Kezee shouted. "Hear me in there? Open up, I say."

"Mother, please."

Al came up the steps with Tommy, who held a face towel filled with ice cubes to his nose. He was whimpering again. Paula pulled the cloth away. There was no mark. It was hardly red. On top of everything else, here was one of her good guest towels all bloody. Al just didn't think.

"What's the story here," Al demanded.

"Boy got himself locked up in there. Y'all need to beat his ass."

"Mother . . . ," Paula said.

Al tried the door. "Open up, son. Come on now."

"He ain't studying y'all."

Al looked at Paula, annoyed. "Why isn't she in bed?" he asked.

"Goes to bed when I feels like it. Just who you think you is standing up in here . . ."

"Boy, you better open this door before I kick it in."

"... talking about 'why ain't she in bed?' Why ain't all *y'all* in bed?"

"I mean it, boy. You open this door. I'm giving you three."

"All hours of the night. I'm an old woman. How I'm supposed to live with all this commotion?"

"One . . ."

"Folks fightin and hollerin."

"Two . . ."

"Slamming doors and running up and down."

"Three."

"Everybody freeze," Paula shouted. "Calm down. Mother's right. It's late. We'll get through this in the morning. Let's all go to bed."

Al threw up his hands.

"Let's go. Come on. To your rooms." Paula felt like a camp counselor. "Good night, Mother. Say good night everyone. Come on."

"Where am I supposed to go?" whispered Tommy.

"We'll make you a nice place downstairs. Come on." Paula opened the linen closet.

"No," he shrieked.

"Why in the hell not?" Al shouted.

"He'll get me."

"No one is getting anyone here. Come on." Paula pulled him to the steps.

"No. You don't know him. He's sick. Don't leave me alone. Please. Please, Mama." He wrapped himself around her. She felt sorry and disgusted at the same time. She looked at Al with the question in her eyes. He mouthed the word "No."

"Just for tonight?"

Al slammed his hand against the door frame. "If you snore, boy, your black butt will end up on the floor. Understand me?"

He lightly swatted his bottom as he scooted toward the bed. "We need to talk," he whispered to Paula.

"About a lot of things. Not now."

"Soon?"

"Real soon."

"I mean it. Watch if his butt don't end up on the floor."

Before they were themselves ready, Tommy lay sprawled across the center of the bed on his back, snoring loudly, his mouth agape.

"Look at that," Al said, disgusted.

"Precious."

"Precious my ass. Hey, boy." He crawled in on one side of his son, rolling him over to stop the snoring.

"Good night," Paula said. She crawled in on the other side.

It had been a long time since either boy had been in bed with them. Stretched out beside her he seemed long and rangy. His limbs were extended as if they were reaching for something and were growing longer to cut the distance. She touched the skin on his back. He was as smooth and dry as paper. He was warm and still.

She heard a rustling. In the dim light she could see Al offhandedly rubbing his hand through his son's hair.

The truck heads north on the highway. The woman watches out the back window.

"This ain't right," she says. She says it to the man with the cotton-puff hair.

"Couldn't be righter," the man says. He drives rigidly. He is nervous.

"No. Not this way," the woman says.

The round brown man shakes his head. "He don't want you no more. He said so."

"No. Not this way." The woman is determined. "Stop. Turn around."

The man pulls off Highway 61.

"You been looking back after him all this time. Do you see him coming after you? Well, do you?"

"Charlie. You think I don't know he ain't coming? I know that. If we don't do this right, I'll never be free. I'll always be tied to him."

The man grimaces. "You're right, of course."

"I'm right."

The man turns the truck around.

Paula woke first. Downstairs she found Tim parked with a book, behind the box of Wheaties and a gallon of milk. He didn't look up.

"Good morning," she said. No response. He casually turned a page of the novel.

"You're the early riser."

He shrugged. He poured more cereal into the bowl.

This game, Paula thought. She set up the coffee maker, let the first cup drip into her mug, then sat down across from him. They would be handsome men, these boys of hers. Or she hoped they'd be. Adolescence could make them over any way it wanted. Already she could see nascent muscles defining themselves on their arms, and a coming-together of facial features. Tim's voice would crack now and then, but Tommy would apparently be blessed. When his voice changed, it subtly slid down an octave. Sometimes overnight.

Except for when they were tiny newborns, she had always been able to tell them apart, and it's possible they had been switched once or twice during those first few months. Maybe this one was the one originally called Thomas, and the one upstairs was the real Timothy. But once she had fixed them, there had been no mistakes. Whether the original Tim or not, this was the one who was . . . what? More fair-skinned (except in summer). Taller? Maybe once. With more square a head? Yes. People were always telling her how they were physically different, but that was not how she knew. This was the one who was . . . stiffer, dignified, less bold, more contained, unique, different from that other person upstairs. Different from everyone else in the world as well. This was the person she needed to get through to now. The person hiding behind that book.

"I'm going to tell you something, and I want you to listen to me." She returned the cereal to the cupboard and the milk to the refrigerator. "Are you listening?"

He was frozen over *The Return of the King*, but she could tell his eyes were not engaged. She closed the book and set it aside. "Are you?"

He sat back in his chair, crossed his arms, and glared at her. She knew that look, that eleven-year-old see-what-a-mean-little-man-I-am-I-don't-have-to-listen-to-your-crap look, a look full of bluster and menace and bravado, all of it false. She could deflate that look faster than a pin prick deflated a cheap balloon. She gave him the same pose. Doing so damped about half of what fire there was left in him.

"Two things you need to understand up front. There's to be no more hitting and no more locking people out."

He shrugged.

"What's that mean?" She exaggerated a shrug. "Where did you get that? Huh?" She knew very well where he got it. She prayed that God would lock in place the shoulder blades of all the males she knew.

". . . mean nothing . . . ," he mumbled.

"What's that you say? You're the big man these days. Can't you even talk?"

"I said it doesn't mean anything."

"As long as you understand my rules."

"He had it coming."

"No hitting and no locked doors."

"If he messes with me . . ."

"No more."

"You don't even listen. You're so busy up there with that old lady you don't even know what goes on around here."

"I think I have a pretty good idea."

"No you don't, because if you did, you wouldn't be sitting here yelling at me."

"I'm not yelling. And tell me all the things go on around here I don't know about."

"I don't have any privacy. Every time I look up there's someone else there, annoying me, making stupid noises. I'm sick of it."

"Did you talk about it?"

He shrugged again.

"I think until you talk about . . ."

"I want my own room."

"That room is plenty big for the two of you. We can re-arrange the . . ."

"I want my own room. You said a long time ago that one of us could move into the guest room."

"Grandma is there."

"I want my own room. Do something about *that*." He grabbed the book and stalked out.

The man and the woman returned to the house above the river road.

"What's this?" the woman asks.

A crowd stood on the sidewalk. A squad car with flashing lights is parked in front of the house.

"Oh my God," the woman says.

The man stops the truck at the curb. He opens the door for the woman and offers his arm.

"What is it?" the man asks.

The crowd makes way for them. "We're sorry, Mrs. Johnson," they say. "Terribly sorry," they say.

The officers wait on the wide porch. From the porch you can see off a ways the river twinkling in the sun.

"Harvey?" the woman says. She knows this officer, knows the people in the crowd. She knows everyone around here.

"Miss Johnson," the officer says. He removes his cap. "Ma'am. There's been an accident."

They held hands and strolled along the levee, tottering on the cobblestones where the pavement had worn away. Fronting the mostly abandoned warehouses of Main Street, this levee seemed a foolish reminder of the past.

"Why don't they just plow this up?" Paula asked. "Put in a park or something."

"You one of them girls got big-city ideas. We simple country folks around here. We don't go for none of that new-fangled stuff."

"I have a lot of big ideas for you bumpkins. Like indoor toilets. Heard of those?"

"No such thing."

"And how bout that lectricity they talking about? Get some lectric lights."

"Hot damn," he said at the top of his voice.

She shushed him, sat him down, giggling, hiding him from a cluster of men in front of the feed and grain store. "They might hear you. Shshsh."

"I own that damn store. Own this whole damn town." He

jumped up and strutted back and forth like a peacock. "That's what my daddy told me."

She shook her head. "He must have been a character."

"Yep. That he was, indeed. Indeed." He picked up a handful of rocks to skip.

"Somehow I can't imagine him and your mom. I mean, I never met him, but . . . know what I mean?"

Al nodded. He walked closer to the river to get a better angle. He drew back his arm and arced out like a discus thrower. The rock sank instantly.

"Damn." He came and sat by Paula on the bank. "Suppose Mother and the boys are OK?" he asked.

"Don't figure there's much we can do if they're not."

He sat forward, resting his elbows on his knees, chin in hand. "Do you ever think things are just totally out of your control? Like the world is spinning along on its merry way, and there is not one damn thing you can do about it."

"You sound like a man needs some religion."

"Saving souls, are you?"

She waved away the idea with her hand. "Me? That's another business I'm retired from."

"Bothered me last night. Not being with you. Not being alone with you."

"Yeah, well, the boys . . . ."

"The boys, my ass. I'm talking about me and you."

She rubbed a hand across her face. She could feel herself reddening the way she always did when he talked this way.

He stood up over her, arms crossed, smiling. "You remember that song, 'Me and Mrs. Jones.'" He sang the first line.

She toppled over, clutching her sides, laughing.

"What is it?" he asked

"I'm your Mrs. Jones now, huh? Look at yourself: you look like Yul Brenner in *The King and I*."

He widened his stance and brought a hand up to his chin. She saw the beginning of an erection through his thin cream-colored pants.

"You better stop messing with me," he said. "I got my eye on you. Did you know that? You and those boys. Did you?"

She straightened herself up, cleared her throat to cover the remainder of the laughter that had instantly become inappropriate. "You're just full of yourself these days," she said.

"You still angry with me?"

"I don't know if I want to discuss that with you."

"Touché. You're still daddy's little girl, aren't you?"

"You're a bastard and big black ape. Don't even think of patronizing me." She started up so she could walk away.

"Sit down," he said calmly.

Despite herself she turned. "Beg your pardon?"

"I said sit down." He said it like a little boy would to a puppy, gently, with a coaxing pat.

She squatted on her haunches, hugging her knees. "You don't own me, you know. You gorilla."

"Yes, as a matter of fact I think I do own you." He put his hands on her shoulders. "Now, why don't we relax. Get comfortable. Can I get you anything?"

Despite her rage, she collapsed beneath the gentle touch. "Yes, let's see. I'll have a martini, and you can get me a gun so I can blow your brains out." She glowered at him.

He sat beside her and draped an arm across her shoulder. "You don't want to do that. You couldn't do it anyway, and what would you do without me? I don't know what I'd do without you."

"There are millions of men out there. They all got what you got, and I'll tell you what: more and more I can live without it."

He whispered in her ear. "They ain't got what I got."

"Ha," she laughed. "You're a dog." She got up and started kicking at his shins. "A disgusting nasty dog."

He dodged her kicks, scuttling up and down the levee just out of her range. He encircled her with his arms, hugged her, and, by kneeling, lowered her to her knees.

"A filthy rutting dog."

"Do you want me to let you go?"

She oozed out of his arms and sat down away from him. "I want to stop playing . . . is this a game? I don't know what's going on anymore."

"As I recall, you and me, we have always been dead serious."

"I feel like I don't even know you anymore."

"It's just me. Al." He sat down and snuggled her neck. "The man of your dreams."

"Change that to nightmares. Whatever you think and regardless of how unimportant you think it is, you can't keep part of your life secret from me. I'll not allow it."

"I think about you all the time. I do."

"I know you too well. You're more slippery than eel slime."

"I want into every part of you: your mind, your hopes, your body, your dreams. I sit in my office and think, I don't want to be here. I want to be at home. In bed. With Paula."

"You've been warned about patronizing me."

"You know what the whole problem is? You're smarter than me. I'm just a simple farm boy from the Midwest. You come along and seduce me with your sophisticated big-city ways. I have to be careful around you."

"You're cute but you're transparent. You think you can use the smoke screen of this election to run your little scam. Your little power trip will blow up in your face. We'll see who gets the last word."

"Let me win. Just this once. What'll it hurt you to indulge me a little?"

"Monopoly, hearts, strip poker, Russian roulette, maybe I might let you win those. *If* you play fair. But not this game."

"You're destroying me." He reached under her blouse to play with her breasts. He kissed at the nape of her neck.

Paula pushed him away. "Feel me up in public. Those men back there looking at us."

"Fuck those men."

"And what if I did?"

"I'd kill you. Then I'd kill the boys, then Mama. Then I'd turn the gun on myself."

"Who'd be left to write the headline?"

"I'd write the story first. MAN DRIVEN CRAZY BY SHE DEVIL."

"You're already crazy."

"And just whose fault is that?"

She put her head between her knees. OK. Here I am, she thought, wandering through the minefield. Miss a step, and I'm dog meat. Or maybe this was more like the fun house.

"Just keep on joking, boy. I'll play your little game any way you want to play it. But only as long as it suits me. And I will win."

"This is no game. I'm dead serious about you."

"You're seriously ill is what you are."

"Yes. Yes, I am. I get these obsessions, you see. You're my oldest and bestest." He knelt in front of her. "All right. You win. I give up. You want my power, here." He pantomimed a knife cutting out his heart. He handed it to her in two full hands. She watched the heart, crimson, dripping, still beating wildly. She pushed it away.

"Where's the rest of it?" she asked. "That's not enough for me."

He waved a finger at her.

"What if I want it all?"

"I think a person should take what she gets."

"And if I refuse?"

He shrugged. He walked away from her, back up the cobblestones in the direction of their house.

She stood up and spied a loose brick. She picked it up and hefted it in her hands. Its corners were worn smooth and it was crumbly from wear and exposure. She could aim that brick at the back of his head, split it open, and dash out his brains right here on this levee.

He turned and gave her a seductive leer. "So. Do you want to do something, or what?"

The brick felt hot and red. She moved her hands together and felt the pieces sifting to her feet.

They spent the rest of the afternoon and the evening at the Rain or Shine Motel on Highway 61 near the bridge to Quincy. Al was gentle and attentive, Paula rough and completely unrestrained. A bite mark straddled his collarbone, and she had clawed one of his shoulder blades. The red marks across his back looked like a message in code.

"I'm not your whore, you know," she said. She was sprawled across his belly like a throw rug. He kissed the top of her head.

"Suppose they're all right at home?"

"Not much we can do about it if not."

"We've been irresponsible parents. And children."

"We'll burn in hell."

"Best just to stay here then."

"Run away: good idea."

"Not away. Just stay here. In this tacky motel. Forever. Which dresser do you want?"

She rolled away and sat up, getting dressed. "Tim wants his own room," she said.

"OK."

"We don't have any other rooms."

"OK."

"You really are a pathetic thing, you know that."

"Yes."

She sighed. "We never settle anything."

He lay spread-eagle across the bed. "You should just do what I do—give up."

She stood over him admiring his open, naked body. He looked clammy and smooth, like an oiled actor in a pornographic film. She stared at him, avoiding his eyes. She snapped her belts and fasteners, fussed with her braids.

"You're right to be afraid of me," she said.

"I hate to be telling you this ma'am, but your husband, Mr. Johnson . . ." The officer is talking. The officer, Harvey. The white county sheriff.

The man with the cotton puff hair sits across from the woman. He takes her hand. They are sitting in the parlor of the house above the river road.

"Go on," the brown man says.

"We found your husband's car. Up the river a piece. Below the river road. He must have missed a corner. Drove through the guardrail."

The woman lets the man comfort her with his hands. She does not need comforting. She looks impassively at her shoes.

"How did this happen?" the brown man asks.

"There were no witnesses."

They sit in silence. The three of them. Through the window they can hear the whispers of the crowd out on the sidewalks.

"A.B?" the woman asks. She looks up. She sees the letter on the mantle. It covers her picture.

"The car landed upside down near the river bank, ma'am. He was dead at the scene. I'm sorry, ma'am."

"Oh, Nobi." The brown man kneels by her chair. He puts his arms around her and rocks her back and forth.

The officer excuses himself and leaves a card on the table. He mumbles something about being in touch.

The man and woman rock back and forth. The man shudders and weeps. The woman pats his back. She is filling up with a bright warm light. Her skin glows. She feels alive. She can feel her throat constricting. The light fills her until she brims over and can feel the tears drip from her chin.

19

TELL ME SOMETHING ABOUT YOUR FATHER, PAULA SAYS. I ask why.

She says, "Oh, its just that your mother and I were talking about old times and she doesn't have a whole lot to say about him."

That's Paula being diplomatic. More likely what my mother does have to say about my father she won't repeat—or better still, she doesn't want to believe that my mother means that hateful stuff. I can just hear her now carrying on about the man. And I don't begrudge her her anger. They had the marriage from hell. I think of my parents as being like one of those battling situation comedy couples, except instead of fighting they said nothing at all. To me they are these old relics from another time—and not too interesting relics at that: the sort of old books and figurines you keep boxed up in the basement, not because you ever want to see them again, but because you somehow don't feel right putting them in the dumpster.

So I tell Paula there isn't much to tell about him, and she thinks I'm holding out on her. She is on this family history kick. Gleaning knowledge from the past. I've got nothing to add, and frankly I think these strolls down memory lane are morose and don't particularly do much for anybody. It's not as if these folks invented peanut butter or were the first to get to the North Pole.

Frankly, I think the most interesting thing about my father is the way he died. When he was fifty-seven years old his car went through a guardrail at a scenic overlook just north of Hannibal. The car was a 1975 Lincoln Continental, one of the designer series, a gorgeous full-powered job, green with beige leather accents. The car landed on its roof in the water, not far from the bank. All four wheels stuck out, and when I imagine this scene, I imagine them spinning the same way an upended turtle waves its legs. When the highway patrol fished the car from the river, my father was still fastened into his seat belt. He hadn't struggled and he was drowned.

So I told her that story, and she said it was tacky and lurid. She says that only a man would bring up what color the car was and the model and year. She misses the point about men like my father. It would be really important to him for people to know that when he went, he went in a sharp-looking car, and not in some piece of junk. If my father were here he would want me to tell her about his car, and to list all the assets he left for me upon his death.

They were: a grain elevator, complete with its own railroad spur, a feed and grain store—regional official distributor for all Cenex products—a small lumber yard, and a two-pump Shell franchise. And, of course, his weekly newspaper, which came with its own in-house semi-modern printing facilities. Also, his house, forty thousand dollars in certificates of deposit, bonds, a delivery truck, and assorted cash.

And he'd want me to mention he left behind the goodwill of his friends and neighbors of River Ridge and vicinity. If I neglected to list all of that he would be genuinely hurt—feel like he had gotten short shrift somehow.

Paula's mother left her a bundle, too. A big bundle she doesn't want to have anything to do with. It sits in trust some-where down in Saint Louis—gathering interest at an often astronomical rate. She calls it the boys' college fund. They ought to be able to buy the damn colleges the way that money grows. We have never been able to have a rational discussion of any kind about her inheritance, so I've given up trying. And when I joke about the things my daddy left me, she gives me this disdainful look—as if I had a two day growth of beard and snot on my face. I figure my father worked hard for his little piece and he sure wasn't ashamed to have it, and now that it's mine, I'm gonna make the most out of it.

It was my grandfather who established and built up these businesses. He expanded them and then taught my father everything he knew. All my father added was the newspaper. Daddy thought being a publisher made him respectable.

I sometimes wonder what it was like for him, growing up back in the thirties, the rich boy in town, despite the depression. It's one of the things the people around here remember about him. They said that little A. B. had whatever he wanted: a car before he was old enough to drive, lots of nice clothes, always a pocketful of money. He told me once his father wanted him to stay away from the local girls: that none of them were good enough for him and that all they wanted was his money. Some of the old ladies around here drop that in the conversation every now and then. They laugh now, though I can tell some of them are still hot about it.

When I was growing up, we had plenty too, though you'd never know it the way my mother and father lived. Except for this big house and a nice new car every year, they weren't for flashing it around. Having money was probably different in my grandfather's day. By the sixties there were more people around who had at least a little of their own, so we didn't stand out as much.

Paula, now she was a *rich* girl, but you'd never get her to admit that. She wasn't servants-and-chauffeurs rich—though I bet her mother could have afforded help if she wanted it. She was private schools, join the right clubs, and never-have-to-worry-about-a-thing rich. And while like a lot of privileged children she dresses down and manifests her share of plebeian tendencies, there's some things you just can't play down. I won't list her expertise. Let's just say she knows her way around the jewelry counter.

Neither of us had to work growing up, unlike my father. The old man who used to work for my father and grandfather, Bud Walters, told me stories about them. He told me that my father worked after school and in the summer, in the lumberyard and in the warehouse. He said that Daddy worked from the time he was eight or nine and that my grandfather did not give him a thing. Daddy toted sacks of grain on his back like a full-grown man. He loaded trucks and cut wood and did everything the adults did. There was a part of me didn't believe all that. He sure didn't have me down there slaving away when I was that age. Maybe he didn't want me to have to go through what he did. Maybe my mother wouldn't let him.

Paula has this sob story about how her mother used to make her work in the insurance office during the summer. She'll break your heart with it, too—what a slave driver her mother was and how little she got paid. We got into a really nasty fight when I asked her how hard could it have been sitting on her butt in an air-conditioned office, and when I expressed the additional opinion that what her mother really wanted was not to have her working but to keep an eye on her, the explosion really began. I almost got put out over that one, but I bet it's true. Helen kept that girl on a micro leash—heaven forbid she should try to go off on her own. Combine that with the fact that she was such a smart girl, and I don't know how she ever got away. She was the best student in the best schools in the city. The only reason she didn't put that good education to some use and end up with some fabulous career—instead of married to me up here in this outpost—is that that short leash kept her from even imagining what she could do. Damn shame. I'm the only one came out good in that deal.

In my father's house education got a lot of lip service, but not much more. My mother, she didn't go past high school, and my father, he had no great love of learning. He was a big believer in the self-made man—which is what he liked to brag that he was (forgetting the years of work his own father had done long before he was even thought of). The only books in this house belonged to me, and for my father the newspaper business was just that: a business. His only interest was in the advertising revenue and the newspaper's ability to promote his little empire and any legislation that might help it grow. He hired others to do the editorial work, and I don't even think he looked at the paper most days.

He used to tell people he'd gone to Culver-Stockton College, but I don't believe it: I think it was segregated. But even if it wasn't he didn't show any signs of formal learning. He even had a degree of some kind he showed off, but I have no idea what it was supposed to be in. I have dug through this house from top to bottom, through the archives at the newspaper and the storerooms at the warehouses, and I have found no indication that my father studied anything: not one paper or grade slip, no class photos, no textbooks. I can't even find the damn diploma.

My parents paid the kind of lip service our folks are always giving education—how you need it to pull yourself up and make something of yourself, and all that mess. It was sort of halfhearted—I never had the feeling they really meant it. Their saving grace with me was the fact that back in the sixties the little schools around here were staffed with these ancient veteran teachers who'd been in the classroom a hundred years and who knew how to make even the toughest customers learn. I wasn't that tough and I bought right in.

Paula, she worries that these boys of ours will fail to come out winners in the educational lottery. The one, that Tommy, bless his heart, he couldn't care less about some damn school. Give him a ball and a bat and he's in heaven. She's on me to talk to them, to tell them they have to bear down, and I do that and then I get that look—the one where they know you don't have the slightest idea what you're talking about, and they yawn and roll their eyes. I'd just as well be talking to the furniture. Spare me.

So she's on me to give her these stories of my father. As if I knew some. I get out this box of photos I saved and hand them to her. There are a few pictures of when he was growing up. Portraits taken at regular intervals. He was one of those people who always looked the same. I can recognize him in a picture that has five years old written across the back in thick black curlicues. He has the same raised brow on the left side, the same off-kilter, sly smile. He was on the heavy side—people who knew him are forever telling me that. You can see that in the photos: the puffy full face, the softness and the extra chins. There are other photos of him from the late 1940s and the 50s. In many photos he is propped up against one car or another. One leg is bent, the foot resting on a running board or wheel well. He wore hats back then, dressy flat-brimmed hats with wide bands, and he wore them at an angle like a gangster. His face is obscured in these old photos. His dark features can barely be seen, but I imagine he is smiling. When you can see his face, he is.

Here and there in the photos are some women. I don't recognize them, and there are no names on the backs. My mother shows up in the fifties. The cars have changed, and the clothes. He is always wrapped around her. He holds on to her like he is afraid she will get away from him. And she always looks like she is being coerced. There are a few photos of her alone. Ones he took, probably. She is posed in front of the car or the house. Her hands shade her eyes from the sun, or maybe she is waving away the flies. All of the pictures are in River Ridge. There are no pictures of them anywhere else. No Chicago, no California, no Cape Cod, no Niagara Falls.

In his entire life my father left River Ridge only two times that I know of: once to go to war, and once to go to Saint Paul—where he found my mother. I was born a little over a year after he came back with her.

Paula studies the photos as if she were trying to decipher some mystery. She asks me all these questions, which she insists I must know the answers to. I make some shit up now and then—she gets on my nerves so bad sometimes. Who are these damn people—how the hell am I supposed to know? Just some people they used to know who are or aren't around anymore. It's like she wants me to tell her that this is the man who invented linoleum and that woman is a famous jazz singer. Like she wants these pictures to be illustrations of some fabulous life, when what they really are are pictures of a man and a woman who worked hard and stayed to themselves. He left every day at seven A.M. and came back at five or later. On the weekends he tinkered with his car and washed it and polished it—he rarely drove it more than a mile. She took care of the house, and sometimes in the summer she would grow a garden. She didn't do any of the typical "mother" things. No baking or sewing or anything liked that. She kept the house clean and she liked to watch TV or listen to the radio. I tell Paula that and she looks at me like I'd killed them.

So I tell her what she really wants is the dirt, and I give her some. I tell her how my parents hardly ever spoke, except to me. And, even though back then I didn't notice how bored my mother was or how all of that hard work seemed to bring my father no joy, I tell her those things, and her eyes fill up with hurt. Then she will leave it alone for while—which makes me glad because I don't want to make it any harder. She doesn't need to know that my father was probably even more remote than I make him sound. We didn't play catch in the yard, build models in the basement, watch sports together, fly kites. He didn't show me how to fix the car, he didn't teach me how to shave. I taught myself, bloodily, with his razor. At supper time he would ask me how my day in school had gone—I expect this is what his own father had done—and I would go through my routine. I could do twenty minutes on what the teacher said and who got in trouble at lunch and how many more sit-ups I could do than anyone else. I turned over my report cards and got cash on the barrellhead for every **A**. Right there at the dinner table. They nodded and smiled. They glowed—a light came on in their eyes when they listened to me. I talked and I talked and they never interrupted, for questions or explanations, for anything. I talked and I talked and I talked. I was naive, but only a little stupid. I didn't know why I should, but I knew to keep talking. I knew to keep on talking and keep on smiling.

I got over it. I don't know how, and I don't know why this kind of story should hurt Paula more than it hurts me. It is mine, not hers.

So I offer her this.

I tell her about the long talk I had with my father the day I was leaving to go away to Mizzou.

I was so anxious to get away from here. I felt strangled by River Ridge, and I expected college to be the beginning of a whole new life for me. The week before freshman orientation I spent packing the things I was taking into a steamer trunk and two suitcases. Mother ironed everything: socks, underwear, towels. I remember she had these big mournful eyes as I packed, and I couldn't even look at her. My father was fluttering around the house much more than was normal for him. He feigned excuses to look for things in my room. He kept checking and rechecking the fluid levels on the Pinto. Then he checked the tires again. The car was brand new—my graduation present. That's another way they'd use their money—expensive gifts. Presents given out without fanfare. They drove me down to Hannibal and I picked it out. My father peeled off the money into the dealer's hand like it wasn't nothing but paper. Hundred dollar bills. I got in and drove home. Money was just something you had around, like crabgrass or teeth. I was the only thing they spent that way on. He wore the same shoes for five years, and she still dresses like a peasant woman. I carried the trunk out to the Pinto and went back in to retrieve the suitcases.

My mother lurked shyly behind doors, just invisible in the shadows beyond the picture window. They were not going with me to Columbia. I didn't ask them and they didn't volunteer. I guess none of us could see the point. Just before I left, my father asked me to come with him.

We got in his car. He was driving a big Buick then, an Electra, I think. He cranked up the air conditioner—it was hot and sticky, as it always is here in late August—and the blast of cold air was as welcome as it was shocking. We drove through town and out Miller's Farm Road. I had no idea where we were going. We didn't go places together. He didn't go places, period. We drove past Miller's place and turned into their lane. He stopped at a gate into the pasture, waved at old man Miller, out, as he often was, just looking at his land, and then we walked to the edge of the bluff. The Millers used to keep goats up there in that pasture—too much trouble to graze anything else. Now it is just a field of alfalfa. They always let people walk around up there. We walked right to the lip.

You can see the whole town from there—reduced to a

simple grid, like a checkerboard. Thirty-six squares, and out beyond, a scattering of houses here and there. The water tower looks like a mushroom from above. My class had painted the year "71" on top. The paint had already faded in the summer sun. Illinois, across the river, seemed formidable, a golden, fertile, empty, endless place. Up there you can see what an accident River Ridge is. How capricious and abandoned.

Daddy leaned back on his heels and said "Well." He stood with his hands on his hips; his big belly jutted out in front of him. His eyes roamed back and forth across the town. He had been mayor for eight years.

"There it is," he said. "Your home." He swept his hand across the town as if he were showing off a prize on a game show. He sighed.

I said I'd miss it, though I knew that wasn't true. It felt like the right thing to say at the moment.

He hunkered down and he began to spin out this story about the town. He did not look at me. His bright eyes and his words were aimed out at the thick summer air above the town.

He said, "When you look out there you might not see anything. You might think it's a dead place, a place didn't nobody care about. Could be that you don't know where you're looking. You have to really see it. It all starts right there at the base of this cliff. That's the heart, you see. And you can see how all the streets seem to be leading to that corner. Down there you can feel it, but you have to be on top of it to really appreciate it."

He said, "I know every person who lives in every one of those houses. One thousand five hundred ninety-seven souls. I know their names. I can tell you when and where they was born, I know how much money they have, where they got it, and how they spend it."

He pointed to a roof on one of the grids: "See that yellow house, two stories, middle of the block, three streets back from

Wharf. Fred and Flora Jenkins. He's forty-three, she's forty-two. She was born in town and he came over from Mexico, Missouri. He's been driving down to the cement company to work, making pretty good money. Bought himself about three hundred acres north of here. Thinking about doing a little farming one of these days. She does sewing out of the house. They never had any kids."

He asked me to pick out any house as far as I could see and told me he'd do the same thing.

"Renfros, Watsons, Simpsons, Turners, Callenders, Harrises, Gregorys, Joneses, Greens, Wahingtons, Fikes," he said, listing a sizable chunk of the families in town. He pointed his hand at their houses, and I expected lightning bolts to surge from his fingers.

He said, "That's my town down there. I don't just mean because I own that (he pointed to the grain elevator) and that (he pointed to the lumberyard) and that and that and that. I mean those are my people down there. I'm their man. They put me in charge. I'll be mayor here the rest of my life if I want to. And I think I will do just that. I like it here. I like those people down there. I like being in charge. Folks down at the county seat want to know what's up, they call me and I tell em. Need a road paved, call me, I get a road paved. Governor wants to turn out the vote up here, he calls me, I turn out the vote. Other things, too. You need to borrow against your crop, I'll lend you the seed. Shake your hand over it. Got a sick child, need a ride to the hospital, got somebody in the county jail, need a few dollars to tide you over til your check comes. I do all of that. That's how a place like this works. You can't keep no secrets around here. Can't hide out. It's the kind of place you come to because you want to know your neighbors. You stay here because what you do matters. You make a difference."

He told me they needed him around here—he was

important to them. He told me he was the person made the town what it was.

"You think about it, boy. This here is your home. I give you everything I've built. When you want it, it's yours. Don't get your head turned around out there. Lots of fancy places and flashy people. Lots of stuff calling your name. But you won't never on God's green earth find yourself in a place like River Ridge. This is it. Right here."

I remember looking out over the rooftops, and when I blurred my eyes I could see the neat geometrical squares—like a quilt—but clear-eyed, I saw that many of the roofs needed patching, and that the streets were buckled and worn. The late summer heat had baked away the life. There wasn't one living thing in sight. It was a movie set, a facade.

And I was anxious to leave. I felt one more minute in this town and I would sizzle and evaporate like a drop of sweat on the sidewalk. Whatever was here was his idea, not mine. I only half believed him anyway—his pomposity, his self-importance. Who did he think he was impressing?

He turned and walked back to the car. He did not signal me to follow him, but I did. We were quiet all the way back to the house. He'd said his last to me.

Back home, I kissed my mother good-bye. He slipped five one hundred dollar bills in my hand the same way he might slip some sort of dirty bribe to a judge, the same way he paid that car dealer. He told me to take care of myself and then drove off in his Buick. I headed in the opposite direction. I drove away from here as if a hydrogen bomb were under city hall. I did not look back, not even in the rear-view mirror.

So I told Paula that story—pretty much that way. I acted it out for her—tried to get some of my father's theatricality into it. Her eyes misted up. What is just plain peculiar to me is touching to her. That's how it is with us. Maybe it's because she never met the man. All she has is those pictures and whatever my mother told her.

"Why did he kill himself?" she asked me.

"Kill himself?" I asked her. And I remembered that that is my mother's version: what she tells herself to make it seem more dramatic and important.

My father drove up and down these river roads like a madman, like he actually did own them as opposed to just thinking he did. What happened that day was that he finally missed the curve, the one he'd slid around a thousand times in his life. And, anyway, suicide you expect from a different sort of man. Not someone like him, someone who had all the answers.

But who knew what his demons were? Not even she did.

The day after his burial my mother ran to Saint Paul where she'd originally come from and didn't come back here until just this summer.

My father's friends gathered around me and shook my hand and told me what a fine man he was. They confirmed his stories about his generosity and his influence. I made up my mind to come home. It was that simple. And here we are.

For Paula, this is not a satisfying story. In her mind there has to be some catharsis, some epiphany that causes our hero to change the course of his life. She believes in karmic intervention and genies in magic lamps.

Me, I believe things go along like they go along and you do what makes the most sense at the time. I came home and here I am still. I don't know if it was the right decision, and I frankly haven't given it a lot of thought.

My father would be pleased I took his legacy and that I've enjoyed and done well with it. I've treated his people fair and kept his good name. That would have meant a lot to him.

20

THAT MOTHER OF YOURS: SHE WAS SOMETHING, wasn't she.

I came down on the plane from Saint Paul for your wedding. Charlie offered to come with me, but I came alone. I had only been back in Minnesota a little while. I was still supposed to be . . . you might say I was still in mourning. It wouldn't have looked right. To come with Charlie, that is. So I come alone.

First time I had been on a plane. Can you believe that? Almost an old woman with a grown child getting married and I had never been on a plane. Al's daddy, A. B., he never wanted to go nowhere. You'd think if he got too far from this town for too long he would up and die. Charlie drove me out to that airport.

"Nobi," he said. "There ain't nothing to it. They do all the work. You don't have to pedal or nothing."

I had seen planes fly most of my life, but I didn't believe they really worked. They called that plane Ozark, painted green and white, and you know how they drive around before they find the spot to take off? Well, we did that for so long I thought that it was just like a big bus and we would drive all the way to Saint Louis. Of a sudden we come rolling along fast and the ground drops away like someone was pulling it. Just like that. Before you have time to even think about it. I was so nervous with the thumping and rattling and roaring and screeching. I thought at any moment the thing would just explode. I thought the wings was coming off. But I looked around and nobody seemed to mind. So I settled in. Real casual. Had me a drink. Paged through my *Jet* magazine. Before I knew it, there I was, on the ground in Saint Louis. One thing about a car—you have plenty of time to adjust to the next place. You can see it coming. But I had just walked up a chute in one place and an hour later I was walking down a chute someplace completely different. Seemed like magic. I was lost. Until I looked over and saw my Al.

There was my boy and there you were, too. He was draped all over you like a cheap fur coat. Looking all mannish, and I thought to myself, could this be the same little boy whose dirty diapers I changed? The one who busted out my screen door sliding down the banister? He was all over you, and he seemed so sure of himself. That's how I knew this marriage would be all right.

Oh, that Junior was always sure of himself. He was the one could get a pick-up game going in the park, or start an exploring club. One time he got a bunch of the little boys together and decided they were gonna walk to Hannibal. Twenty miles, whatever it is, up and down those hills. He got them together, lined them up, and off they went down the road. I didn't say nothing. Figured they'd turn around and come back when they got hot and tired. Couple of hours go by and them other mothers get on the phone asking me where their children is. Send them home for supper, they said. They knew everybody was at Junior's because Junior always had something going on. Course hadn't nobody given permission to go on no walk. Cept me. So I get in the car, drive on down to get em. There they was. Five miles out, down past where the new high school is. Just strolling along throwing rocks at rabbits. Each one had a stick and was dirty as a coal miner, and you know they didn't get that dirty just from walking. I pulled that car over, opened the door and they got in. I turned around and drove home. Nobody said nothing. That's how boys are. Get into stuff and expect Mama to save em. I have no doubt theyd've walked all the way—all night if need be—and not thought a thing of it. But Junior was forever doing stuff like that. Big plans. Impulsive. It's a good thing for the mamas of all the boys in this town that he always meant well. You know what I'm saying? Get one of them hellraisers in charge and you got a mess on your hands. Not that he didn't raise a little Cain now and then. All boys do. But I don't think he was ever spiteful for course. He always meant to do right.

Here I was, face to face with my boy first time in a long time. I felt shy of him. Almost afraid of him, and so small. I didn't know how to act. We were together at his daddy's funeral. That's where we got out of balance. Junior was organized and helpful. Even when I didn't want or need any of his help. He'd be, Oh, Mama, can I get a drink for you? Or, Why don't you just go lay down and let me get this. And all the time, of course, I couldn't have cared less about that boring old funeral and that boring old dead man in the box. It was all I could do to look like I was even interested in all that mess. People saying, "Poor thing, she's in shock." Shock my behind. I was ready to get the hell out of there. Sounds shameful, don't it? I ain't shame. If only you knew.

I remember you at that funeral. It's comical to look back at it. First time you spent any time around me and you was more afraid of me than a mouse of a cat. Sour old thing like me. Sitting up there in your little black dress and your big African hair. You didn't know what to do. I could tell you was afraid to get in there and touch my things, but all the while you couldn't wait to get your hands in my china closet. Here I didn't even have nothing real fancy like your mama. A woman knows when another woman is looking at her things, and I just might have jumped on you for pressuring me. It was my right, but, no, I wouldn't have. I told Junior right then and there that you could have it all.

Just as you two was headed back to Columbia, he said, "Mama, if you need me I'm taking Paula back to school for finals. I'll be right back to be with you." I told him to take me directly to the bus station. I said to stop fussing and take me right to the Greyhound. I was going home. He looked at me hard. I couldn't tell whether he was hurt or if he just didn't believe me or what.

"Mama, I'll be right back to help you with the house," he said.

"You do what you want with it. I don't want none of it," I told him.

"You're just upset," he said. "You come and lay down for a while." Fool boy had never seen me lay down in my life.

"I'll call me a cab then," I told him. He backed down. I don't know what he did with you, cause I didn't see you no more till that time at the airport. He put me in the car and drove me to Quincy, where the bus runs more often. All the way there he didn't say nothing to me. But I could tell he was about to explode. I don't know if he was disgusted or if he just gave up. He never said anything.

"Will you come to my wedding?" he asked me.

I nodded. I couldn't look at him. I wasn't shame. I just . . . He patted me on the hand and I got out, got on my bus, and went home.

Next time I seen him he was at that airport wrapped around you. I didn't know how we'd get along, but he was all smiles. Had a big kiss for me. It wasn't on account of seeing me he was so happy. Y'all was love drunk. In love with everything. But that's OK. I pretended like it was for me because it felt so good. We picked up my one suitcase. That big ugly pasteboard thing, tan with brown leather trim. Let's see, that was its fourth trip, counting the time Mama came up from Mississippi with it.

He slung that raggedy suitcase in the back seat of his car

and put me up in the back with it. That's how important I was on that trip. You trying to be so sweet—making small talk, asking me how my trip was. Junior, he's being a dog—feeling you all up on your leg while he's trying to drive. That was quite a show, I'll tell you.

To be honest, I was relieved when y'all turned me over to your mother. I knew she was gonna be something as soon as Junior pulled up in front of that big fine house down in the city. I lived in a good-sized house, too, but this was special. Didn't expect to see no rag opening up the door to one of these joints. I wasn't disappointed. Your mama, she looked like she spent all day at the beauty parlor, getting facials and manicures and make up. But I know that wasn't it. She had spent her whole life like that. It was second nature to her. It's just what she was. A perfect lady. She had on that gray suit and white blouse. Everything looked like it was made just to fit her. She greeted me and took both my hands. Said how pleased she was to meet me. I felt like a queen.

That was the last I saw of you and Junior. Didn't see much of you at all except for at the wedding. Cept for that one time. You remember? You got kind of short with your mother cause she was showing off her things. Excuse me for bringing that up. It stayed with me. I know you were excited about the wedding. Your mama did go on a bit—showing off this thing and that thing. You went off on her, girl. Said she was embarrassing you. You got kind of rough with her, and that was a nervous moment for me. It stuck with me.

After you did that, a funny thing happened. Helen stopped fussing so much. Over the wedding, at least. Not that there was much to fuss over. Everything was planned down to the last crossed **T**. That afternoon before the rehearsal dinner, she and I took off. I don't know where you children were. She left some secretary in charge, a tall girl with a pink sweater. We got in her car and she showed me her city.

What a funny town. She seemed to be driving out of her way to make sure every street we saw was as pretty as a picture. I wasn't that simple. I'd seen pictures. I'd been in Saint Louis once or twice over the years. I knew about all the burnt-out store fronts and all them filthy tenements. We didn't see none of that. Your mama made sure my eyes were only soothed. Down past all those big houses along the park, out through Ladue. She showed me the house just off the freeway, must have a hundred rooms in it. Told me was a wealthy old colored gentleman owned it. A doctor and inventor, and he was single. She told me not to get any ideas cause she had her eyes on him herself.

I guess she didn't know about my other arrangements.

We stopped our tour down at the Arch and she parked by that little old church. We linked arms and tottered across the grass like a couple old ladies. We held on because under the grass the ground was lumpy, like the earth had been dropped in big chunks and left to sprout. Felt like we was walking on a field of potatoes. When we reached the other side we felt like we'd really done something.

Helen walked across the big plaza. She stood underneath and swept her arm over her head.

"This is our crowning glory," she said. I wished I'd made a picture of her right there, her arms all up in the air and that silver circle framing her against the city.

I looked up and I felt my own head spin and I wanted to faint. We did not go up in that thing. We were both too scared. But we stood there staring at it for a good long time.

Then we went to lunch. You're right about your mama. She didn't go for no fancy places. We went to a Howard Johnson's by Forest Park. She'd been there a lot, I could tell, cause they knew her in there.

"For two, today," she announced when we went in, and do you know them white ladies in there hopped to it and set her up her regular place as quick as you please. Though you knew she'd been there every day, she got out her glasses and skimmed over that menu like she'd never seen it before.

"These shrimp are kind of expensive, don't you think?" she said.

"Oh, yes," I agreed, but I rolled my eyes behind my menu. Wasn't nothing on there more than $6.95. Her with that house and the most expensive things in the world. I got the message. I ordered a little salad and a dish of ice cream.

I have never been fussy about food.

Over lunch she told me about your daddy. She said they got married late in their lives, and that she regretted all the missed years. She said she knew if she could just go back and turn the right corner, ten, fifteen years earlier, she would have all of those other years with him too. She also said that despite the money he had left and the opportunities it had given her, she would have traded it all for just one more day with him. She made him sound like a very fine man. I know you don't remember him much.

She hardly asked me about my life at all. Out of respect for my mourning period, I know, but also it seemed like she trusted me somehow. Like she didn't need to hear more than she already knew.

She ate daintily, like a bird. She took small bites, seemed to savor each morsel. Just a small bowl of chowder, she had, and a dish of vanilla ice cream. I would have taken her for a woman with an appetite. I guess I was wrong about that.

We finished lunch, and before we went back to your house,

we stopped by her office. We took the elevator up and entered a hall full of frosted glass doors.

"This is The Fuller Insurance Agency," she said. Wasn't nothing I saw but a door with some gold letters on the glass, but Helen, you could tell she was proud of it all. She seemed even taller. She stood there beaming, spread her arms open wide with that purse hanging over her elbow. I could tell she expected a response.

"It's very nice," I said, and she said, "Do come in." She led me into what must have been her own office. It seemed sort of old and depressing, like it hadn't changed in forty years, same as where I used to work when I worked for the army. Them big old green filing drawers. Not one colorful thing in the place.

"I'll show you the rest of the setup after I let them know I've arrived. She pushed a buzzer and said 'I'm here.' Harsh like that, she said it. Then she pushed another button and said it again.

"Wouldn't want to catch anyone sleeping on the job," she told me. "It'd be a shame to have to turn someone out on a day we're supposed to be celebrating."

She gave them a minute to get themselves together. We looked at your father's picture while we waited. "That's my Herbert," she said. He looked like a million dollars up there—like the most important Negro in town.

We went into the next office. There were six or seven colored fellows in there and a young lady.

"Gentleman," she said. "Meet my daughter Paula's soon-to-be mother-in-law, Mrs. Johnson of River Ridge, Missouri."

I was already going by Miss Kezee by that point, but that was OK. I was never gonna see any those folks again. She introduced each man in turn, and I shook their hands. She seemed to have trouble remembering the young lady's name. They clustered around your mother and made a big fuss. She was so charming.

She laughed at each one's jokes. She joked back. One man—he looked like the oldest one there—produced a present wrapped in silver foil and white ribbons.

"For Miss Paula," he said. "From all of us. Tell her we remember her fondly." I got the feeling it was important that your mama see their present.

"Thank you all so kindly," she said. "Of course, we'll see you at the wedding tomorrow."

Every one of them men said "Of course," and though I didn't check, I bet they all showed up, too.

"If we may?" another gentleman said. He produced a bottle of champagne.

"On our special day? Why of course," your mama said. The man popped the cork and we drank champagne out of coffee mugs. Your mother took only a little and gave a toast.

"To my beautiful daughter," she said.

"Yes, ma'am," and "All right," and "Here, here," they said. We touched cups, everyone but Helen. No one touched hers. She held her mug high and nodded to each one. They made little bows to her.

Paula, I have never met a woman like your mother. I have never seen a woman treated that way. She had those people's lives in her hands. You could just tell. If she snapped her fingers, they jumped. We women don't get much of that kind of power in this world. Oh, there are few of them—Golda Meier, Indira Ghandi. Some new ones they got out there that I ain't been following. But you get round a woman like that and it's like it starts to rub off on you. Coming out of that office, I felt high as a mountain. She was regal. She was a queen, and I was one too.

It sounds funny to say that you could get close to someone so fast. I don't know that anyone could get close to your mama. Not to a cool strong woman like that. But I felt like I did. On the morning of the wedding we helped each other dress just like we were schoolgirls. Your mama came over to your room a couple of times, but I guess you weren't having none of that.

"I can never help her," she said to me.

I'd bought a dark blue dress—me supposed to be in mourning—but I had a light blue chiffon with me, too. A real pretty mother-of-the-groom number. Your mother insisted I wear it. She said, "Today is a day when there will be only joy."

"I have a good feeling about this," she said to me.

I did too. A good feeling about our children.

Did you notice . . . no you couldn't have. Your mother and I walked each other down the aisle. We did. Them usher boys walked behind us just as useless as they could be. She and I strutted ourselves down that aisle as proud as hens. We sat down together. On my side of the church.

The woman stands at the river. Alone. She feels younger now. Not alone. She is not supposed to be here. They will be waiting for her back at the house. The big house above the river. Her son. A girl. Others. They want to console her. She does not need consoling.

She takes the letter from her purse and the matches. She sets her purse on the cobblestone river bank, strikes a match, holds it to a corner of the letter. She holds the flaming paper over the water. The black-inked curlicue script crackles and shrivels away. The wind above the river carries the ashes with it. She drops the last of the scraps and they spin in and out as the water laps the old levee.

She picks up her purse, turns, and walks back toward what used to be her house.

"I already forgot," she says over her shoulder.

Paula was reclined across the end of the bed listening to her mother-in-law's story. Miss Kezee had drifted off for a minute—turned her head to the side and closed her eyes and snored lightly. She was in and out like that a lot of the time. Maybe old people did that. Maybe it was par for the course.

She couldn't remember having noticed where her mother had sat at the wedding. She had not noticed much that day at all. Miss Kezee was right: she had been love drunk, and intoxicated besides, feeling that day as if she was at the top of the tallest drop of a roller coaster. Something was going to happen, something exciting and something good.

Her mother-in-law's head jerked as she came awake. She looked around for a minute, confused. But only for a minute.

"OK, Mother?"

"You were sure gone a long time yesterday. You and Junior."

"Yes, ma'am." Paula smiled. "We have some things to work out, you know."

"Don't mean to get in your business, though you know I'm always willing to listen. Are you satisfied? You got everything under control?"

"You know how it is. There's always things to work on."

"Takes time. Takes time." She cleared her throat with a disgusting hacking sound. She rose from the bed, went to the tall dresser and began rummaging through a drawer. "We done a good job yesterday, didn't we? The boys and me. Spent the whole day. Didn't nothing catch fire. Didn't nobody get killed. Left everything where it belonged."

"Sorry we took so long. Things got . . . complicated."

"Put it out of your mind. We done good, didn't we?"

Paula nodded in agreement. "Everything was wonderful. Thank you for keeping an eye on them. What are you looking for?"

"I'll find it. It's here somewhere." She rummaged noisily

through a high drawer. A half slip floated to the floor followed by a knee sock. Paula had never seen either of them before.

"I'm doing much better, don't you think?"

"Definitely. You're settling in here, too, I can tell."

"I'll never settle here. Found it." She stopped her rummaging. She turned and faced Paula with a blue velvet box in her hand.

"I appreciate all you've done. I wanted to tell you that."

Paula waved her hand. "Nothing. I haven't done anything."

"Yes, it is too something. But enough on that. We both know what I want to talk about." She came and sat beside her. "Time to talk about my restless soul." She laughed.

"I don't think you're ready to go anywhere, Mother."

"Lord better have mercy on us, you and me. We'll go another round or two about this before it's settled. Might be few harsh words pass between us. We're strong. We can take it. This is just my opening shot."

"You been shooting since before I put you on that plane."

"All right, then. Just letting you know my intentions."

"I heard you the first time."

"So you did," Miss Kezee said. "Anyway, before the battle gets too hot . . ." She handed Paula the box. The velvet was worn smooth from handling, and the brass framing where the top and bottom met had tarnished. It had taken on the aged-pine smell of old furniture. Paula looked at her mother-in-law.

"I wanted to give you something," Miss Kezee said. "I don't have much. I was gonna go out and get you something. I set out once or twice to do just that, but I got off track."

"I know this box." Paula whispered that.

"I'm an old woman. Ain't got bread to eat. But I wanted you to have something. Go on now. Open it up."

She snapped up the lid. The jade earrings pinned into the

velvet were the shape of tear drops. "Where did you get these?" Paula gasped.

"Familiar are they? They should be. Your mama gave them to me. You probably saw her with them."

Paula trembled. Her breath came in hot spurts.

"Your mama gave them to me at your wedding. Said they weren't her kind and that she wanted me to have them. Can you imagine? Beautiful things like these. Must have cost her a pretty penny."

Paula fingered the stones. They felt the same. Delicate and just this side of too heavy. They blurred.

"She had so many nice things, your mama did. One less thing couldn't have meant much to her. I wore them all the time myself. They were Charlie's favorites. They went good with my coloring. See." Miss Kezee picked up one of the stones and held it to her ear. "See how pretty." She held the earring next to Paula's cheek. "Perfect," she said.

Paula sniffed, holding in the trembling the best she could. She shook her head. "I can't take these," she forced out.

"But I want you to have them. I don't wear much jewelry anymore. I want you to have something to remember me by."

Paula kissed Miss Kezee on the forehead. "Silly, silly thing. How could I forget you. You're not going anywhere. Not for a long time."

"You so sure, are you? Well, others have made that mistake about Xenobia Kezee. We shall see."

21

$\mathcal{P}$AULA COULDN'T REMEMBER WHETHER TO TAKE THE Kingshighway exit or North Florissant exit to get to the cemetery. She never spent much time in that part of Saint Louis. Their kind of people didn't live there anymore. That's what her mother would have said. Funny that her mother should be spending eternity here now. She remembered hearing somewhere that this cemetery had once been white only. There would be many unhappy dead people here besides her mother.

She had wakened the boys early and told them they would be going on a little trip. She'd left Al at home with his mother. She would be fine on her own, but there was no telling. At a moment's notice she could regress back to any of her previous states. Old people had as many ways as cats had lives. They changed moods the way some people changed clothes. For all she knew, right now Miss Kezee was chasing her son around the house with a pistol. Or perhaps she had him down in the parlor, charming him with stories about his long dead ancestors. Most likely she was up in her room, sitting in the rocker, in front of the TV, and Al was downstairs typing, reading, pacing, brooding, the distance between mother and son fixed. Neither of them cared to have it otherwise. She was angry and sad to think about it.

Al was in seclusion. He and Walter had spent two fruitless days figuring some way around the coin toss. There was none. Poor man. Despite his seeming recklessness, he was not the sort who ever really liked to leave anything to chance. He only played when the odds were tipped to his advantage. He'd pass on even odds every time.

During breakfast he had sighed and stared wistfully out the window. He was begging her to ask him about it, but she wouldn't give him the satisfaction. She got her boys together, packed a picnic lunch, and dug around a filing cabinet for a map to her mother's burial plot. From the kitchen table he followed her with pathetic, almost hungry eyes. She handed the lunch bag to Tommy and told the boys to go wait in the car. She plopped herself down hard on his lap.

"Ouch," he said.

"So?"

He sighed.

"And so what are you gonna do with yourself all day, little boy?"

"Are you sure you're coming back?" he whined.

"Give me one good reason why I should?"

"I got your reason right here." He kissed her neck and felt under her blouse. "Will you bring me a present?"

"Don't hold your breath."

"Only til you come back. Are you sure you want to do this?" She nodded.

"I'll come with you if you want."

"Already got two men. Couple of strong fighting types. Real good-looking men, too."

"Where'd you find them?"

"Right here in the neighborhood where I find all my men." She kissed him on the forehead and then rubbed away the mark. "Gotta go." She gathered her purse, keys, the map. She turned back to Al. "About tomorrow . . ."

He shifted his weight and diverted his eyes.

"I know: you don't want to discuss this with me," she mocked him. "That's only true when you want it to be true.

Right now, I got something to say, so you might as well listen up."

He glared at her, harrumphed.

It was her turn to shrug. "Be a big boy and take your medicine."

He made to get up.

"What are you gonna do, plug your ears and hum? You might as well sit there. I will talk and you will listen. Now, later. I got time."

"Means so much to you, go ahead."

"I don't need your permission. You see, I finally cut through the bullshit. You and this political thing. For you it's just a mind game. Moving around lines on a map, changing numbers in a book, going on and on and on about your ideas and your schemes and your plans. I got big news: there's real people out here. That's something you'd rather not sully your hands with. I know it for a fact, because if you did, you'd be dealing with the real folks right here under this roof. Your mother. Your sons. That's the stuff you *really* don't want to discuss with me, but your good thing just came to an end. I won't be your one-woman department of domestic affairs. After today, no more free rides."

He stared at her, a cross look on his face. "That's it, then? That little pop psychological snapshot."

"You are so cute when you're obtuse." She pinched his cheek and he swatted her hand away. "Listen up: You and me are up at the front line these days. Pretty soon there'll be no one left to hold our hands and tell us it'll be OK. Nobody's gonna fix anything for anybody anymore. Except you and me."

"Grown-up time at last, eh," he said, leaned into a door jamb, rubbing at his chin. "Any other day-brighteners before you go?"

Mocking his pose, she crossed her arms and widened her stance and put on a crooked smile. "Two more things. First: I hope you lose. You want to know why?" She waited for a response.

He shrugged.

"Coward. I wasn't gonna tell you anyway."

"That must be the other thing."

"It should be, but, it's this: I hope you get whatever you want. I want only the best for you." She left the room and started up the staircase.

"Smart girl like you must know that's contradictory," he shouted after her.

The multiple panels of drapery obscured the light from outside. She pulled back a layer and the room took on a faint pink glow.

"You awake, Mother? It's morning."

Miss Kezee snored lightly.

"That's OK. You sleep in. No harm in a good sleep-in." She smoothed the comforter over her. She saw that the water pitcher was low and filled it at the bathroom tap. Al was standing at the bottom of the steps wearing his pajama bottoms. His open robe revealed his broad bare chest. He was staring up at her, so she waved at him.

She set the replenished pitcher on the nightstand, felt Miss Kezee's brow. "Stubborn old woman. Think you're gonna tell somebody what to do. Ha! You got another think coming." Her forehead felt warm. Her temperature was hard to keep down, but the doctor said to expect that. Keep her quiet, he said. Force those fluids. "You are not going anywhere, my dear. No walking trips, no nursing home. No Saint Paul. Not for a long time. You're staying right here, you understand me?"

Miss Kezee continued her snoring. It sounded like sandpaper against wood.

"Long as we're clear. You belong right here."

Al was still waiting at the bottom of the steps. "Hope I lose, huh?" He had his hands on his hips.

She patted his flat brown stomach. "The best for you. Only the best."

The boys had been good most of the time in the car. By the time they reached Saint Charles they had eaten the food she had packed for the day. Two sandwiches each, all the chips, and everything else but the fruit. That was OK. They could stop for burgers afterwards. Eating had always been some sort of competitive thing, a long-standing part of their feud, even before full-scale war was declared. Tommy was the aggressor. If Tim took a cookie, Tommy took two, then Tim two more, and so on until the whole bag was gone. They could go through two pounds of Chips Ahoy in five minutes. Given enough food they would eat themselves to death.

"There had better not be one crumb on that seat," she had said as they approached Highway 70.

Saying so almost caused the only trouble she had. A stray Baggie became a featherweight football in a game of pass the blame. It threatened to explode into a riot until she swerved the car wildly from shoulder to shoulder. She alternately braked and accelerated, made shrieking noises so that it seemed that she had actually lost control of the car. A Honda honked and veered out of her way. She screamed and shrieked, zoomed the van into the gravel parking lot of an abandoned fireworks stand. She braked sharply and rocks spewed from behind. She jumped out and ran in front of the van, and facing them through the windshield, she bent over and screamed some more, pulling at her hair and pounding her arms at her sides. She screamed until her throat hurt and she had trouble getting her breath.

When she turned from the car to catch her wind, she saw that an older white couple was watching her from a vegetable stand at the end of the lot. She waved at them primly, straightened her clothes and returned to the van, pulling onto the road quickly.

What those people must be thinking. What all white people thought, of course, and now it was confirmed: we are crazy.

She saw in the rearview mirror the boys frozen into their individual bucket seats. They were melting slowly now, from their rigid seat-clutching horror, collapsing against the head rests, their faces gone from panic to awe to disgust.

When Paula looked again Tim had crossed his arms, enraged, a hard look of defiance on his face.

"Really, Mother," he said. "That was so embarrassing."

"Really," Tommy seconded.

"Those people were looking right at us."

"They probably took down our license plate number." Tommy shuddered and cringed.

"Sorrreeee," she said. What a couple of fussy old fogies they were. Even in his immaturity, Tommy played by the rules. His clutter was structured clutter. His silver Transformer only sputtered when it flew, never when it rolled, and the G.I. Joe Jeeps were designed only to climb bodies or steps, but never furniture. And, even more rigid, Tim begrudged Tommy every bit of his constricted fun.

"You boys need to lighten up," she said. She felt like a hypocrite: after all, where had they learned to be such tight-asses? From her and Al.

Maybe.

"Let's all try to take it a little easier," she added as an afterthought.

She followed the map to a rise in a newer part of the cemetery, near a rear entrance. She vaguely remembered the hill, the view of the city off to the southwest.

"Here it is," she said. She directed the boys to a wide, pewter-colored marble headstone. Plain, double-arched. Tasteful, of course. Her father's name on the left, her mother's on the right. Two doves, heads intertwined, crowned the stone in raised relief. She had never seen her mother's name on the stone. Mr. Wade, the funeral director, had sent her a picture that she had somewhere. She ran her fingers across the letters. Their roughness contrasted with the polished surface of the background.

"This is it," she said.

The boys stood back reverently, close to the drive, arms clasped behind their backs with their father's wide stance. They looked festive in loud summer clothes—bright Hawaiian-print shirts, tank tops, baggy white shorts. The clothes in no way matched the solemnity of their expressions.

"Come closer," she ordered. In tandem they sauntered forward. Though the ground had long since settled, and in neither case had it begun to subside, the boys seemed to sense the outline of the graves. They kept a corresponding distance.

Paula sat and rested one shoulder against the cold marble. The sun, high in the sky to the south, had not heated this side of the stone.

"Are you supposed to do that?" Tim asked.

"Don't see anyone around here to stop me. Except you two. Come and get comfortable."

"This place is creepy," Tommy said, shuddering visibly. He dropped to his haunches, still six feet from the headstone.

"Oh, come on. You guys go play in that River Ridge cemetery all the time."

"Not all the time," Tommy said. "Only when there isn't a moon. And you have to make sure you carry a cross and a lucky charm."

Tim rolled his eyes. He walked around in a wide circle behind the stone. "You said we were visiting relatives," he sneered.

"These are my relatives. These are my parents. Herbert and Helen Fuller."

"Gross," he said. He wandered the row, looking at some of the other names.

Paula squared her back against the stone and drew her knees up. The coolness of the marble seeped through her blouse, and she became aware of an interruption at her mid-back. Part of the inscription—the dates, perhaps. Tim paced up and down the row of graves, but never further than fifty yards or so down the rise. He was tense and skittery; he skirted the stones widely as he squinted to read the names. Faithfully, Tommy squatted at the foot of her father's grave, off-handedly waving the gnats from his eyes.

"So, did we know these guys, or what?"

"You saw Mother a couple of times when you were little."

Tim circled from behind a grave on her left. "What is it lately with these relatives. First we don't have any and now here they come, out of nowhere."

"We always had them. You lose track sometimes."

"Like Grandma," Tim went on. "Here she comes all of the sudden. What's the story on her? She gonna be here forever?"

"Until she gets better. And for as long as she wants after that. Yes, forever, if she wants.

"She won't live forever. Everyone in the family is going to have to adjust, and it won't always be easy. But, really, it won't be bad if we can get it together."

"Great." He picked up a stick and threw it.

"Better tell him, Mom," Tommy warned. "You shouldn't throw things in the cemetery. It's bad luck."

"Shut up."

"Gentlemen . . ."

Tommy scooched up closer to his mother. She put out her arm and gathered him in by the headstone.

"Hey you," she called to Tim. "Land somewhere."

He appeared over the top of the stone and Tommy

jumped. He was dribbling pieces of grass and dried leaves on their heads.

"Scared you," he taunted.

"Grow up," she said, holding onto Tommy, just in case. "You: sit down somewhere. Somewhere where we can keep an eye on you." He went and sat in Tommy's former place at the end of her father's plot.

"Are we gonna stay here all day long?"

"Yeah, you said we could go to the mall."

"A little while. For me, OK?"

"Are you sad, mom?" Tim asked.

"It was her mom and dad."

"I know that, fathead."

"Sad isn't really the word, though that's part of what I feel. I also feel everything else I ever felt about them, too. That might not make sense, I know. And it's not like they are really here in this place. I mean, we know what's left here is just whatever is left of their bodies."

"Yuck," both boys squirmed.

"Come on, guys. If you think that's the part that gets you— the moldy old skeletons—you've been watching too many zombie movies."

"Can any of it get you?" Tommy asked, wide-eyed. Tim shook his head in disgust.

"Well," Paula said. "There was a time I'd've been quick to say 'no,' but now . . ."

Tim jumped up. "Here comes one over the hill."

Tommy started, moved even closer to Paula, relaxed when he saw his brother laughing.

"Sit your fool self down," she said.

"Gotcha again."

"And if they were to come, what makes you think they'd mess with some demons like you? Huh?"

Tommy turned and fingered the numbers on her father's inscription. "1962," he said.

"A long time ago."

"You remember him?"

"Not hardly at all. I was just a little girl when he died."

"And let's see: 1984. Say, where's the place for you on here?"

"You can put your daddy and me in shoeboxes in the backyard. That would be just fine."

"With Yertle," the boys said together. Yertle: one of a series of pre-salmonella-ban box turtles, none of which had ever lasted longer than a few weeks.

"I don't think you'll fit in a shoe box, mom," Tommy said.

"Sure I will. We'll use one of yours. With those big feets you got, I won't even need to go on a diet."

"1984," said Tim. "So, what about her? What was she like? Was she like you?"

"I wouldn't say that. But she was something else."

22

ℐ GUESS YOU MIGHT SAY I WAS KIND OF DIFFICULT WHEN I was growing up. I wasn't a bad girl. I didn't do things like drink and run around with a lot of different boys. I never stayed out all night. I was willful, though. I could be contrary. If Mother said black, I said white. If Mother salted the food, I said it was too salty. If she didn't salt it, I'd say it was bland. The thing is, I wasn't doing it just to be annoying. A lot of times we just didn't agree.

She was an extremely picky person. Everything had to be done her way. I don't think I ever got to pick my own clothes, not until I was in high school. By then we had to wear uniforms, and still she always had a comment. The skirt is too short. It hangs funny on you. Don't wear those socks with that. It was a long time before I could defy her and go my own way. It was hard. If you didn't go along with her plans, her feelings were hurt. It got to where I didn't care.

I went to a rather exclusive high school, here in the city. A Catholic girl's school: Rosati Kane. We weren't Catholic, but it was a very good school. They worked us hard all the time. A lot of wealthy girls went there. Their parents drove them in from all over the area because it was such a good program. There were poor girls there, too, on scholarship, but everybody treated everybody pretty fair, really. I mean we knew that you had to be pretty smart to have gotten in, and you had to work hard to stay. It was competitive. We looked down on girls who weren't smart enough to get in and on girls who flunked out. Me too, I think. I was kind of snobbish that way. Somehow around those smart people it seemed OK.

I did everything there: I went to three or four clubs, and I was in all the plays. I even went to the senior prom, even though I wasn't going out with anybody at the time. Everybody was going so I asked my friend, Steve. You boys remember him? He and his friend came to visit us last year. He was my buddy, so I asked him if he would escort me. He said "Yes." He came all the way from D.C. during his finals. That's what a friend'll do for you.

Now, this prom stuff really wasn't my thing. Us smart girls, we didn't go in for a lot of girl stuff, but I'd gotten myself into it. I had the date. I just had to get ready. I didn't have any idea what to do. I turned to the expert: Helen Thomas Fuller. I asked her to help me get ready for the prom.

Her eyes lit up. She wrapped her arms around me, almost killed me in a bear hug. You'd think I'd asked *her* to the prom.

She didn't do anything halfway. Over spring vacation she closed the office and flew me to Chicago to buy my dress and shoes and bag. We went up on Michigan Avenue, the big shopping street up there. We spent two days going from store to store—from Marshall Field's to Carson's to these little boutiques.

If I tried on one dress, I tried on one hundred. That is no exaggeration. I had very little fashion sense: the dresses all looked good to me. We went to a shop called "Nina's Place." Nothing but fancy dresses. A woman sat Mother down and got her a cup of coffee. "We'll look at the pinks and the blacks," Mother said. The woman—she must have been Nina—said "Very well, Mrs. Fuller." She took me to the dressing room and got to work. She had whole racks of pink and black dresses, just my size, too. I swear, every dress I came out in Mother said was

"Not quite right." She wanted this one a little narrower in the skirt and that one with a lower back. Nina kept whipping them out. She had everything back there.

"Let's see it with a bow." "Put the bow on the side." "Does it come with a sequined bodice?"

I would have worn any of those dresses. They were all the same to me. But Mother had ideas of her own.

"A girl like you needs something beautiful, but simple. We don't want to draw attention from your face."

There was one dress that I actually kind of liked. A strapless hot pink with a slit up the side. It was a happening dress.

"Absolutely not," Mother said. No daughter of hers was going out dressed up like a Las Vegas showgirl. No way. She told that Nina that as far as she was concerned, pink still meant pink, nothing hotter than strawberry ice cream, and when she got answered back—woman tried to tell her about the latest style and all that—you better believe we got out of that store. Mother didn't take back talk from sales help.

Later that day we finally settled on a very simple black dress with a wide silver belt at the waist. After all that trouble and all that work it was the most basic dress in the world. I wanted to say something about the fact that it was so plain, but before I could, she cut me off.

"Wait till you see what we do with this. You'll love it."

I hoped she was right.

We bought black pumps at Marshall Field's. A small square purse, too. So far there was nothing to die over. I had to say something. Cautiously, of course. You had to be careful with Mother. She heard any criticism as ingratitude, pure and simple.

"That isn't too ordinary?" I asked her. I waited until we were on the plane coming home, waited till she had a chance to relax and get herself something to drink.

"I'm not finished," she said. I asked her what she was going to do, but she just told me I'd have to wait. She wouldn't budge an inch.

The week before the prom I noticed her eyeing me a lot. Every time I looked up, there she'd be, staring at me. Staring at the top of my head, really. I knew what her problem was, but I asked her anyway. She came up behind me and started pulling through my hair with her fingers.

"A damn shame," she said.

"Not this again," I warned her. We had been at a stand-off about my hair, she and I, for over a year. I had cut it the way I liked it, in a big blown-out afro. It was out to here. Mother knew better than to start in with me about it. I had it cut without her consent, and it wasn't up for discussion. She hated that hair. She never said so to my face, but she didn't miss an opportunity to get her digs in. One time we were driving through Forest Park and she saw a sister with hair even bigger than mine. "Look at Gertie over there," Mother said. "Hair looks like a rat's nest." Then she gave me a sly dirty look. She had a hundred ways to let you know how she felt.

So she's standing there picking at my hair. God, I hated that. I wanted her to stop. I asked her what she thought she was doing.

"What a shame all your lovely hair is gone," she said. "I think I've got an idea."

I thought, God help me. I told her to get her hands out of my hair and get the idea out of her head. She told me to play along. Told me I just might like it. I told her I'd play along with anything that didn't involve grease and a pressing comb.

She told me to trust her. "I've never been wrong before," she said.

I don't know, by that point I was just exhausted with all the preparations. I just let her take over the whole thing.

After school on Friday she took me to a beauty shop downtown. Took me over to a guy she called Mr. Geoffrey. Well, first of all, that was new to me: a man hairdresser. Before I cut it off, Mother had always fixed my hair. Or we went to a woman on the south side who used to do us both down in her basement.

Mr. Geoffrey was about six feet five and as thin as a two by four. Mother whispered something in his ear, pointed to a picture in Ebony, and right away it was, "Yes, Mrs. Fuller," "Of course, Mrs. Fuller," and all this giggling behind his hand. To this day I have never seen anything like the way service people would cater to Mother.

She didn't bother telling me what she had in mind. She went away and Mr. Geoffrey got to work. What seemed like an hour later, after a lot of clipping and washing and more clipping, he spun me around and said, "There. See."

My hair was as short as yours is. Can you believe that? Shorter, maybe.

Behind me, in the mirror, Geoffrey and Mother were carrying on, saying things like "Tres chic" and "Foxy." I was stunned. I didn't know whether to laugh or to scream. I looked so different. And I felt I had been . . . violated.

"Don't you just love it," Mother kept saying. "It is perfect for her. Just perfect."

I got up and walked out. I didn't speak to her for the rest of the day.

The next morning—the morning of the prom—Mother was waiting for me at the breakfast table. I knew she was hurt because I had acted so badly at the salon, but I didn't care. I knew she wouldn't say anything. She was too proud. She sat and stared at me. I hate that, don't you? When someone sits and stares at you. A little smile came over her face. It drove me crazy. I snapped.

"All right. Just say it," I said. "Whatever you're thinking, just say it."

Her smile got even bigger and she started shaking her head.

"You won't trust me," she said. "You won't ever trust me. I wasn't born out in some alley. I know things. I've been around. I know what I'm doing."

"I look like a boy," I whined, though I didn't really believe it. I'd gotten over the shock and I knew I looked OK. Shoot, I looked good. Better than ever.

She crossed her arms and smirked at me. Like all mind readers, she could see right through me.

"No one will ever mistake you for a boy, my dear," she said, . . . think that's funny, do you? I never thought she was funny back then, but now I know I was wrong. She was always saying sarcastic stuff. Stuff I know now that she thought was funny. Back then, it always got on my nerves. She was forever criticizing the way people looked and the way people talked. I always thought she was criticizing me. A lot of the time I think she was. But, I don't know . . .

That night, after she'd gotten me into the dress and arranged what was left of my hair so it was as good as Mr. Geoffrey had it, she took me to her room and sat me down at her dressing table. Now, in the first place, my mother's room was off-limits. She never told me, like your dad and I tell you guys to stay out of our stuff, but it was as if that room had a force field around it. I knew I wasn't to go in there, and the funny thing was, I never wanted to.

She went into her closet and came out with a gorgeous brown box, the size of a small TV set—you've seen it. I have it in my room now. It's mahogany, and back then it looked like she polished it every day.

"Here they are," she said. She pulled from the box three pieces: a silver necklace inlaid with pieces of turquoise, and earrings to match.

Well, anyway, she put the necklace on me and then snapped on the earrings. She sprayed me from her bottle of

"Joy"—very expensive stuff, I must tell you. She said my father gave it to her.

She walked me over to her closet. She had a three-way mirror in her room, right there in the closet, just like in Famous Barr. She spun me around twice. I couldn't believe it. It was like a different dress. It was like a different me.

She was behind me, and we stood there together for a very long time. She clutching my shoulders. Her eyes filling up with tears. It was the first time in my life that I got it. The first time that I actually understood what all of the shopping and primping and fixing up garbage that other girls did was about. It was about the girl in the mirror. I put my hands on my hips and winked at myself. I was that fine.

In that mirror was also the only time I think I had ever seen my mother and me together. I can still see her there. By me, behind me.

"You have to trust me," Mother said. She stepped away and let me have the mirror to myself. But I turned and looked at her. We didn't say anything.

That was as close as we got, the two of us. Whatever else, I know for that one minute I was everything she wanted me to be. And it didn't make me unhappy. I looked at her and wanted to tell her "Thank you." And "I love you." But we didn't do that sort of thing, she and I.

Still I needed to do something for her, something to tell her how I felt. I could only figure on buying her something. I knew she liked nice things but it was impossible to please her. I spent a whole day at Northwest Plaza looking at everything, trying to decide what to get her. I looked at crystal and silver and linen and clothes and candles and knickknacks and furniture. She had already bought herself everything on earth. I ended the day in the jewelry store, desperate. I never wore much jewelry and neither did she. I was looking in the earring case when I saw them. I thought they were perfect for her. Little jade teardrops. I spent quite a bit. Over a hundred dollars. I gave them to her one night after supper. "For helping me so much last week," I said. I couldn't even say "Thank you" then. She took the box from me and opened it. She did not look up at me. She just sat and looked at them for the longest time. She was crying. In a minute, she excused herself and went to her room.

I don't know if she ever wore them. Here they are. See. You can touch them if you like. Aren't they pretty? Perfect for me. They found their way back to me. I think she knew they would.

You know, I love you guys. Mother and I never said that to each other. We didn't always treat each other very well. Sometimes—a lot of times—she drove me absolutely crazy. That doesn't mean I didn't love her.

I want us to do better. She would expect that, just like she expects me to be here, paying my respects and telling you stories about her.

I agree with her. I think you should know about your people. We wouldn't be here if it wasn't for them. I don't know everything about them, but I know some things.

Now, Daddy, I hardly remember, but Mother talked about him all the time. She said he . . .

23

$\mathcal{H}$ERE, FROM THE FRONT ROOM OF THE HOUSE MY grandfather built, out the picture window, down a hill through the woods, you can see the Mississippi River. I have never taken it for granted and have always been surprised to see it there. Sometimes I gasp when I see it: what is that thing? Often I just sit and watch the water. I don't know why.

My mother is asleep upstairs. Or awake watching TV. I have not checked on her and I probably won't. She is fine. If I fuss over her—tuck in her bed or bring her something to drink—she acts as if she'd rather I didn't. So I won't.

It's quiet here in the house, and I quite like it. A big old house like this has done most of its settling, and the only noises are the ticking of clocks and the quiet hum of the refrigerator. Paula wanted to know what I was doing with myself today. The usual, I told her. Check in at the store and the paper and what have you. We of "the owner class"—as Walter calls me—spend most of our time driving here and there to look at our things and make sure they are still where we left them. So I did that, and everything is in its place, doing what it's supposed to be doing.

So I sit. And think.

Paula says it is a crazy thing about me—sitting and thinking. She will stand in front of me and snap her fingers and do the old "Earth to Al" routine. She accuses me of being a thousand miles away.

She's off today visiting her mother in the cemetery in Saint Louis. How crazy is that? A woman she fought her whole life to get away from. Crazy and silly and morbid, but she is like that—prone to weirdness. On the surface she seems normal, but really she believes in good luck charms and Santa Claus and miracles. That's why I love her. She likes to pretend like she's sane, but she guards her eyes when a black cat approaches, changes her stride to adjust to the cracks in the sidewalk. But she wouldn't give me credit for noticing.

She says to me, "I hope you lose," and then, "I hope you get whatever you want." Cryptic, riddlely shit like that. She wants me to lose because I closed her out of the election, and she wants me to have whatever I want so she can have it both ways. That's how she'd like the game to be played: with all the cards in her deck, and her the dealer and the rulemaker, too. She is brilliant, but sometimes there is a loose wire.

Once, going to the Muny in Forest Park, she made me drive all the way around the park to avoid Hampton Avenue. "I don't like that street," she said. I didn't ask her why. Could she possibly have a rational reason?

She believes if we read our boys the right kinds of books, feed them properly, speak softly and smile, they will turn into decent men. And, of course, be protected from the shitload of superstitions she carries charms against.

I say feed em and give em a warm place to sleep and they'll be whatever they want to be. So far so good. There are better kids out there, I guess, but many many worse ones. I don't expect they'll become ax murderers or thieves. If they do, I'll feel bad, but I won't take it personally. Those sobbing courtroom parents: those people are pathetic. I'll get em a good lawyer—because that's how the system works—and I'll wish em good luck. That's about it.

Maybe I'll grow sentimental in my old age.

I do care about them, even though she thinks I don't. If I thought there was something I could say or some button I could push—something I could do to make their lives turn out perfect, I'd do it in a flash, without a second thought. But I don't believe in such buttons, and there are no magic words. It's them against the cards. You play what's dealt you and you draw from the top of the deck. Straight up and no do-overs, and so be it. The Johnsons have always played a good strong game.

Soon they'll be grown up and gone. I imagine they will both move away. It's a quiet place and too small probably for those two: they'd go crazy if they stayed. They still seem so pre-formed to me. I try to imagine their lives, and what I see are those baby calendars with the infants wearing firemen's hats and baseball mitts. So much will happen to them in the next several years.

Who knows, maybe they will be firemen or baseball stars. Or maybe they'll get some of those consulting jobs where you make nothing but paperwork. They could live in fancy reno-vated townhouses in an area of Saint Louis their mother knows to be dangerous. Or be Air Force pilots—I can see Tommy as one of those guys. He'd shave his head and embrace obnoxious right-wing ideologies about spreading the American way to the unenlightened. He'd come home for the holidays and we would have these monstrous screaming fights while the turkey gets cold. Paula will put her foot down and insist that we have a civ-ilized meal for once, so after supper just us men will sneak down to the tavern and continue the fight over some beers. I will wonder how someone like him came to be a member of this family.

They could be the types who live in three-bedroom brick ranch-style homes in sprawling suburbs with good schools. Barbecue on the weekends and gossip over the back fence. They may carpool. They'll get degrees and licenses and certificates and endorsements and mortgages, have marriages and jealousies and affairs and successes and failures.

But they won't stay in River Ridge.

Paula and me, I think down the line we'll have to get us a project of some kind. We'll start a candy factory, get our own husband-and-wife TV ministry. The reverend Al and P.D. I'll preach the gospel of money, and Paula will review for America her mother's prescriptions for the good life: brush twice a day, don't invite strangers into your home, keep a hanky handy just in case.

We'll get us one of those big campers and travel around the country to the national parks and other such tourist traps. We'll put on one of those bumper stickers that brag as to how we are squandering our children's inheritance. When we pull up in front of our sons' houses they will die of embarrassment. We will kidnap the grandkids, spend lavishly, produce erotic home videos, become circus clowns.

We'll probably stay right here and run these raggedy old businesses right into the ground. Despite me, they seem to self-perpetuate in their own marginal way. As we keep saying to each other, we aren't getting rich, but we are . . . comfortable.

Paula tells me to focus. Says that she—we—need me to be present. Can I help it if my mind goes from one thing to the next?

Here it goes to the election. The coin toss.

Tomorrow. City hall. 12:00 noon. Heads, I am the mayor. Tails, I am not.

It's fucked.

Still, as much as I don't like it, I am a fatalist, too. Like my father. What is going to happen is going to happen. We might as well get on for the ride.

If I had gone to the library instead of the bookstore I would have missed Paula. My father went to Saint Paul instead of

Memphis and he met my mother. Take a different route, leave a little later, look the other way: there are infinite possibilities in every life every day.

Everything might as well turn on a damn coin toss. Though it's not often this . . . literal.

Heads or tails, things will be different tomorrow night, and Paula says, therefore, we will be dealing with a whole bunch of shit on her list.

Bring it on, I say. What can I do besides take what comes? I'll do what I can and I'll do what I want.

"I need you to be more present," she says, and so I will try to be. Paula and these boys, they are my rocks, my anchors—without them I'd be off in space, doing God knows what. I'd be one of those men in the movies who drifts from town to town and gets into things with the locals before he moves on. I'd freelance.

And I'd like that. I would like to be freer, too.

Some days.

Some days, too, I feel like I am some new kind of being, something that has found its way here and is trying to figure out the game. I'm out here in the middle of America, a vast and open and confusing place. If there are rules, no one has bothered to tell me about them. And there's this Paula. She claims to know a thing or two. So I have to trust her, I guess.

Tomorrow I'll stand up by that judge with my wife and my kids at my side. I'll shake hands with everyone, be an all-around good sport. I'll smile and be generally brave and pleasant, and when that coin flies through the air, I promise I will not flinch.

And afterwards I will try to be more present.

If only they'll tell me what in the hell that's supposed to mean.

24

$\mathcal{M}$ISS KEZEE HAD STUBBORNLY SETTLED ON HER BLUE dress—the old-ladyish one that she always wore and that hung on her like a rag and that Paula hated. Arguing was pointless: Paula gathered the dress over her head and fastened the back.

"There," she said. "I still think the pink would be better."

"Did I ask you?"

Paula threw up her hands, turned and fussed with her own braids in the mirror.

"You rushing like you in a hurry," Miss Kezee said.

"Al wants us there at four. Wants 'the whole crew there,' he says. He took the boys with him."

"We got time. Sit a spell."

Paula flopped down in the rocker the same way one of her boys would. She thought she heard a snap—didn't know if she'd prefer it were the old chair or one of her bones. She picked up the *TV Guide*, flipped through its pages. Then the *Essence*, then the *McCall's*. She eyed her mother-in-law, sitting, knees to the side on the window seat, peering through the draperies.

"I'm gonna ask you something, Mother. Promise you won't go off on me."

Miss Kezee laughed. "I don't make those kinds of promises, girl. You oughta know by now. I'll go off whenever I feel like it."

She flipped through a few more pages of the magazine.

"Go on then," Miss Kezee prompted.

"All right." She closed the magazine and leaned forward on the rocker. "Why are you so anxious to get away from us? Tell me why you won't stay here with your family."

"Ooh wee, you are looking to get burned today." She laughed, and Paula averted her eyes.

"Forget it, then," Paula said.

"I intend to forget whatever I don't want to be bothered with. Let me set you straight on a few things. The first bit a smart girl like you ought have figured out by now. What I'm doing don't have nothing to do with you all. See me: this seventy-five-year-old woman sitting here?"

"How could you be only seventy-five if . . ."

"Getting awful close to that fire today, aren't you. This woman you see here, me: I got my own home. I like living in it. Got a home and a life, such as it is. There's nothing more to it."

"And this house?"

". . . is your house. Look around here. Look at everything you got: floors and ceilings and all the beautiful things in be--tween. Doesn't matter who made it or whose it used to be. It's yours now. My being here don't change that. No, I will not tell you what makes me want to get out of here. Why? Because I'm the only one left who knows and my time in this life is almost over. If I tell you, the story lives on and I don't want that. I want the sorry mess gone forever."

"Things were that bad?"

"A lot worse things happen to people every day all over the world. Big evil things. A person'd go crazy thinking on the badness in this world. You know we been blessed, don't you?"

"Yes, ma'am."

"There's all that big evil in the world, but then there's little evil too. Little nasty things people do to each other. The lies and thefts and all the spiteful things folks do. In their own way they're just as bad. Come from the same source. I got me a package so big. As my gift to the world I'm taking it with me when I go."

"You're a tease," Paula said. She cranked the rocker back and forth and riffled through some pages.

"Think so? Just keep trying me, then . . . sit still, girl. You ain't sat still for a second all day. What's the matter with you? You nervous?"

Paula swept the pile of magazines from her lap, got up and flopped on the bed. "It's this . . . chess game your son and I been having. Well into its second decade."

"Playing games, are you? You acting like a woman about to lose."

"My mother didn't raise a loser. I got my eye on the next move. Whichever way it goes today, I got him. Just wish I knew how that coin was going to land."

"It'll come out one way or another, I suspect."

Paula rolled her eyes. Full of pointless homilies, as usual— garbage that on television passed for council from a wise old sage, but in real life, sounded like the pablum it was. She wasn't sure this was an old person's thing. Maybe they all spouted homespun sayings and cryptic wisdom. She didn't know. Miss Kezee was her only old person thus far in life.

"Yeah," Paula said. "I guess it will come out one way or another."

"Always does," Miss Kezee punctuated. Always with the last word, she.

"Y'all was gone a long time yesterday. Left me and Junior here alone."

"I wanted to spend some time with my boys."

"Uh huh."

"We went down to Saint Louis. I showed them around a bit."

"You have a good day? Do all you set out to do?"

"It went very well," she said. And it had. She didn't expect miracles, knew not to look for changes overnight. They had taken the opening step down a long, long road. She didn't know where that road came out, but so far . . .

"That's a nice town, Saint Louis. Not like Saint Paul, but it's nice enough. I'll have to get me back there one of these days."

"I'll take you. We'll make a day out of it."

"I'll see how it fits into my plans."

Paula shook her head. She was up against the master.

"Let's go. I got to go," Miss Kezee said. "And I got a stop I want to make on the way."

"You and your stops."

"No skin off your nose. You can indulge an old woman, can't you?"

"Let's do it," Paula laughed.

"Open that closet and grab a bag, will you."

"A bag of what?" Paula laughed. She couldn't imagine what the old woman would be hauling around in some bag. Then she saw the suitcases. "What is this?" she asked.

"My bags. Grab one."

"I don't understand."

"For a smart girl, sure is a lot of stuff you don't get. Bus out of Quincy at five. Best get moving."

Paula wiped at tears which seemed to be rolling across her cheeks. "Why? Why today?"

Miss Kezee handed her a handkerchief. "Stop your blubbering girl. Sent for me a ticket. For today. Let's go."

"I'm not blubbering. I'm . . . surprised. I didn't expect . . ."

"Listen at you. How long I been sitting up in here telling you I'm going. OK. Today I'm going."

"But . . . the election . . ."

"Well. Like I said. It'll come out one way or another. You

coming or am I calling a cab." She pushed past Paula and picked up a shoulder tote. "Grab that old heavy one. What I don't need is my back going out on me when I'm traveling."

"You have to hurry, Mother. We can't be late."

Miss Kezee had bent forward just where the river lapped the shore. She seemed to be working something loose with her foot. Every now and then she wiped her forehead with a handkerchief. It was ninety-eight degrees, humid: even someone as powdery dry as Miss Kezee had beads of sweat running at her temples.

The sun on the water gave the illusion of stillness. Only now and then a churned-up piece of driftwood sent lifeless waves rippling to the shore, their power sapped by the sun.

"Mother."

Today the river smelled like freshly turned earth after a heavy rain. It was filthy, overwhelming, revolting, and appealing at the same time, alive. You could understand the Baptists—how they wanted to get in, be submerged, go under and come up cleansed. Its scent saturated the air, gave the humidity a corporeality, and surrounded you. This close to the river, Paula thought, and you might as well be in it.

Miss Kezee picked up a stick and began working at the object at her feet. She gave up, tossed the stick in the river, almost toppled in after it.

"Be careful there."

That river could pull you in faster than a vacuum cleaner picks up loose dirt. All that business about hocus-pocus and magic and the father of the waters, well, there weren't any phantoms here. There was only the power of hundreds of millions of gallons of water every hour, pushing and grinding and rolling and swirling by. It was real power, a force all its own. Water that washed through corn fields in Iowa and down rooftops in Illinois, over oak leaves in the Wisconsin summer, over a face, over a child's face. Over her children's faces. Water that carried a little bit of all that life. A little of the story. All the stories.

Power.

Real power.

I'm comin, girl. I'm comin. Hold your horses just one damn minute. I like this old river. Always liked it. Always lived close by. Here or there. I know a lot about it. It knows a lot about me. Good and bad both.

Letting go.

Just a little bit.

It's time.

I'm gonna let go, Charlie. Let go of some of this part. Just a little. It'll be OK. I'm sure of that. It's for the best. I know.

Yes, it is. I ain't afraid.

Whatever happens. OK?

I'm on my way. Charlie. Today. You come travel with me. Will you do that?

You will?

Yes, you will.

Left, out of town on Highway 61, Paula started through a checklist: what needed to be said to whom, what bandages to be put where, what fires—if any—would need to be put out.

"You sure you got everything, Mother?"

"I don't, you'll send it, won't you."

"Of course."

Since it was Monday afternoon there wasn't too much traffic. Paula whizzed around one or two cars with Iowa license plates. This road was always popular with Iowans driving back and forth to Saint Louis. The clock on the dashboard said three

fifty-five. She'd miss the coin toss. And so what? This little . . .
annoyance, anomaly, aggression—whatever he would call this
trip—well, it could be the end of the round, or the beginning of
a whole new match. Damn coin toss didn't have a thing to do
with it.

"Me and my Charlie come this way. Right along this very
road."

"Is that a fact?"

"Yes, ma'am. Remember it as clear as a bell. Never told you
much about my Charlie, did I?"

"No, ma'am."

"Well, let me tell you . . ."

And she began telling, and Paula listened and laughed and
let the hot asphalt roll beneath them. She'd call him when they
stopped for the night. Hell, the way she was feeling they might
drive all the way up tonight. She'd give it a couple of hours and
see how the old lady did. Al, he'd fume and stew—let him. The
big baby. She'd say some sweet things, knock him right off his
little perch. She'd let him whine or crow—whichever. She had
his number. Here's the old lady going on with that fish story
again.

"Nobody cooked a fish like my Charlie. Nobody."

"I'll just bet."

"Whatsa matter with you, girl. Turn off for Quincy's back
there. You don't pay attention."

"Thank you, Mother. I know where I am."

DAVID HAYNES was born in St. Louis, Missouri. He earned a B.A. in English from Macalester College and an M.A. in liberal studies from Hamline University. A teacher for fifteen years, Haynes helped plan and implement an experimental, high-tech school in St. Paul, Minnesota, called the Saturn School of Tomorrow, where he was an associate teacher of humanities from 1989 to 1993. He is currently a teacher-in-residence for the National Board for Professional Teaching Standards.

Haynes is the author of *Right By My Side* (New Rivers Press, 1993), a novel that won the 1992 Minnesota Voices Project and was selected by the American Library Association as one of the best books for young adults of 1994. His short stories have been published in journals and anthologies, and two were read and recorded for National Public Radio's "Selected Shorts." He won the 1985–1986 Loft Mentor Series, the 1989 Loft International Residency, and the 1989 Lake Superior Contemporary Writers Series Regional Writers Contest. Haynes is working on a new novel, which will be published by Milkweed Editions in 1996.

Designed by Wendy Holdman.

Typeset in Minion by Stanton Publications.

Printed on acid-free Liberty

by Quebecor Printing.

More fiction from Milkweed Editions:

Larabi's Ox
Tony Ardizzone

The Clay That Breathes
Catherine Browder

A Keeper of Sheep
William Carpenter

Winter Roads, Summer Fields
Marjorie Dorner

Kingfishers Catch Fire
Rumer Godden

The Importance of High Places
Joanna Higgins

Persistent Rumours
Lee Langley

Ganado Red
Susan Lowell

Tokens of Grace
Sheila O'Connor

The Boy Without a Flag
Abraham Rodriguez, Jr.

Confidence of the Heart
David Schweidel

Cracking India
Bapsi Sidhwa

The Crow Eaters
Bapsi Sidhwa

Aquaboogie
Susan Straight

Justice
Larry Watson

Montana 1948
Larry Watson